Destructive Messages

CRITICAL AMERICA

General Editors: Richard Delgado and Jean Stefancic

The Color of Crime: Racial Hoaxes, White Fear, Black Protectionism, Police Harassment, and Other Macroaggressions
Katheryn K. Russell

The Smart Culture: Society, Intelligence, and Law
Robert L. Hayman, Jr.

Was Blind, But Now I See: White Race Consciousness and the Law
Barbara J. Flagg

The Gender Line: Men, Women, and the Law
Nancy Levit

Heretics in the Temple: Americans Who Reject the Nation's Legal Faith
David Ray Papke

The Empire Strikes Back: Outsiders and the Struggle over Legal Education
Arthur Austin

Interracial Justice: Conflict and Reconciliation in Post–Civil Rights America
Eric K. Yamamoto

Black Men on Race, Gender, and Sexuality: A Critical Reader
Edited by Devon Carbado

When Sorry Isn't Enough:
The Controversy over Apologies and Reparations for Human Injustice
Edited by Roy L. Brooks

Disoriented: Asian Americans, Law, and the Nation State
Robert S. Chang

Rape and the Culture of the Courtroom
Andrew E. Taslitz

The Passions of Law
Edited by Susan A. Bandes

Global Critical Race Feminism: An International Reader
Edited by Adrien Katherine Wing

Law and Religion: Critical Essays
Edited by Stephen M. Feldman

Changing Race: Latinos, the Census, and the History of Ethnicity
Clara E. Rodríguez

From the Ground Up:
Environmental Racism and the Rise of the Environmental Justice Movement
Luke Cole and Sheila Foster

Nothing but the Truth:
Why Trial Lawyers Don't, Can't, and Shouldn't Have to Tell the Whole Truth
Steven Lubet

Destructive Messages

How Hate Speech Paves the Way for
Harmful Social Movements

Alexander Tsesis

NEW YORK UNIVERSITY PRESS
New York and London

To Sasha

NEW YORK UNIVERSITY PRESS
New York and London

© 2002 by New York University
All rights reserved.

Library of Congress Cataloging-in-Publication Data
Tsesis, Alexander.
Destructive messages : how hate speech paves the way for harmful
social movements / Alexander Tsesis.
p. cm. — (Critical America)
Includes bibliographical references and index.
ISBN 0-8147-8272-8 (cloth : alk. paper)
1. Oral communication—social aspects. 2. Hate speech. 3. Racism.
4. Freedom of speech. I. Title II. Series.
P95.54 .T778 2002
320.5'6'014—dc21   2002004197

New York University Press books are printed on acid-free paper,
and their binding materials are chosen for strength and durability.

Manufactured in the United States of America
10 9 8 7 6 5 4 3 2 1

Contents

Acknowledgments

I am deeply indebted to Richard Delgado and Jean Stefancic, who first encouraged me to write this book. I profited enormously from their advice and congeniality. Their commitment to social justice has left a deep imprint on me.

This work arose from my article, "Empirical Shortcomings of First Amendment Jurisprudence," 40 *Santa Clara Law Review* 729 (2000). I am grateful to Santa Clara University for giving me permission to reprint parts of the article here. All sections have been greatly expanded, and my approach here is more multidisciplinary and comprehensive. The comments I received on that article reverberated into the book. Steven J. Heyman helped further my understanding of Justice Oliver Wendell Holmes's relativism and its consequences on his First Amendment jurisprudence. Christopher M. Murray edited the article in great detail, improving the grammar and style. Kenneth M. Obel, Kevin M. Mulcahy, and Maryam Javaherian also line edited the article. Gregory D. Gilson offered some interesting philosophical points.

Over the course of several years, James Lindgren, Sheldon H. Nahmod, and Richard W. Wright have encouraged my writing. I am deeply grateful to them for the hours of conversation and helpful advice.

Several persons helped me understand the various manifestations of racial and ethnic animus. In particular, Robert F. Berkhofer Jr.'s immense knowledge of Native American culture and his good humor found their place into various portions of this book. Thanks also go to Ronald N. Satz for sending and discussing his articles on the Indian policy of President Andrew Jackson. Moctar Teyeb put a human face on Mauritanian slavery by courageously speaking out against that brutal practice. Joshua T. Katz reassured my mind about some etymological aspects of coining "misethnicity" throughout the text.

Several others aided me through the writing process. In particular, my parents who stimulated in me the love of knowledge and individuality. Shannon Verner line edited the entire work and encouraged me with her friendly personality. Norma I. Reyes and Thomas A. Doran who placed me in a friendly work environment. Andrew E. Taslitz offered structural and substantive advice that helped me clarify my outline and fill in the blanks. Gil Rabinovici guided me to neurological resources. I am also grateful to Jennifer Hammer, my editor at New York University Press, for her support and ideas on this work. I received important insights into foreign law from Martin Weiss, Jarno Syrjala, Blake Redding, Akash Kara, Mariann Orencsák, Jan Jayanto, Lasse Qvigstad, and Marc Wey. Thanks is also due to Carolyn Sherayko for her concentrated effort in creating the index.

My greatest friend has been my loving wife, Sasha, whose ideas were invaluable to this project and whose character never ceases to inspire me.

1

Introduction

Freedom of speech is critical to the growth and maturation of societies and is a much vaunted benefit of living in the United States. However, that freedom has not always led to the collective improvement of all citizens. History is littered with examples of harmful social movements, in various countries and cultures, employing violent racist rhetoric. Such hate-filled ideologies lie at the heart of human tragedies such as the Holocaust, U.S. slavery in the antebellum South, nineteenth-century Indian removal, and present-day slavery in Mauritania.

Propaganda is essential for eliciting widespread cultural acceptance of exclusionary and supremacist ideologies. When hate speech is systematically developed, it sometimes becomes socially acceptable, first, to discriminate and, later, to oppress identifiable groups of people.[1] Racialist rhetoric has been effectively harnessed to formulate and spread racism on national and even international scales. This book focuses on the emergence, elaboration, and reinforcement of stereotypes. It explores the effects of misinformation that is disseminated with the express purpose of persecuting targeted minorities. Specifically, I deal with expressions denigrating members of historically oppressed racial and ethnic groups ("outgroups"). I do not here discuss other forms of verbal abuse that have time and again fueled discrimination against women, gays, and lesbians. Bigots have rationalized all these biases through threads of thought that are subtly woven into the fabric of everyday language.

Speech plays a pivotal role in communicating ideas—both progressive and regressive. Over time, the semantics of a language will mirror the historical development of a people. The context of phrases and the subtle nuances of demonstrative messages can contain the kernels of a cultural worldview. Traditionally accepted perspectives permeate the unconscious and form an often unquestioned social "reality." Prejudices that reflect collective outlooks gradually find their way into laws.

People intent on maintaining power manipulate stereotypes that echo their followers' preconceptions. Orators and authors strategically exploit imbedded cultural meanings not just to create grammatical sentences, but also to persuade their audience. They use repeatedly uttered, dogmatic imagery to influence attitudes toward particular groups of people. Large audiences more readily recognize tenets when they draw on deeply held beliefs. This book uses historical examples to demonstrate these concepts.

Hate speech and the prejudice it fosters deny individuals fundamental rights like autonomy and tranquility. I use the term "misethnicity" to describe institutionalized hatred of ethnic groups. "Misethnicity" is divisible into two Greek words. The Greek infinitive "*misein*" (μισειν) means "to hate." It appears as the prefix in words such as "misogyny," meaning the "hatred of women." Ethnicity is a common English word. Its root "*ethnos*" (εθνοσ) has a rich origin: it dates back at least to Homer, who used it to refer to a unique nation. In ecclesiastical Latin, *ethnicus* came to mean "heathen." Eventually, the term became associated with identifiable groups of peoples who were outside the mainstream: "ethnic minorities." I use a broad definition of "ethnic group" to refer to people with the same cultural, historical, linguistic, or ancestral backgrounds. "Misethnicity" is sometimes preferable to "racism" and "ethnocentrism." "Racism" is the diminished respect and unequal treatment of peoples based on their biological particularities. "Ethnocentrism" is the sense of superiority of one's own ethnic group. "Misethnicity" is more specific in recognizing that ethnic prejudice is a groupwide hatred. I delve into the psychology and sociology of these issues in Part II of this book and give a more refined explanation of the term there.

Misethnicity is deeply nestled within conventional practices. By drawing attention to the centrality of language in perpetuating discrimination, we may be able to dislodge some deep-rooted racist thoughts and behaviors. Charismatic leaders can harness subtle and explicit misethnic statements to instigate active or complicit participation in hate crimes. Expressions such as these create an atmosphere of combustible intolerance: "Most Indians are drunks, but he's a hard worker"; "He may be a Jew, but he's not greedy"; "I'm usually careful around blacks, but he can be trusted." These statements reflect the same animosity as their more flagrant counterparts: "Indians are drunks," "Jews are greedy," and "blacks are dangerous." Studying the linguistic development of misethnicity and its relation to socially destructive conduct is critical to realizing, anticipating, and thwarting its potentially catastrophic consequences.

Scholars like Richard Delgado, Jean Stefancic, Mari Matsuda, Charles Lawrence, and Kimberle Crenshaw have exposed connections between misethnic language and political and social hierarchies. Their works show how hate speech is used to stifle minority voices. *Destructive Messages* goes a step further by illustrating, through empirical examples and sociopsychological analysis, how racist and ethnic slurs become ingrained in conventional language and in herd mentality.

Books about the power and ramifications of unbridled hate speech seldom discuss sociohistorical factors like the ones detailed here. At most, they devote part of a chapter to slavery, segregation, and similar systematic oppressions. A noteworthy exception to this is Gustav Jahoda's lengthy examination of disparagements about primitive peoples in *Images of Savages*.

Historic analysis is crucial because it exposes the association between hate propaganda and discriminatory actions. Oppressors justify inequities by making their targets out to be less than human, unworthy of fair treatment or even of the mercy ordinarily shown to animals. Outgroups are portrayed as sexually depraved demons or unruly, childlike savages and the victims themselves are blamed for their own problems or destruction. Negative stereotypes and ideological schemas, designed to rationalize power in the hands of dominant groups, precede crimes against humanity such as genocide. Many lives may be ruined before the views of those who rebuff popular prejudices trickle into the community conscience. Even societies striving for equality, steeped in natural rights theory, and vigilant against intolerant majorities are not wholly immune from becoming havens for supremacists promulgating aggressive ideologies.

Pondering the effectiveness of anti-Semitic and racist messages brings into stark relief the dangers that purveyors of hate pose to representative democracies. Scrutinizing the foundations of genocidal hatred in Germany and of dehumanizing and devaluing dogma in the United States yields abundant information about how, particularly in times of social and economic unrest, hate speech builds upon established ideologies. By understanding the progression from hatred to destruction, we can know better how to prevent misethnicity from being exploited by provocative rhetoricians intent on generating dangerous social movements. Studying how unjust political movements, such as the National Socialist party or the Confederate Nullificationists, manipulated cultural stereotypes is instructive in avoiding future calamities.

In spite of the numerous manifestations of discrimination in the United States, including slavery and Indian removal, most Supreme Court precedents on inciteful speech do not acknowledge its potential to ignite broad-based support for injustices. Instead, the Court maintains that virulent bigotry is protected by the First Amendment so long as it does not call for imminent unlawful actions. The freedom to express even macabre wishes against minorities is thought to add to dialogue, to be cathartic, and to protect minority rights.[2] Such justifications for the constitutionality of hate speech fail to recognize that for much of American history discrimination existed side by side with the First Amendment. The same Constitution that safeguarded speech also legitimized slavery.[3] The drafters of the Constitution did not incorporate any protections for their slaves' speech rights. Rather, they envisioned the First Amendment as a constraint against the censorship of the "political, scientific, and artistic discourse that they and their class enjoyed."[4] Even after the passage of the Thirteenth Amendment and the end of slavery, speech continued to play a role in spreading ethnically divisive views.

The Supreme Court has found few exceptions to the constitutional prohibition against legislative restrictions limiting instigative speech. In assuring people the freedom to express their views, the Court has focused on preserving speakers' liberties while neglecting to consider the negative impact of hate speech on targeted outgroups. Recent events, such as the Littleton, Colorado, shooting spree and Benjamin Smith's deadly rampage in the Midwest, call for a reevaluation of current free speech doctrine.

The book is divided into four parts. Part I presents an empirical survey of the role that ideology plays in the development and perpetuation of ethnic intolerance. Chapter 2 evaluates the effects of anti-Semitic speech in late nineteenth and early twentieth century Germany. The chapter shows how, through time, anti-Semitism influenced social consciousness until it led to disenfranchisement, imprisonment, forced labor, and attempted genocide. Chapter 3 analyzes how racist speech contributed to the entrenchment of black slavery in the United States. I contend that pro-slavery arguments, made in the context of a prejudiced society, undergirded the conceptual framework that supported hereditary servitude. Chapter 4 contains an account of depictions used to disparage Native Americans. I discuss the dehumanizing effect of rhetoric asserting the cultural inferiority of aboriginal Americans. Popular utterances about native peoples shaped colonists' views and provided them with rationalizations for the policy of Indian massacres and removal from their native lands.

Chapter 5 focuses on contemporary issues, beginning with some details on a pressing present-day injustice: black slavery in Mauritania, which continues to destroy thousands of lives. Moving on to recent U.S. encounters with hate speech, I first examine the spread of destructive messages over the Internet and the inadequacy of commercial filtering software in checking their proliferation. I then discuss the role that videos and pamphlets played in recent hate crimes such as Timothy McVeigh's bombing of the Oklahoma federal office building. I end with some insights into the inroads that white supremacist groups have recently made into U.S. politics.

Part II identifies psychological and sociological issues behind scapegoating. Chapter 6 analyzes the centrality of prejudiced speech in forming misethnic personality traits. It also relates how historical images of the "other" impair character development of both perpetrators and victims. I explain how misethnic invective elicits emotional and motivational responses, thereby easing guilt about groupwide mistreatment and injustice. The primary concern of chapter 7 is with the social forces that give rise to and reinforce outgroup stereotypes. It examines why societies so often resort to discrimination, despite its destructive consequences.

Part III discusses jurisprudence and public policy matters. Chapters 8 and 9 evaluate U.S. Supreme Court decisions on the constitutionality of criminal statutes that penalize the expression of bigoted messages. My critique concentrates on Justice Oliver Wendell Holmes's dissent in *Abrams v. United States*, which created the "marketplace of ideas" concept; Justice Antonin Scalia's majority opinion in *R.A.V. v. St. Paul*, with its blanket prohibition against content-based regulations; and *Brandenburg v. Ohio*'s "imminent threat of harm" standard.

Chapter 10 deals with theoretical foundations that, I argue, should be intrinsic to a representative democracy. I approach this topic from a rule consequentialist (deontological consequentialist) perspective. I contend that social contract obligations require governments both to protect fundamental rights and to increase social well-being. I conclude that hate speech, which augments the rights of the majority at the expense of the minority, weakens the sinews of a well-ordered society. If social welfare is measurable by the degree to which society helps maintain its residents' fundamental rights, speech that is detrimental to achieving that end must be restricted. Chapter 11, then, confronts the conflict between democratic ideals and hate speech.

In chapter 12 we study the laws of several countries that have recognized the harms of hate speech and have enacted criminal laws prohibiting bigoted incitements. Chapter 13 begins with a framework for a public policy checking the propagation of hate speech and ends with two alternative criminal causes of action.

My argument that hate speech should be criminally restricted arises from the injuries provoked by widespread stereotypes and popular prejudices. While hate propagandists defend their own right to free speech, they seek to suppress minority voices from influencing political and social thought, serving the cause of inequality. This is antidemocratic. Oft-repeated, sweeping labels dehumanize victim groups and represent them as deserving of violent action and unworthy of empathic treatment. Orators can more easily sway followers to persecute persons based on their race, national origin, or ethnicity once it becomes socially acceptable to degrade them using these salient characteristics.

Each of us, in our civic capacities, has a responsibility for safeguarding democracy and justice. Our social duty is not only toward our own ethnic or racial groups. We must guard vigilantly against unfair treatment of each individual, for historical examples show that heinous crimes can be committed anywhere misethnicity has donned the raiment of acceptable dialogue. Misethnicity eventually becomes so deeply rooted in cultural thought and folklore that it countenances barbarities even when they are against the perpetrators' economic and national well-being. Armed with empirical lessons from past injustices and a wellspring of compassion for victims, we can assure that our innate interest in human rights resounds in policy and legislation. Stories of intolerance and suffering can be "interpretive devices" for deciding which social institutions are detrimental to public tranquility.[5] I conclude that, to prevent crimes against humanity, narrowly tailored laws should be adopted prohibiting the dissemination of misethnic stereotypes that are intended to elicit crimes against outgroups.

I was born in the Soviet Union and immigrated to the United States with my parents. We fled that country because of the systematic anti-Semitic barriers we encountered there. I can clearly remember sitting on my father's shoulders at the age of four, when we lived in a communal apartment and one of our neighbors repeatedly calling my father a *zhyd* (a

Russian word that is significantly more pejorative and inflammatory than "kike"). My father asked him not to be so callous around a child. Even before I was aware of my Jewishness, I knew that Jews were derided.

In 1974, when we immigrated to the United States, we lived in one of Chicago's public housing projects among a racially mixed group of people. I soon realized the hardships misethnic speech causes other minorities. Instrumental in this process of sharpening my sense of empathy were Richard Wright's *Black Boy* and Robert Berkhofer's *The White Man's Indian*. Throughout my studies, I have been struck by how hate speech aimed at one historically derided group tends to harm society as a whole, not just the victims. This book, I hope, will go some way toward both understanding how hate propaganda instigates active discrimination and providing some useful solutions to avoid those risks.

PART I

Historical Lessons about the Dangers of Hate Speech

History shows that when bigotry develops over an extended period of time, it often leads to crimes against humanity. Hatreds directed against members of a community significantly influence peoples' perspectives, attitudes, and interpersonal relations. Preconceived notions about vulnerable minorities influence how they are treated. Misethnicity is developed, popularized, and spread by speech that represents outgroup members as symbols and embodiments of evil, rather than as individuals. The persecution and total annihilation of outgroup members are, then, rationalized by the fervent desire to rid society of undesirable and supposedly deleterious groups.

2

The Heart of German
Anti-Semitism

The Nazis successfully harnessed a racist ideology that grew out of ancient religious teachings. During the late nineteenth century, these ideas took on a biological aspect supporting racial superiority. The German experience is instructive because it demonstrates how broadly disseminated disparagements can gradually influence a nation to persecute a minority.

Anti-Jewish sentiment had simmered in Germany since medieval times. It was then common European lore that Jews poisoned wells, caused the Black Death, and ritually murdered Christian children. They were also blamed for the Crucifixion. In the Middle Ages, during crises and times of religious zealotry exemplified by the Crusades, the Jews' legal rights were curtailed. They stood out in the German social landscape: living in Jewish ghettos, they were forbidden from owning real property or practicing their religious rituals. Their practices were considered satanic; barred by law from numerous professions, they turned to money lending. Germans considered Jews to be the enemies of Jesus Christ and therefore treated them as an outgroup. In fact, in some religious circles, persecuting Jews was considered a religious obligation.[1] Myths about Jewish insidiousness fueled pogroms against them. For several hundred years, stories spread through German lands purporting that Jews desecrated and tortured the communal host, which Roman Catholics considered to be the transubstantiated body of Christ. Hatred gnawed the German populace until the myth culminated in massacres of more than three thousand Jews between 1298 and 1301.[2]

The plethora of religiously based myths about Jews continued to influence German interrelations with them. Historical anti-Semitism developed the vulgar yet beguiling ideology that Jews are materialists, willing to sacrifice anything, even God incarnate, for the love of money. Christian belief in the obligation to renounce worldly pleasures was contrasted with the greed that supposedly permeated Jewish religious and political interests. It was commonly believed that Jews had calculatingly renounced Christianity to pursue their selfish interests.

During the Reformation, attitudes toward German Jews hardened even more. Martin Luther's doctrines reverberated in the volitions of millions of his followers. Part of his message was directed at Jews, and his doctrine lay at the heart of many populist social movements. Along with his calls for religious renewal came hailstorms of religious intolerance.

Luther's letters and pamphlets proclaimed that Jews are the enemies of Christ who were spawned by the Devil and deserve retribution. As one observer pointed out: "Luther's anti-Semitism clearly had a religious and not a racial foundation, but it cannot be denied that it provided each successive Protestant generation with . . . sanction for animosity and persecution."[3]

Early in his break from the Roman Catholic Church, Luther had preached tolerance toward Jews, but with time, unable to win them to his brand of Christianity, his attitude changed considerably. Three years before his death, in a book entitled *On the Jews and Their Lies*, Luther advocated a fanatical hatred for Jews. "First . . . set fire to their synagogues or schools. . . . Second, I advise that their houses also be razed and destroyed. . . . Third, I advise that all their prayer books and Talmudic writings . . . be taken from them. . . . Fourth, I advise that their rabbis be forbidden to teach henceforth on pain of loss of life and limb."[4] Luther further urged that "they be forbidden on pain of death to praise God, to give thanks, to pray, and to teach publicly among us and in our country."[5] Lutheran anti-Jewishness took medieval concepts a step further toward ascribing an innate evil character to Jews. We will see later in this chapter that when the Nazis first came to power, they periodically invoked Luther's teachings to justify passing anti-Semitic laws and racial policies.[6]

The Enlightenment of the eighteenth century signaled a departure from religious anti-Jewishness to the advent of an even more dangerous, secular variety. Germans blamed Jews for controlling economic and cultural life. This line of thought developed into the myth that Jews secretly conspired to dominate the world and persecute non-Jews. In response to this unsubstantiated allegation, German towns passed discriminatory laws prohibiting Jews from settling there and practicing various professions. I do not mean to imply that all German Enlightenment thinkers were anti-

Jewish. Some, such as Gotthold Ephraim Lessing, the author of *Nathan the Wise* (1779), were not. But the German intellectual landscape was dominated by *völkisch* ideology that reacted against the slogans of the 1789 French Revolution—liberty, fraternity, and equality—by extolling authority, martial order, and self-sacrificing nationalism. German ideologues called for the sacrifice of individualism and liberalism for the sake of the national community and the state. Obedience to powerful leaders, Teutonic courage, and rigorous discipline became entrenched in German mores. Jews were portrayed as dangerous to this *völkisch* order, parasitical on the German nation, and self-interestedly capitalistic.

In the late nineteenth century, widespread negative Jewish stereotypes built on this popular rhetoric and its manifestation in the social consciousness, thereby making it possible to enlist social, religious, and intellectual support for discriminatory laws. Both the political right and left advanced their ends by exploiting contradictory views about Jews. In the 1850s, Wilhelm Riehl expressed his contempt of Jews because he regarded them as the proletariat of German society. On the other hand, Karl Marx claimed that Jews were at the root of capitalism. Marx therefore conceived of a proletariat revolution as the "emancipation of society from Jewry."[7] Jews were, consequently, the pariahs of both extremes of German political thought.

In spite of vehement opposition, German states made civil rights progress at the urging of liberal political parties, whom Otto von Bismark was forced to placate for supporting his unification plan. Among the southern states, civil rights were granted to the Jews of Baden in 1862 and Württemberg in 1864. Jews received complete legal emancipation in northern Germany on July 3, 1869, with the passage of a law lifting all civic restrictions based on their religious status. When Bavaria allied itself to the Northern German Federation during the Franco-German War (1870–71), it too granted Jews civil status. Judeophobia was by then so entrenched that its adherents refused to concede the civil rights victory. Anti-Jewish sentiments and *völkisch* drives were soon directed at the liberal parties, whose leaders, Eduard Lasker and Ludwig Bamberger, were Jews.

The windfall of receiving equal citizenship was tainted by a wave of virulent Judeophobia following the Reich's first financial crash in 1873. Otto von Glogau, a journalist, gained notoriety by exploiting what he believed was the most commonly held belief of anti-Semites: that Jews were responsible for economic suffering. He provided a conceptual framework for the acceptance of Jew-hating through several articles published in the widely circulated periodical *Die Gartenlaube (The Bower)*.[8] "Today the social question," he wrote in 1876, "is essentially the Jewish question. All other explanations of our economic troubles are fraudulent cover-ups."[9] Glogau's catchy slogans about "Jewish high finance" resonated with the long-standing belief that Jews were selfish materialists. His articles, read throughout the country, made conventional in German households the view that Jews were "a physically and psychically degenerate race—commanding the globe by means of mere cunning and slyness, usury and shoddy dealings."[10] Along with the accusation of Jewish bad faith in financial dealings, Glogau threw in the charge that Jews sought to undermine native German culture. Later, politicians seeking votes incorporated his doctrine into their speeches.

Anti-Jewish thinkers developed and popularized expressions and catchwords in order to more effectively disseminate their misethnic *weltanschauung*. Wilhelm Marr was the first to coin the word *Antisemitismus* (anti-Semitism) in the 1870s in his work, *Der Sieg des Judentums über das Germanentum (The Victory of Judaism over Germandom)*.[11] The book quickly went through twelve printings and dispersed across the country the notion that Jews were innately "antisocial." Marr used the term "anti-Semitism" rather than "anti-Judaism" to imply that Jewish evil traits were the result not of their religion or isolation from German society, but, rather, that Jews were inherently tarnished. As he saw it, Germany was at great peril from the Jews since they were at "war [against] all ideals" and sought "the transformation of everything to merchandise."[12] Marr jarred his readers by declaring that the enemy, whom he identified as the whole "demonic" Jewish race, had already conquered German civil and political institutions.

> You have elected the foreign rulers into your parliaments, you are making them legislators and judges, you are making them dictators of the financial system, you have surrendered the press to them . . . what do you really want? The Jewish people is flourishing [*wuchert*] with its talent and you are beaten.[13]

The Jews had supposedly won because Germans allowed them to infiltrate society. They ruled the world by manipulating the press and financial institutions. To curtail this imagined power, Marr advocated taking measures such as boycotting Jewish businesses. Marr's dogma made discrimination more respectable among Germans and was an important step on the road to the Final Solution.

Antisemitismus became an effectual rallying cry for gathering individuals and organizations into an ideological, racial, and political camp. "Anti-Semite" was an accolade, denoting someone who was self-sacrificing, nationalistic, and lacking capitalistic motives. Marr resolved to take advantage of the social climate, which was permeated by anti-Jewish sentiments, to further his ambitions. As with any other successful demagoguery, Marr's ideology had a provocative, activist component. He understood that an anti-Semitic platform could win support, even when it was not tied to other political issues. During the 1879 elections he won conservative financial backing to found a journal, *Deutsche Wache* (*German Guard*), for disseminating his anti-Semitic teachings. Marr called on fellow Germans to "Elect no Jews."[14] *Deutsche Wache* also provided Marr with a forum to gather support for the Antijüdischer Verein (Anti-Jewish Society), which soon changed *jüdisch* to *semitisch*, becoming the Anti-semitenliga (Anti-Semitic League). Thus, the term "anti-Semite," connoting someone who opposes Jewish world dominance and supports German ideological restoration, was set into motion. Marr refined ancient, anti-Jewish sentiments into a doctrine that regarded Jews as so unalterably evil that they had to be excluded from German society and politics.

Several other misethnic speakers developed anti-Semitic followings during this period. Anthropologists began analyzing data about the skin and eye pigmentations of Germans and Jews to discover distinguishing marks between Aryans and Semites. Using pseudoscientific research, they helped popularize the dogma of Aryan superiority over other races. Racialist scientists of the nineteenth century, such as Alfred Ploetz, the founder of the Society for Racial Hygiene, made eugenics and "racial hygienics" intellectually legitimate. So that, while Nazi doctors later expanded this research, adding data through gruesome experiments, they contributed little to their predecessor's racial ideology.

Adolf Stoecker, a court preacher from Berlin, was the first politician to realize the effectiveness of anti-Semitic slogans. He first ran for political office in the nationwide Reichstag elections of 1878 before he resorted to overt misethnicity. Running on the Christian Socialist Workers' party ticket in a thoroughly unsuccessful campaign, he counseled his few followers to keep autocratic church rules and called for an economic policy that would reconcile workers and the state. On that platform, Stoecker received less than 1 percent of the vote.

Stoecker realized that in the developing xenophobic climate, he had appealed to the wrong audience. He was aware that during the campaign his supporters had urged him to speak about the Jews and their perceived role in Germany's socioeconomic problems. They often resorted to racist slogans to silence his opponents. He delivered his first clearly anti-Semitic, and most influential, speech in September 1879, when running for the Prussian Chamber of Deputies. Entitled "What We Demand of Modern Jewry," the speech displayed the opportunism of an aspiring politician and the conviction of a Jew hater. He began with Glogau's catchy aphorism, "The social problem is the Jewish problem." His audience quickly grasped his message because it was grounded in age-old ideas. Jews were outsiders, aliens in the midst of the Germans; therefore it was legitimate and necessary to enact legislation restricting Jewish economic progress to protect German interests. In the same speech he asserted: "The Jews . . . remain a people within a people, a state within a state, a separate tribe within a foreign race." Stoecker was instrumental in making discrimination seem like an acceptable way of dealing with Jews and gaining votes: "If modern Jewry continues to use the power of capital and the power of the press to bring misfortune to the nation, a final catastrophe is unavoidable. . . . It will not be easy to curb Jewish capital. Only thoroughgoing legislation can bring it about." The Jews, according to him, were a disease, a "cancer" among the German people which threatened to spread if Jewish civil rights were not curtailed.[15] Based on the warm reception to his speech, Stoecker altered his second campaign for political office and breathed life into his political career.

Stoecker won the election of 1879 by attracting the vote of the discontented *Mittelstand* (middle class)—peasants, small farmers, small businessmen, and artisans—all bound together by a common devotion to anti-Semitism. They believed that urbanization, factory-made products, and large companies threatened their livelihoods. These they thought were in Jewish hands. Support of Stoecker reflected the desire to blame others for their inability to compete in a changing economy. As a leading authority put it: "Cut loose from village and small town, Stoecker's voters blamed their troubles on the mysterious financial power of the Jews. It was easier . . . to blame the ancient enemy rather than face their own inability to compete in the new national market."[16] Although the National Socialists were not yet in existence and would not gain political dominance for another fifty-four years, anti-Semites were beginning to develop a diverse coalition.

Another proponent of German identity who got his start during the early years of political anti-Semitism was Paul de Lagarde, an acclaimed biblical scholar and Orientalist. His contribution to the increasingly reactionary social climate was the advocacy of German imperialism, known as *lebensraum* (living space). Lagarde spread some of the seeds for World War II, pushing for German expansion to the East and propounding the legitimacy of a war with Russia to obtain Poland, the Balkans, and lands on the Black Sea. The victors would set aside useless land in the east for Slavic survivors of such a war. These ideas seemed ridiculously unrealistic until the National Socialist party, whose members had internalized them in their youth, gained power and went about trying to fulfill Lagarde's megalomaniacal aspirations.

In 1887, Lagarde, who became a hero of the anti-Semitic movement, called for the seizure of all Jewish credit and banking facilities and for the expulsion and physical destruction of Jews. "Every Jew is proof of the enfeeblement of our national life and of the worthlessness of what we call Christian religion," he wrote. Lagarde considered Jews to be "usurious vermin" for whom there could be no compassion: "With trichinae and bacilli one does not negotiate, nor are trichinae and bacilli subjected to education; they are exterminated as quickly and as thoroughly as possible." He preached that Jews carried "decay and pollute every national culture, they exploit the human and material resources of their hosts, they destroy all faith and spread materialism and liberalism."[17] Lagarde's ideas festered in popular German culture for more than sixty years, until, at the peak of anti-Semitism, Hitler carried Lagarde's dogma to its lethal conclusion by urging Nazis and their sympathizers to murder Jews. The Nazis found Lagarde's ideology such an important indoctrination tool that they distributed an anthology of his works to German soldiers.

The writings of Heinrich von Treitschke also illustrate the vigor and endurance of German anti-Semitism. Treitschke was among the prominent professors at the University of Berlin, where his lectures were attended by future schoolteachers, military officers, and prominent politicians. He legitimized academic anti-Semitic propaganda, passionately arguing that Jews should be excluded from governmental bureaucracy, law, and German education. In his popularly acclaimed *History of Germany in the Nineteenth Century* (1879), Treitschke criticized Jewish emancipation and blamed the Jews for the anti-Semitic responses that their presence aroused in the German people. He distanced himself from Enlightenment thought as "in reality Jewish hatred of Christianity and Jewish cosmopolitanism" and downplayed Jewish army involvement in the War of Liberation.[18]

Treitschke further expostulated his brand of misethnicity in periodical pamphlets. In an article entitled *Ein Wort über unser Judenthum (A Word about Our Jewry)*, he characterized the anti-Semitic Berlin Movement as a "passionate movement against Judaism" (*"leidenschaftliche Bewegung gegen das Judentum"*). The article, published in the distinguished *Preussische Jahrbücher*, showed that Treitschke was of basically one mind with the expanding anti-Jewish agitation.[19] In an even more influential article, *Unsere Aussichten (Our Prospects)*, published in the same periodical in 1879, he coined a slogan that gradually led German society down the path from intolerance, to oppression, and then to genocide. *"Die Juden,"* Treitschke boldly proclaimed, *"sind unser Unglück!"*[20] ("The Jews are our misfortune!"). This catch-phrase became a painful dart with slow-acting poison stuck into the heart of Jews. Heinrich Class, who in 1908 was to become president of the political Pan-German League, attested to the power of Treitschke's destructive messages when he wrote that the phrase "became a part of my body and soul when I was twenty years old; it essentially influenced my later political work."[21]

What began as isolated bigotry became, by the 1890s, embedded in polite German culture. Many Reichstag deputies, such as Otto Böckel who was elected in 1887, argued that Jewish property should be confiscated and distributed to the German poor. The same year, he published *The Jews—The Kings of Our Time (Die Juden—die Könige unserer Zeit)*. One of Böckel's campaign slogans was *"Judenfreiheit!"* ("Freedom from the Jews!"), yet another nineteenth-century slogan the Nazis later adopted. His party, the Anti-Semitic People's Party (Antisemitische Volkspartei), won five Reichstag seats in 1890. Hermann Ahlwardt, who was elected in 1892, aired his anti-Semitic views two years before in his book, *Despairing Struggle of the Aryan Peoples with Jewry*. By 1893, anti-Semitic political parties had a sixteen-person faction in the Reichstag. These successful forays by fringe political parties led major parties such as the Conservatives to adopt anti-Semitic platforms in order to increase their popularity among the middle class.

The importance of misethnic propaganda in developing mass movements had already become evident to major political figures. It was reasonably foreseeable to campaign strategists that virtually any program—whether it be the Christian Socialists', the Roman Catholics', or the Conservatives'—all of which exploited anti-Semitism for political gain—would boost their standing from an infusion of widespread racism. Among the most successful and astute at the art of hate speech was Theodor Fritsch. The leader of the Reichshammerbund, an umbrella organization of nineteen propaganda groups, he realized the importance of deliberate and systematic dissemination of anti-Semitism. Fritsch set out to convince his listeners of the moral corruptness of the Jewish character, against which it was imperative to be on guard. Jews could not be reformed by any means, not even by religious conversion. To be consistent, Fritsch claimed Jesus was an Aryan. In 1932, the year before his death and Hitler's assent to power, Fritsch demanded that the purity of German blood be maintained, that interactions between Jews and German Christians be forbidden, and that all social relations between Jews and Germans be terminated.

Anti-Semitism also spilled into university organizations, influencing the attitudes of future leaders. The Union of German Students and the Academic League of Gymnasts enjoyed large-scale support among students and provided a forum for spreading racism to budding intellectuals and teachers. One of the students' often-repeated complaints was that Jews enrolled in secondary schools and universities at a higher rate than their proportion to the population, increasing competition in the job market. Libraries contained extensive collections of anti-Semitic literature for popular consumption. In sum, anti-Semitism permeated Germany at the turn of the century.

An English-born writer, Houston Stewart Chamberlain, was as instrumental as his father-in-law, Richard Wagner, in spreading anti-Semitic nationalism. Chamberlain's *Foundations of the Nineteenth Century*, published in 1899, considered only a pure Aryan race capable of strong culture, while mixing with lower races caused social chaos and ruin, as it had in Rome. The *Foundations* was fertile ground for anti-Semites searching for doctrinal sustenance. Chamberlain, who became a naturalized German in 1916, employed Social Darwinism to distinguish and valuate different human races. Natural selection was a necessity for the German people, whom Chamberlain counseled to breed for racial purity. Among the races who mixed, Jews were a special case because in them, Middle Eastern intermixture had resulted in an evil race. Germany, he believed, was too tolerant to aliens, which meant that, "our government, our laws, our art . . . , practically all branches of our life have become more or less willing slaves of the Jews. . . . The Indo-European, moved by ideal motives, opened the gates of friendship: the Jews rushed in like the enemy, stormed all positions, and planted the flag of his [*sic*] . . . alien nature."[22] Jews employed cosmopolitanism and Enlightenment ideals against Germans, denying racial differences in order to destroy civilization.

Anti-Semitic ideology continued to spread into German consciousness, while politically it still posed no imminent danger. In fact, anti-Semitic parties only mustered eleven Reichstag seats in 1903, compared to sixteen in 1893. Germany's defeat in World War I reversed that trend, creating an atmosphere conducive to scapegoating. Before then, Marr, Stoecker, and Fritsch had followings among the middle class but were unable to gain broad-based political support. But the years of anti-Jewish pamphlets, periodicals, and books did not go for naught. They had made it ideologically acceptable for politicians, editors, academics, scientists, and laymen to blame Jews for Germany's social, economic, and moral troubles. The difficulties facing post–World War I Germany only aggravated these circumstances. Politicians and their minions often blamed Jewish entrepreneurs for the rise in inflation and shortages of vital goods. These accusations contributed to the periodic looting of Jewish businesses. Evangelical preachers also blamed Jews for Germany's postwar misfortunes.

Searching for someone on whom to assign blame for the military loss, hyperinflation, and terms of peace, ideologues hit upon the teachings in the pamphlet entitled *Protocols of the Elders of Zion*. An abundance of anti-Semitic articles and pamphlets were circulating throughout the country after the war, but none had as devastating an effect as the *Protocols*. It helped propagandists shore up support for their anti-Semitic and anti-Masonic explanations as the causes of Germany's disaster.

The *Protocols* combined old world myths about "the Jews" with the turmoils of the time. The work endeared itself to the masses by refurbishing age-old anti-Jewish slanders while confronting modern dilemmas. Examining its power over the German mind offers a study in the ease by which demagogues can exploit long-established group libels to inflame the masses and gain their support. "The *Protocols of the Learned Elders of Zion* reflects in theory the practical transition of a primarily religious prejudice that later becomes a social sentiment into a new political worldview."[23]

The *Protocols* became one of the most infamous and effective anti-Semitic works. Purportedly made up of the minutes from a fictitious 1897 meeting of Jewish elders in Berne, its chief premise was that the Jews were conspiring to crown a Jewish ruler who would reign over the world and enslave Christians.

Gottfried zur Beek, whose real name was Ludwig Müller von Hausen, published the first German edition of the book in 1920. It went through thirty-three editions by 1933, the year Hitler was appointed chancellor. The pamphlet first appeared in Russia in 1903 and was written by the *okhrana* (the tsar's secret police). The poorly written document charged that the Jewish elders intend to achieve world domination by spreading revolution, liberalism, and socialism around the globe. It claimed that Jews were unscrupulous in their methods: "We must not stop at bribery, deceit and treachery when they should serve toward the attainment of our end."[24] By subverting faith in authority and belief in God, it went on, the people's will to resist would be undermined. Meanwhile, Jews would manipulate financial markets to drive up prices. These means would allegedly enable the Jews "to absorb all the State forces of the world and to form a Super-Government."[25] Once they enthroned the King of the Jews, he would demand absolute obedience from his Christian bondsmen. The Protocols thus combined the ancient myth of Jewish financial control with the nineteenth-century fear of political upheaval to create a powerful document that helped unite disparate anti-Semitic groups. As Fritsch expected years before, Judeophobia proved an effective tool for bringing together religious, intellectual, and political forces, thereby augmenting the power of misethnists.

The London *Times* exposed the *Protocols* to be a forgery in August 1921. The *Times* proved that most of the pamphlet was copied from a satirical attack on Napoleon III entitled *Dialogue aux Enfers entre Montesquieu et Machiavel*, by a French lawyer named Maurice Joly. The *Protocols* replaces Napoleon with the Elders of Zion to add an anti-Semitic flavor to the text. The *okhrana* lifted over 180 passages, comprising 1,040 lines out of a total of 2,560, without alteration from the *Dialogue*.[26] In 1926, Binjamin Segel wrote a book denouncing the *Protocols* and warning that "if we do not move quickly to choke off the roots of the superstitious belief in the *Protocols* who can assure us that it will not continue to befog the understanding of simple men, poison their hearts, and pervert their common sense for decades, perhaps for centuries to come?"[27] But no refutation put the brakes on its distribution and acceptance in the marketplace of ideas.

Segel's predictions were right on the mark. The book served as a catalyst for pogroms in Russia and for even worse in Germany, where the Nazis made it required reading. It distracted attention from the governmental sources of social woes and drew support away from political movements seeking basic reforms. The *Protocols* helped fuel xenophobia, authoritarianism, and fears of political innovations and cosmopolitanism. It was crucial to the gradual progress of misethnic indoctrination that eventually led to mass extermination. The influence of the *Protocols* contributed to the enactment of laws prohibiting Jews from participating in German public life. Jews were portrayed no longer as just united against Germany but against the whole world, which they sought to entrap in their tentacles. Anti-Semites now accused Jews of scheming behind the scenes of every loss and tragedy that befell nations and individuals. The *Protocols* raised anti-Semitism to a fever pitch, implying that the only way to end the misery of economic distress, the loss of traditional values, and the intermixture of Aryan blood was to abridge the Jews' human rights, to separate them, and ultimately to eliminate them.

An eyewitness account, written the same year the *Protocols* was published in Germany, describes the frenzy the work produced there:

> In Berlin I attended several meetings which were entirely devoted to the *Protocols*. The speaker was usually a professor, a teacher, an editor, a lawyer or someone of that kind. The audience consisted of members of the educated class, civil servants, tradesmen, former officers, ladies, above all students, students of all faculties and years of seniority. . . . Passions were whipped up to the boiling point. There, in front of one, in the flesh, was the cause of all ills—those who had made the war and brought about the defeat and engineered the revolution, those who had conjured up all our suffering. . . . I observed the students. A few hours earlier they had perhaps been exerting all their mental energy in a seminar under the guidance of a world-famous scholar. . . . Now young blood was boiling, eyes flashed, fists clenched, hoarse voices roared applause or vengeance. . . . German scholarship allowed belief in the genuineness of the *Protocols* and in the existence of a Jewish world-conspiracy to penetrate ever more deeply into all the educated sections of the German population.[28]

Hitler claimed to have read the *Protocols of the Elders of Zion* in his youth; the book informed and reaffirmed his impressions about Jews. Hitler's earliest mention of the immensely influential book occurred in a speech given in August 1921 about rising German inflation. Following the *Protocols'* claims, he told the audience that inflation was brought on by the Jews as part of their plan for world conquest. Heinrich Himmler, who directed German National Socialist propaganda from 1926 to 1930 and later became *Reichsführer* of the *Schutzstaffel* (better known as the SS), poured out to his diary the influence of the *Protocols* on his life. He considered it "[a] book that explains everything and tells us whom we must fight against next time."[29] Himmler's anti-Semitic readings in 1921, shortly after he joined the paramilitary *Einwohnerwehr*, also included Chamberlain's work *Rasse und Nation* (*Race and Nation*), which inspired him to write in his diary, "It is true and one has the impression that it is objective. . . . These terrible Jews."[30] According to Heinrich Class's diary, Lagarde, Chamberlain, and the writing of a French diplomat, Count Arthur de Gobineau, laid the groundwork for Class's anti-Semitic legislative proposals.[31] So it was that books, pamphlets, and magazine articles, first published at and before the turn of the century, influenced the thoughts and actions of anti-Semites for decades.

Images of Jews as aliens and enemies, residing inside the nation and undermining it from within, permeated culture and language. Propagandists not only made anti-Semitism acceptable, they made it respectable. Yet these slogans rarely posed an immediate danger to the Jews. Before the Nazi ascent to power, German violence against Jews was relatively rare when compared to the harsh realities in East European countries such as Russia and the Ukraine. During the late nineteenth century, influential and articulate persons and anti-Semitic groups impressed their ideas on the consciences of ordinary people and future rulers, causing resonating harm. The Jews, above any other minority groups living in Germany, were the most visible and convenient scapegoats for Germany's problems. They had been characterized as villains for centuries, and influential misethnists had derogated them for decades. In this context, anti-Semitism not only served as a political rallying cry, but a unifying force that appealed to all elements of German society and united them as no other ideology could. Judeophobia appealed to the sense of community not just of Germans but to Germanic peoples living throughout Europe. It called on Aryans to unite against the worldwide menace to their racial being. German leaders were the product of their times, educational system, and linguistic imagery.[32] Galvanized by a common hatred and long-standing, misethnic ideology, charismatic leaders were able to gather a populist movement for the discrimination, isolation, and destruction of Jews.

The Nazis succeeded in obtaining national prominence where other anti-Semitic organizations had failed because they were determined to destroy the republic and organized their minions to achieve that purpose. Nazi use of anti-Semitism was not only a strategic decision but a passionate conviction shared by the vast majority of Germans.[33] The Nazis equated all opposition movements—socialist, liberal, communist, humanitarian, cosmopolitan, individualist, democratic—to the Jewish cabal. Orators and writers developed catchy political slogans based on time-worn accusations, thereby gathering a diverse set of adherents: leading historians supported the view that Jews were destroying German culture, scientists wrote to prove misethnic hypotheses about the racial inferiority of Jews, and popular print brought anti-Semitism into average households. Propagandists bombarded Germans with anti-Semitism and came to accept Jews' blameworthiness as an indisputable fact. It did not happen overnight but took time to become part of the social conscience.

Yet, another crucial ideological development led to the attempt to murder all Jews, the so-called Final Solution: racialist ascription of nonhuman characteristics to Jews helped justify the concerted effort to exterminate them. Such a program could not be sold to the public without first divesting Jews of their humanity. There were simply things that one could not do to other people. As long as Jews were recognized as men, women, and children, they were endowed with certain rights which had to be recognized. This is where Lagarde's dehumanizing twist to anti-Semitism was essential to the Nazis: if the Jew was a parasite, a microbe, a bacillus, then he or she had no human rights nor legal or ethical demands to ask of the Aryan.

Statements of Nazi leaders make clear how much these views influenced the masterminds of national socialism. On one occasion, Hitler spoke of the development of his own thought: "I discovered the Jew as the bacillus and the ferment in social decomposition."[34] Propaganda Minister Joseph Goebbels wrote in November 1941 of his observations in the Vilna Ghetto: "The Jews are squeezed together here, horrible figures, not to be looked at even less to be touched. . . . The Jews are the lice of civilized humanity. They have to be exterminated somehow; otherwise they will continue to play their tormenting and troublesome role."[35] Likewise, Himmler, on April 24, 1943, told the SS-*Korpsführer*:

We were the first to really answer the race problem by action, by the race problem we naturally did not mean anti-Semitism. Anti-Semitism is exactly like delousing. The removal of lice is not an ideological question, but a matter of hygiene. Thus anti-Semitism is not an ideological issue, but a matter of hygiene, which will soon be behind us. We are almost deloused, we have only some 20,000 lice left, and then it will be ended in all of Germany.[36]

The Nazis were deeply committed to destroying Jews, and they enlisted ordinary people in their cause.

Much of the Nazi propaganda was built on slogans developed decades beforehand. Julius Streicher, who published the savagely anti-Semitic newspaper *Der Stürmer*, ordered that posters be placed throughout the Third Reich with Treitschke's inflammatory message, "The Jews are our misfortune!" The Nazis made reading Treitschke's works mandatory and distributed booklets with his quotes to German soldiers. But Streicher's anti-Semitism is traceable even farther back in time. Before judges sentenced him to death by hanging, he "told the Nuremberg tribunal that Luther . . . had long before said what he himself had to say about the Jews, and much more sharply."[37] The Nazis developed and systematized animosity against Jews that had been developing many years prior to the advent of the Third Reich. By the time they came to power, linguistic casuistry had become dogma.

The Final Solution began sometime in 1941; however, this plan was in the making for years prior to its commencement. National Socialists had advocated this goal even before Hitler became German Chancellor in 1933. On November 24, 1938, the SS periodical *Schwarze Corps* announced the plan to exterminate ("*ausrotten*") and annihilate ("*vernichten*") all Jews.[38] Moreover, Hitler told Czechoslovakian Foreign Minister Chvalkovsky on January 21, 1939, that "we are going to destroy the Jews."[39]

Hitler's diabolical plan and its implementation should be compared with Luther's ominous directives of how to deal with Jews. Take, for example, Luther's advocacy of the burning of synagogues; nearly four hundred years after his pronouncement, when ancient anti-Jewish sentiments were at their apex, the Nazis and their sympathizers did just that. During the night of November 9–10, 1938, known as *Kristallnacht* (Night of Broken Glass), frenzied crowds throughout Germany—stirred on by years of anti-Semitic propaganda that had become part of their psyche—set fire to a hundred synagogues, destroyed shops and houses, raped Jewish women, and killed Jews indiscriminately. Furthermore, following

Luther's ideas, the Nazis denied that Jews were members of a distinct religion and denied Jews the right to practice Judaism.

By the time the Nazis came to power, the malevolent vitriol that German leaders and thinkers spewed against Jews had become entrenched in German culture. The Nazis were not elected in a cultural vacuum. Hitler could not have come to power and guided the Final Solution without the support and compliance of hundreds of thousands of Germans. Years of anti-Semitic indoctrination prepared Germans for Hitler's plan. The most basic ethical principles, such as the one adjuring people not to kill innocent humans, were broken down by centuries of contempt directed against Jews. Synagogue burnings, physical attacks, and participation in mass deportations became acceptable for Germans in large part because prior anti-Semitic rhetoric had dulled their consciences.

The widespread participation of ordinary Germans makes it impossible to support the notion that they were unwilling, nonautonomous pawns. Much of the German infrastructure participated directly in oppressing and murdering Jews. Daniel Goldhagen recently pointed out that while the extermination and processing camps were primarily in Poland (Auschwitz, Sobibor, Treblinka, Majdanek, Belzec, Chelmno), the Nazis built a network of labor camps within Germany. Berlin alone housed 645 labor camps, and in the Hesse region, located in west-central Germany, 606 camps supplied Aryan industrial needs.[40] Major companies enthusiastically made death camps efficient at killing, while railway workers were intimately involved and knowledgeable about the inhumane treatment of Jews who were transported to the East. Physicians and healthcare workers willingly experimented on healthy human subjects and saw scientific value in torture.[41] Judges, magistrates, and lawyers maintained and practiced a form of "justice" that included the administration of the infamous Nuremberg laws.

The German experience contradicts the view that only speech posing an immediate threat of harm is dangerous enough to warrant statutory censure.[42] To the contrary, the most dangerous form of bigotry takes years to develop, until it becomes culturally acceptable first to libel, then to discriminate, and finally to persecute outgroups.[43] The Nazis were able to accomplish what nineteenth- and early twentieth-century anti-Semitic parties could not—the establishment of an autocratic government committed to excluding and murdering Jews—only after extensive and prolonged racialist agitation. The German experience constitutes one example among many of the instrumental role hate speech assumes in the development of a social psyche willing to tolerate massive inhumane treatment of outgroups. Over time, misethnic religious and secular beliefs catalyzed a murderous ideology, supported by the majority of the German public. Early German ideology, which denounced Jews for not adopting Christianity, gave way to an even more combustible view that attributed to them an implacable and biological evil.

3

Endearing Racism in American Minds

Like the theories of Jewish inferiority, pseudoscientific views about blacks played a significant role in their oppression.[1] Unfortunately, only a sparse historical record details the evolution of hate propaganda against blacks and its effect upon their enslavement. Nevertheless, sufficient information exists to piece together the role hate speech played in justifying the institutionalization of hereditary servitude. A historical analysis is particularly important for understanding how black slaves and freemen came to occupy a lower social rung than whites.[2] Long-held views and declarations referring to blacks as a subspecies of humans, mentally inferior, sexually predatory, and savage, perpetuated and supported American slavery.

Over one hundred years before the British colonized America, European commercial centers such as Sicily, Spain, and Portugal were deeply enmeshed in the African slave trade. In 1619, when slavers first imported blacks into British Virginia, many of them, along with aboriginal Americans and whites, were indentured servants. After serving a period of indenture, they became freemen, capable of owning property. Based on the scant available documents, this apparent initial symmetry in treatment and the ensuing institution of exclusively black slavery indicates that racial discrimination only gradually became ingrained in colonial perceptions. Colonial manipulation of language was essential to this process. The first Virginia census designated persons with African ancestry "Negroes," in some cases, they were referred to by race alone without being named, already indicating some degree of dehumanization and objectification. The terminology helped stratify colonial society by distinguishing them from whites.

The ideological roots of racism, which made their way across the

British channel to England and across the Atlantic to America, were well developed before slavery was systematically employed in the colonies.[3] Europeans and American colonists relied on racial dogmas to justify the subjugation of blacks. Legal slavery only gradually seeped into the laws of the British colonies. During the 1950s and '60s, several historians, including Carl Degler, Winthrop Jordan, and Oscar and Mary Handlin, conclusively demonstrated that slavery developed slowly and was not widely accepted in colonial society until the eighteenth century. The linguistic casuistry of changing blacks from humans to chattel did not happen overnight; it took protracted socialization to deprive blacks of their civil rights. Both the ideology of race prejudice and the abject position into which blacks were placed reinforced stereotypes about their supposed inferiority.[4]

Preachers, politicians, newspaper writers, and businessmen waged a concerted effort to win the colonies' support for slavery and to establish laws protecting it. Slavery touched on virtually all aspects of colonial life. Eventually it became so overbearing a subject that the desire to retain it, coupled with states rights claims, played a vital role in bringing about the United States Civil War. Its advocates made slavery a socially acceptable institution by linking it to salvation and defining Africans as subhumans. Southerners were willing to die for slavery only after it had endeared itself to their minds through repetitive socialization. While blacks were considered unworthy of the most basic of human rights, slaver-traders believed themselves to be God's servants, bestowing Christian religion and meting out God's punishment on African heathens. Thus, they deemed slavery to be a divine institution, both redeeming and just.

Written works preaching Christianity's recognition and approval of slavery were common before and during America's colonial period. Their authors regarded blacks as spiritually inferior to whites. As early as 1578, the explorer George Best put forward his view that black skin color was a curse inherited by Ham's progeny. His scriptural support for black spiritual inferiority emerged as an ideological bud that blossomed into hereditary slavery laws. That slavery did not become legally permissible until 1660 indicates that these destructive messages preceded state-sanctioned discrimination. Best began his argument by arbitrarily deciding that Noah's family was white and,

> by course of nature should have begotten . . . white children. But the envie of our great and continuall enemy the wicked Spirite is such, that

as hee coulde not suffer our olde father Adam to live in the felicite and Angelike state wherin he was first created . . . so againe, finding at this flood none but a father and three sons living, hee so caused one of them to transgresse and disobey his fathers commaundement, that after him all his posteritie shoulde bee accursed.

Best went on to posit that Ham's son and "all his posteritie after him should be blacke and lothsome, that it might remaine a spectacle of disobedience to all the worlde. And of this blacke and cursed Chus[, who was Ham's son,] came all these blacke Moors which are in Africa."[5]

The earliest printed dispute about the merits of slavery appeared in an exchange between the anti-slavery theory of Samuel Sewell in *The Selling of Joseph* (1700), which argued against appraising blacks and Indians as cattle, and John Saffin's reply (1701). In his *Brief and Candid Answer*, Saffin supported slavery on the basis of the puritanical view that God had ordained differing "degrees and orders of men."[6] The predominant Calvinist view in early eighteenth century New England held that, as God's elect, whites had a religious right to own slaves. Its advocates held that mercy toward slaves meant instructing them in Christian doctrine but not emancipating them. For example, Cotton Mather, a prominent theologian, wrote in his diary that the slave given to him was a blessing from heaven.[7] The same year, 1706, Mather published a pamphlet advocating the Christian instruction of slaves, for "[w]ho can tell but that this Poor Creature may belong to the Election of God! Who can tell, but that God may have sent this Poor Creature into my Hands, that so One of the Elect. . . . Teach your *Negroes* the *Truths* of the Glorious Gospel."[8] Likewise, Anglican preachers justified the ownership of humans by directing masters to give their slaves religious instruction and to teach them the duty of obedience to their masters. Ministers did not hide their convictions from whites or blacks, telling both master and slave congregants that blacks were the accursed children of Ham. Preachers were essential in the highly religious puritanical culture for implanting the belief that black inferiority and involuntary servitude were part of God's will and plan of Election. Slavery, it was believed, was the atonement of Ham's children for the sins of their father.

Thus, the movement to convert slaves, while seemingly benign, also sustained the institution of slavery. While this organized effort helped improve the living conditions of slaves, it failed to question whether slavery was indeed part of the divine order. Preachers called on slaves to abide by their masters' commands and on owners to bring up blacks in Christian instruction and care for their physical well-being. This somewhat improved slaves' quality of life but did nothing to end the inequitable relationship between them and their masters.[9]

Some slavers denied their slaves religious instruction. These owners were divided into two camps. One side believed blacks were incapable of obtaining salvation because they were subhuman, while another opposed sermonizing to blacks for fear that slaves would then seek equal church membership. The first camp included those who argued that blacks and Native Americans should not be converted to Christianity because they were so different from Europeans: "[A] disingenuous . . . *Position* hath been formed;" wrote Morgan Godwyn, "and privately . . . handed to and again, which is this, That the *Negro's*, though in their Figure they carry some resemblances of Manhood, yet are indeed *no Men*."[10] Seeing these conditions in 1730 when he was visiting the colonies, Bishop George Berkeley said at the Society for the Propagation of the Gospel that "an irrational contempt of the blacks, as creatures of another species, who had no right to be instructed or admitted to the sacraments—[has] proved a main obstacle to the conversion of these poor people."[11] This Christian, pro-slavery attitude was persistent. Just before the American Revolution, Theodore Parsons wrote in support of slavery, taking it as undeniable and unquestionable "that the removal of the *Africans*, from the state of brutality, wretchedness, and misery . . . to this land of light, humanity, and Christian knowledge, is to them so great a blessing; however faulty any individuals may have been in point of unnecessary cruelty, practiced in this business."[12] These views propelled the forces of slavery; they had a significant effect on human lives. Colonists heard these doctrines since childhood, and they became a part of their perspectives about the appropriate treatment of blacks.

Anti-slavery ideas did not persuade most colonists to abandon the institution of slavery. Opposition to it in the colonies is traceable at least to the Reverend Morgan Godwyn's 1680 pamphlet, *The Negro's and Indian's Advocate*. Quakers were the chief proponents of abolition. The founder of Quakerism, George Fox, publicly argued, in 1671, that black servants in Barbados should be treated decently during the term of their servitude and eventually be freed. Likewise, in 1682, William Penn, in "Articles of the Free Society of Traders," advocated that black slaves should be freed after fourteen years.[13] The Society of Friends opened its meetings to blacks and urged masters to bring them. Numerous Quaker pamphlets, such as *Testimony against the Antichristian Practice of Making Slaves of Men* (1733) and *All Slave-Keepers that Keep the Innocent in Bondage, Apostates* (1738), were published in the early eighteenth century.[14]

The Methodists, too, played an important part in appealing to congregants against maintaining hereditary servants. John Wesley, the founder of Methodism, propounded against slavery in *Thoughts of Slavery* upon returning to England from the colonies in 1774. Methodism forbade its members from dealing in slaves and excluded slave owners from its ministry. The split between Northern and Southern Methodists took place because of their disagreement about whether slavery was a sin or sanctioned by the Bible.[15]

The words of religious theorists who advocated tolerance did not alter overall American relations with persons of African descent. Although they had truth on their side, abolitionists did not turn dominant social forces to their way of thinking. To the contrary, public oral and written defenses of slavery fixed the practice in colonial conduct. In the marketplace of ideas, pro-slavery thought won out. Later in this chapter, we will see how religious defenses of slavery continued to influence inequality for years after their introduction.

When blacks began converting to Christianity, supremacists developed a secular doctrine: now, blacks were innately defective in character and mentally subordinate to whites.[16] Such a linguistic framework gave further justification for retaining slavery, and the conceptual schema made it more respectable to treat blacks brutally. Blackness was cognitively connected with slavery and slavery with blackness. Racial differentiation was combined with ethnocentrism. Pro-slavery orators regarded blacks as intellectually and physically below white humans. They were also thought to have different psychological and emotional responses. Slave dealers justified separating families on the supposition that blacks did not have the same affinity for relatives as whites. Numerous colonial laws denied blacks the right to be educated in order to keep them docile. Most slaves did not know enough to show themselves capable of lucid thinking, and, untrained in the art of politics, they were unable to organize advocacy groups or mass rebellions. Differences in skin color, religion, culture, and appearance were therefore associated with a natural subordinacy.

Eventually, racial distinction came to be the chief attribute that was linked with slavery. In ancient times, everyone was subject to the terror of being stolen and forced into slavery; however, since the expansion of slavery in the sixteenth century, no Europeans have been hereditarily enslaved. In America, slaves were always people of darker color. Slavery was supported by hate propaganda, proclaiming white excellence and the supposed racial baseness of blacks. The state became complicit in this social hierarchy. Whites relied on state power to bolster their attitudes and enact laws enforcing them. The proponents of legislation supporting slavery disseminated the fiction that blacks were chattel property. The contradiction of a position that viewed people as property, on the one hand, and held the highest regard for human liberty, on the other, was not enough to destroy the institution.[17] In response to natural rights theorists who argued that all people are naturally equal, white supremacists enlisted theories purporting blacks' innate physical and mental inferiority.

Racial stratification served a central role in competitive U.S. society. Since blacks were thought to be essentially subservient, many whites believed they had a mutual interest in subordinating them. They all had a right to property, and if they did not already own slaves, then blacks were potential property, the right to which they would not allow to be abridged. By characterizing blacks as naturally inferior and biologically different, whites thought themselves justified in exploiting blacks as beasts of burden. But misethnic degradation was not exclusively economically motivated, it also served as a psychological crutch to affirm whites' self-esteem and sense of self-worth. Cotton Mather, who affirmed that blacks "are Men . . . and not Beasts" and pled that whites apply the golden rule in dealing with them, nevertheless considered them stupid in relation to their Christian instructors: "[T]heir *Stupidity* is a *Discouragement*. It may seem, unto as little purpose, to *Teach*, as to *wash an Æthopian*. But the greater their *Stupidity*, the greater must be our Application."[18]

Assaults on the humanity of blacks carried even worse repercussions than Mather's statement because they justified cruel treatment:

[T]hose who are concerned in the Man-Trade . . . have, some how or other, a Kind of confused Imagination, or half formed Thought, in their Minds, that the *Blacks* are hardly of the same Species with the white Men, but are Creatures of a Kind somewhat inferior: I say it is reasonable to suppose so; for I do not know how to think that any white Men could find in their Hearts, that the common Sentiments of Humanity would permit them to treat the black Men in that cruel, barbarous Manner in which they do treat them, did they think and consider that these have rational immortal Souls.[19]

This exposition of supremacism, written in 1762, was based on contemporary doctrines.

Several authors differentiated between whites and blacks by classifying Africans with simians. One anonymous author began his diatribe by painting numerous tribes with the same scurrilous brush, "the Negroes on the western cost of Africa, are the most stupid, beastly race of animals in human shape, of any in the whole world. The brutality, nastiness, indolence and other *criminal* propensities of the Hottentots, are a convincing proof of the truth of my assertion." These unsubstantiated generalities were followed by a self-aggrandizing assumption, "I would subdivide the Africans into five *classes*, as 1st, Negroes, 2d, Ourang Outangs, 3d, Apes, 4th, Baboons, and 5th, Monkeys . . . There never was a civilized nation of any other complexion than *white*."[20] Such arguments were not solely statements of opinion. They were intended to perpetuate the institution of slavery by justifying the denial of fundamental rights to persons with African ancestry. The same author considered the slave trade a "generous disinterested exertion of benevolence and philanthropy, which has been the principal means of heaping wealth and honours on Europeans and Americans, and rescuing many millions of Africans . . . and even compelling them to the enjoyment of a more refined state of happiness."[21]

Edward Long of Jamaica, reacting to the anti-slavery movement, coupled this line of thinking with a perverse twist. Long wrote that orangutans had sexual relations with African women. "[O]uran-outangs . . . sometimes endeavour to surprize and carry off Negroe women into their woody retreats in order to enjoy them." He believed orangutans and blacks had comparable proclivities: "The amorous intercourse betwen them may be frequent . . . and it is certain, that both races agree perfectly well in lasciviousness of disposition."[22] Long popularized the comparison of blacks with apes and helped develop it into scientific jargon. His ability to spread the imagined hereditary connection between humans and simians indicates the power of speech. Although Europeans had been aware of dark-skinned Africans for millennia and learned of apes around the Renaissance, no one had seriously suggested a biological connection between the two before the 1770s.[23] Once fixed in lay and expert minds, the image degraded blacks and made legal reform even more difficult.

Long also highlighted blacks' supposed incompatibility with the fictional white species. He wrote that Africans were correctly depicted in literature as having an "odious and despicable character; as proud, lazy, deceitful, thievish, addicted to all kinds of lust, and ready to promote them in others, incestuous, savage, cruel, and vindictive, devourers of human flesh, and quaffers of human blood, inconstant, base, and cowardly, devoted to all sorts of superstition; and, in short, to every vice that came in their way." Long determined that blacks were "incapable of making any progress in civility or science." He believed them devoid of any systematic morality or moral sense, barbarous with their children, having "no taste but for women." The attribution of these derogatory characteristics, cannibalistic practices, and heathen qualities identified all blacks as bestial and incapable of becoming civilized. Long concluded that "[t]hey are represented by all authors as the vilest of human kind, to which they have little more pretension of resemblance than what arises from their exterior."[24] Bernard Romans, a cartographer who also living during the Revolutionary age, wrote that "trechery, theft, stubbornness, and idleness" were part of the natural attributes of African blacks.[25] Arthur Lee, a Revolutionary hero, held similar points of view about blacks. In opposition to Adam Smith's attack on slave owners' malevolence, Lee showed his supremacist colors, writing that Africans were "a race the most detestable and vile that ever the earth produced. On the contrary . . . the inhabitants of the colonies are descended from worthy ancestors . . . a human, hospitable, and polished people."[26] Although Thomas Jefferson intellectually realized that slavery was unjust, during the course of his life he nevertheless augmented the number of slaves he owned. In part, Jefferson did not emancipate them because he believed blacks were "inferior to whites in the endowments both off body and mind. . . . This unfortunate difference of color, and perhaps of faculty is a powerful obstacle to the emancipation of these people."[27]

Attributing physical, mental, and moral inferiority to blacks was a convenient way to explain away social inequality. Beginning with the premise that everyone is created equal, as Jefferson wrote in the Declaration of Independence, mainstream America drew the illogical conclusion that all members of the group in power were equal and others were not. And that group consisted of white males. "In the South all men are equal," said Senator Albert G. Brown during debates on the Kansas-Nebraska Bill. "I mean, of course, white men; negroes are not men, within the meaning of the Declaration. If they were, Madison, and Jefferson, and Washington, all of whom lived and died slaveholders, never could have made it, for they never regarded negroes as their equals."[28]

There were, of course, compassionate whites with an eye for humanistic values, acknowledging the dignity and worth of the entire community rather than an elitist few. But their efforts were not enough to change American racial stratification.[29]

Supremacist literature constructed a reality that permeated American society and its Constitution, which countenanced blatant inequality. Expostulations on black inferiority helped create a social climate that tolerated and condoned chronic discrimination even though it so contradicted the aspirations of the American Revolution. Unable to reconcile slavery with the ideals of personal autonomy, rhetoriticians defined Negroes as subhumans to justify excluding them from the fruits of democratic republicanism.

The concerted efforts of business and agrarian interests to degrade blacks to the status of beasts of burden resulted in social norms that countenanced treating them as little better than domesticated animals. While downplaying black intellect, writers of the time conceded their physical prowess and even exaggerated it in order to more easily find excuses or taking advantage of them. If they had attributed equal intelligence to blacks, it would have undermined the premises of hate speech; but extolling the black body for its strength and stamina was similar to praising the bodies of cattle or mules for their power and endurance.

The process of divesting blacks of their humanity began in Africa, where slave traders treated them like animals, herding and buying them in open markets. Slaves were regarded in predominantly physical terms. The daily operations of plantations, with their owners' interests in wealth maximization, reinforced this mentality, since blacks were evaluated and esteemed in terms of their productivity. Masters branded their slaves with their initials to assure that they and everyone with whom they came in contact would perceive them not as people but as movable property. Buying, selling, trading, and lending slaves went on much like any livestock transaction: bargains were struck, prices were set, and values were determined by capacity to work for their owners' enrichment. Slaves became a form of property recognized by the Constitution. Slave owners then obtained legal justification for their inhumane practices.

Little concern was given for the lives of blacks, as evidenced by the unsanitary, despicably cramped, and often lethal conditions that they were forced to endure during transport from Africa through the Middle Passage.[30] The widespread belief that Africans were subhumans impacted how whites treated them. The adherents of legitimizing racist discourses were raised in a society which denied that blacks were worthy of basic human rights. This belief translated into actions. For instance, slave traders did not treat Africans with even minimum respect. A letter from the Guinea Company to Bartholomew Haward, dated December 9, 1651, exemplifies the callous treatment of African captives: "Put aboard you so many negers as yo'r ship can cary and for what shalbe wanting to supply the Cattel, as also to furnish you with victualls and provisions for the said negers and Cattel."[31]

Contemporary ideology had significant, life-changing consequences on the victims of racism. Considering blacks a different species than themselves, slave traders had no scruples about ignoring the emotional sufferings inflicted upon captives separated forever from their family members. Lacking compassion for those whose lives they robbed, apologists of slavery believed that, "[w]ith regard to the separation of husbands and wives, parents and children, . . . Negroes are themselves both perverse and comparatively indifferent about this matter."[32] Parents were often separated from children during purchasing frenzies. The heart-wrenching scenes elicited no mercy from the captors. The laws of many states made slaves' offspring the "property" of slave owners, lending exploitation an air of legitimacy through legal sanctions.

Plantation owners must have daily seen the spuriousness of their views, and yet the prevailing ideology so powerfully affected them that they could overlook the most glaring realities. Blacks worked, spoke, cried, and laughed like whites. Daily interactions between whites and blacks clearly indicated their common humanity. The urge for freedom was so evident in blacks' conversations and relations that it caused in whites a fairly constant fear of slave rebellions. The personhood of their slaves must have been evident, but widespread prejudices helped them put on blinders to the injustices of racial stratification.

Slave society gave no recognition to the black family. Virile black men were used like bulls and studs, even hired out by masters for breeding with female slaves on other plantations. Black women and girls were in particular danger; often they were the objects of predatory sex acts by slaveholders. Southern whites believed that the chief purpose of black unions was to multiply the number of their slaves. In some states, slave codes prevented blacks from entering into contracts and, since marriage is a contractual relationship, blacks were not permitted to marry there. Even where marriages between slaves were lawful, owners could dissolve the unions by selling one of the spouses. Most owners were more interested in their financial situations than in sustaining stable family units. Often, family cohesion was complicated by the separate ownership of wives and husbands. In those circumstances, a slave owner desiring to keep a family together could not prevent the other owner from deciding to sell one of the spouses to a distant plantation. These decisions were the outward manifestations of a doctrine that advocated maintaining differing moral norms toward whites and blacks.

The black slave trade was a vestige of ancient despotism that continued to sway European minds in spite of philosophical, political, and cultural advances. The underlying injustices of slavery denied fundamental rights and contented lives to a group of people solely based on their skin color. They were denied access to the means of accomplishing their hopes and aspirations, not for lack of necessary qualifications, but because of a prevailing dogma. Whites abridged their slaves' autonomy rights, forbidding them to make decisions about essential aspects of their lives. They forbade slaves to marry whomever they chose, to associate with friends, neighbors and spouses, to pursue their choice of professions, and to travel. Hate speech was the means for spreading supremacist sentiments and attitudes. Once pro-slavery theories took on systematic structures, they were used time and again and had long-term consequences, ultimately rending American society into warring camps. As one of the greatest historians of the pro-slavery movement, William S. Jenkins, put it: "The foundation for each branch of the pro-slavery theory was laid during this formative period, and in the years to come the many hackneyed arguments were applied over and over against in varied form."[33]

Teleological views also gained prominence in the pro-slavery movement. They represent an interesting example of how self-serving injustice can be expressed in academic-sounding rhetoric. During a debate held at the 1773 commencement at Harvard University, one of the interlocutors argued that slavery was ethically justifiable based on act utilitarian and racial superiority grounds. The speaker took it as axiomatic that the happiness of the community members was the epitome of social accomplishments. From this premise, he reasoned that it was ethical for the majority to increase their welfare and liberties by diminishing the freedoms of minority groups.[34] Consequentialist thought was also popular in the upper echelons of political circles. Governor Stephen Miller told the South Carolina legislature in 1829, "Slavery is not a national evil; on the contrary, it is a national benefit. The agricultural wealth of the country is found in those states owning slaves, and a great portion of the revenue of the government is derived from the products of slave labor."[35] Similarly, Thomas R. Dew asserted that it was important to perpetuate slavery since manumission might be economically disastrous for the whole South. To the economic argument Dew added supremacist overtones, asserting that free blacks were less productive than slaves since they were "worthless and indolent . . . the very *drones* and *pests* of society . . . [their] worthlessness and degradation will stimulate [them] to deeds of rapine and vengeance."[36] These types of act utilitarian rationales justified the perpetuation of slavery because it supposedly maximized the wealth of their proponents. In this scheme, minority rights were sacrificed for the happiness of the majority. The lives of one group of people, they believed, could rightly be sacrificed for the satisfaction of the group holding the reins of power.

Slavery's apologists in the United States also denied that abolition was legally possible here. Many argued that the Constitution reflected a compromise between Southern and Northern interests. The South conceded some of its states-rights claims because it was assured that the institution of slavery would remain untouched by the national government. It was therefore unconstitutional, so the argument went, for the federal government to meddle with the peculiar Southern institution. No provision for the abolition of slavery was ever written into the Constitution. In fact, some of the signatories of the Constitution owned slaves before and after the Philadelphia convention; therefore, slavery's defenders believed, they must have expected to retain the property right to continue owning them. Strict constructionists claimed constitutional provisions, and the protections under the Bill of Rights applied only to those people who entered into the political compact and to their posterity. Africans were not then part of the body politic, had nothing to do with writing or ratifying the Constitution, and therefore had no claims to its protections and guarantees. Another school of thought conceded that the Constitution protected men's natural rights. It justified curtailing blacks' fundamental rights by maintaining that blacks were not "men" under the Constitution, otherwise the framers would have freed them.

Abolitionists advanced counterarguments to these positions, speaking in terms of emancipation rather than conversion. Many of their ideas were based on natural rights theory, which had made fly the sparks of the American Revolution. They believed everyone, regardless of his or her race, had an inalienable right to liberty, which no government or individual could abrogate. It was evident that slavery contradicted the principles on which the new nation stood. Abolitionists maintained that "[l]iberty is the right of every human creature, as soon as he breathes the vital air. And no human law can deprive him of that right, which he derives from the law of nature."[37] Similarly, David Cooper, a Quaker from New Jersey, insisted in 1783 that blacks and whites shared equally in the immutable laws of nature.[38] Some legislatures enacted these principles. Rhode Island passed emancipation provisions in June 1774. Three years later, the Massachusetts assembly declared that slavery was a "disgrace to all good governments, more especially to such who are struggling . . . in favor of the natural unalienable rights of human nature."

Leading American Revolutionaries, such as James Otis, who led opposition to the Stamp Act; Thomas Paine, the author of *Common Sense*; John and Abigail Adams, the second president and his First Lady; and Gouverneur Morris, one of the chief architects of the Constitution, argued against maintaining innocent people in bondage. Former President James Madison, a slave owner himself, recognized that slavery was corrupt and inhumane. Manumission societies spread their views throughout America. Future Supreme Court Justice John Jay presided over the New York Society for Promoting the Manumission of Slaves. Elder statesman Benjamin Franklin in 1787 was elected president of the Pennsylvania Society for Promoting the Abolition of Slavery, the Relief of Negroes Unlawfully Held in Bondage. The same year, at the constitutional convention, George Mason argued against continuing the slave trade.[39] None of this, however, was enough to dislodge the power of plantation owners and slave traders whose interests prevailed in spite of and in opposition to the lofty ideals of the Revolution. Although abolitionism had prominent advocates, slavery continued to flourish and entrench itself in U.S. society. The inductive lesson from this is that the widespread availability of egalitarian and humanistic ideas does not always bring about social well-being and equal rights. Influential persons with financial and psychosocial stakes in slavery dominated the politics on this issue. Truth about the equal humanity of whites and blacks was iterated in the printed and oral exchange of ideas but was not enough to end the institution, particularly given the long-standing beliefs about black inferiority that had been ingrained over several generations.

The predominating belief held that blacks were outsiders, living, eating, and staying warm at the mercy of their owners. Even free blacks were subject to the whims of states that could revoke and grant them political rights as it suited the interests of powerful whites.

Religious arguments for black hereditary slavery, which we first encountered in the late sixteenth century, continued to dominate popular discourse in the years leading up to the Civil War. Their persistence indicates the long-term effects of hate propaganda once it has spread into common discourse. In the antebellum United States, religious dogma resembled that which was established before the Revolution. Thomas Cooper of South Carolina College published a pamphlet in 1825 defending the institution of slavery by drawing attention to the lack of proscriptions against it in the Bible. He further supported the right to own slaves based on slavery's recurrent appearance throughout history. Biblical justifications of slavery also continued to flourish. Thornton Stringfellow, in *Scriptural & Statistical Views in Favor of Slavery* (1856), cited biblical passages to show that slavery was an institution sanctioned by God. At the threshold of war, Benjamin M. Palmer championed slavery from the pulpit. His view was that Providence had instructed the South to

conserve and to perpetuate the institution of domestic slavery as now existing. . . . [F]or us . . . the duty is plain of conserving and transmitting the system of slaver . . . we hold this trust from God, and in its occupancy we are prepared to stand or fall as God may appoint. . . . [Duty] establishes the nature and solemnity of our present trust, to preserve and transmit our existing system of domestic servitude, with the right, unchallenged by man, to go and root itself wherever Providence and nature may carry it. This trust we will discharge in the face of the worst possible peril. Though war be the aggregation of all evils, yet, should the madness of the hour appeal to the arbitration of the sword, we will not shrink even from the baptism of fire.[40]

Even after suffering defeat at the hands of the Union Army, John Saffin, a colonial Congregationalist, continued invoking the puritanical creed of Election to excuse the practices of slavery. Saffin referred to chapter 12 of Apostle Paul's first epistle to the Corinthians for the following conclusion: "God hath ordained different degrees and orders of men, some to be High & Honourable, some to be Low and Despicable," some to be masters, "some to be born Slaves, and so to remain during their lives."[41]

Religious stereotypes reinforced and strengthened racism for centuries after their introduction. Religious doctrines, propounded by fallible people, are often unquestionably believed because of their allegedly divine origin. Blacks did not look like the stereotypical European image of Jesus, who, although a Middle Eastern Jew, was depicted by artists as white. People closer to the prototypical images of Jesus, which of course were figments of artists' imaginations, were considered closer to God's image and likeness. All those people were white males. Misethnicity was part of a broad conceptual construct in which the full humanness of blacks was denied because they did not match the popular image of the children of God.[42]

Just as with racist religious views, antebellum pseudoscientific ethnographies, which did so much to imbibe Southerners with a sense of justice in their cause, were based on seventeenth- and eighteenth-century beliefs about the existence of *Homo sapien* hierarchies, with whites on the top rung and blacks on the bottom. The hereditary circumstances of blacks were painted in bleak and unalterable terms. When propagated by persons with scientific backgrounds, ethnology took on an aura of experientially proven fact. This school of thought deemed Negroes to be members of a different animal species that was behaviorally, intellectually, and physically inferior to whites, the same argument Edward Long had made in the eighteenth century. Likewise, Josiah C. Nott, a physician from Mobile, Alabama, in *Two Lectures on the History of the Caucasian and Negro Races* (1844), maintained that whites and blacks were from the same genus but comprised unalterably different species. As blacks could not change their skin color, regardless of the climate where they lived, neither could they alter their primitive ignorance, regardless of how civilized their surroundings.

The notion of an immutable black subserviency to whites fostered an atmosphere of hopelessness for the future prospects of blacks. Bigots could rely on this view to excuse their discriminatory actions and blame blacks' degraded circumstances on their nature. The ideology created not only a system of beliefs that changed people's perceptions, but also influenced their behaviors by limiting the range of duties owed to creatures they thought unworthy of human compassion. George S. Sawyer, a protagonist for racial species plurality, went so far as to question the value of dealing fairly with blacks at all: "We would not decry or discourage missionary labors among them, if they can by any means ameliorate their condition. . . . But we fear that they are 'casting their pearls before swine.'"[43] Scientific experiments were organized to study black bodies, brains, organs, and physiognomy. Just as Long before him, Samuel Cartright, in 1857, compared black people with simians. After joining his voice to the argument that blacks were a "different species from the man of Europe or Asia," Cartright went on to disparage black intellectual abilities through racialist conjecture: "[T]heir faces are proportionally larger than their crania, instead of smaller, as in the other two species of the genus man." Cartright also advocated the premise that blackness was a permanent biological handicap that permeates persons of African descent.[44] Scientists like Samuel G. Morton believed Negro brains to be smaller and lighter than Caucasians'. Louis Agassiz, one of the leading nineteenth-century biologists, also did much to mislead public opinions about blacks: "A peculiar conformation characterizes the brain of an adult negro. Its development never gets beyond that observable in the Caucasian boyhood. And, besides other singularities, it bears a striking resemblance, in several particulars to the brain of an ourang-outang."[45] The writings of prominent scientists bolstered misethnicity. False scientific findings were used to confirm the plural theory of mankind and justify the paternalistic self-righteousness and misguided benevolence associated with black enslavement.

Ethnological rationalizations validated and reinforced beliefs about black inferiority. They sought to show that blacks are intellectually and developmentally inferior to whites and then to derive the non sequitur that blacks do not have the same innate rights to live unmolested, autonomous lives. Ethnologists were following a long tradition begun in 1701 by Judge John Saffin, who waxed poetic in his commitment to institutionalized slavery:

> Cowardly & Cruel are those Blacks Innate,
> Prone to Revenge, Imp of inveterate hate.
> He that exasperates them, soon espies

Mischief & Murder in their very eyes.
Libidinous, Deceitful, False & Rude,
The Spume Issue of Ingratitude.[46]

Supremacists on both sides of the Mason-Dixon Line denied blacks opportunities, claiming they were innately incapable of any but the most base sentiments and actions. Thomas R. R. Cobb, who later became a general in the Confederate Army, wrote that blacks did not even have natural sentiments for their children or spouses: "His natural affection is not strong, and consequently he is cruel to his own offspring, and suffers little by separation from them. . . . Fidelity to the marriage relation they do not understand and do not expect, neither in their native country nor in a state of bondage." The Negro character, Cobb continued, is lascivious, and blacks are prone to rape.[47]

Prominent leaders spread misethnic myths and snuffed out all hope of a truly equitable society. Common people clung to their words to confirm the conviction that as whites they were naturally better than blacks and had God-given rights to dole out whimsical punishments, separate families based on economic considerations, and prevent the development of any creative impulse not exploitable by the white majority.

Politicians employed both religious and scientific arguments to maintain power and preserve Southern institutions. They saw slavery as fundamental to the Southern identity. The fairness of slavery was no longer an issue for them. In their form of doublespeak, it was abolitionists who sought to deprive Southerners of their natural right to own property, not they who had so deprived others of fundamental liberties. The "positive good" theory of slavery emerged as a leading form of persuasion that galvanized pro-slavery forces. Charismatic leaders spewed this doctrine to the masses, who swallowed the hateful morsels. It gave them a common cause for which to act and invoked their sense of patriotism to the South and to the centuries-old institution their ancestors had done so much to establish. By cauterizing the present to the past, the supporters of racism became an indoctrinated and emotionally charged force with which the North would eventually have to reckon.

William Grayson, who served in the U.S. Congress, argued that slavery subdued blacks' "savage heart."[48] John C. Calhoun, who at various times served as Secretary of State, Secretary of War, Vice President, and Senator, epitomized the positive good theory. He merged age-old racist ideology coupled with the charisma necessary to sway popular opinion.

"[I]n the present state of civilization," he said in a speech directed against abolitionist petitions,

> where two races of different origin . . . are brought together, the relation now existing in the slaveholding States between the two, is, instead of an evil, a good—a positive good I fearlessly assert that the existing relation between the two races in the South . . . forms the most solid and durable foundation on which to rear free and stable political institutions.[49]

Calhoun combined the fictitious view of biologically distinct races having varying physical and intellectual abilities with the self-serving conclusion that it was better for whites and blacks that the latter be enslaved in the United States than free in Africa:

> [T]he European race has rapidly increased in wealth and numbers, and, at the same time, has maintained an equality, at least morally and intellectually, with their brethren of the non-slaveholding States, [meanwhile] the African race has multiplied with not less rapidity, accompanied by great improvement, physically and intellectually. . . . To destroy the existing relations, would be to destroy this prosperity, and to place the two races in a state of conflict which must in the expulsion or extirpation of one or the other.[50]

The idea that deprivation of human rights profited Africans was recurrent in his speeches: "Never before has the black race of Central Africa, from the dawn of history to the present day, attained a condition so civilized and so improved, not only physically, but morally and intellectually."[51] Furthermore, in a clear case of verbal obfuscation, Calhoun presented slavery as one of the Union's free institutions.[52]

The supposed economic windfalls of slavery were also part of the proslavery dogma, and Southerners' dread of falling materially behind their Northern neighbors enlisted passionate support. Southern industry functioned on the sweat of slaves. Even those who did not own any slaves thought they had an interest in the institution. The folk belief in the economic benefits of slave labor turns out to have been as spurious as all other dogmas built on misethnicity. Rigorous contemporary studies indicate that slavery was economically inefficient and regressive. Pioneers in this field, such as Cassius M. Clay, Hilton Helper, Frederick Olmsted, and John Cairnes, differed in their approaches but agreed that the underlying problems of slavery brought on a fundamental depredation of Southern economy.

To contemporary pro-slavery proponents, however, slavery looked economically necessary and socially and morally justifiable. South Carolina's Governor James H. Hammond unapologetically argued before the U.S. Senate that white civilization was allowed to benefit from an unrecompensed black workforce: "In all social systems there must be a class to do the menial duties, to perform the drudgery of life. That is, a class requiring but a low order of intellect and but little skill. Its requisites are vigor, docility, fidelity."[53]

A particularly influential tenet of antebellum hate speech was the belief that slavery contributed to overall equality. This theory, like so many others, measured social well-being by the majority group's welfare, failing to take into account overall good, which includes in its equation respect for the individual rights of persons regardless of whether they are members of the majority. The thought was that even poor white people with no slaves had an interest in maintaining slavery since they or their children might one day be slave owners. Thus, many Southerners thought they had an actual or potential property interest in slaves. This line of reasoning probably got its start from Calhoun's 1820 response to John Quincy Adams's attack on slavery. Calhoun spoke of slavery as producing "an unvarying level among" whites. By the middle of the century, that ideology had taken off and was commonly argued within the halls of Congress. In 1842, Representative Campbell of South Carolina warned about the course the South might take against attempts to end slavery, portending the Civil War. He addressed himself to Adams's repeated assaults on the gag rule, which forbade anyone from arguing against slavery on the floor of Congress. Slavery, Campbell believed,

> produces equality and nurtures a spirit of liberty among the citizen population of a country. . . . Where domestic slavery does not exist, menial and domestic offices are performed by a portion of the poor among the citizen population; and this degradation of a few affects the respectability of the entire class to which they belong. . . . [T]he free-born and laboring poor, although perhaps more virtuous than their rich neighbors, are treated as inferiors. . . . Equality among its citizens is the cornerstone of a republic . . . an entire exemption from the performance of menial and degrading offices produces equality.[54]

Likewise, Congressman Henry Wise of Virginia contended that "[t]he principle of slavery was a leveling principle; it was friendly to equality. Break down slavery, and you would with the same blow destroy the great Democratic principle of equality among men."[55]

Jefferson Davis, the future Confederate president, also held the view that whites were lifted to a state of equality through the degrading treatment of blacks:

> I say that the lower race of human beings that constitute the substratum of what is termed the slave population of the South, elevates every white man in our community. . . . It is the presence of the lower caste, those lower by their mental and physical organization, controlled by the higher intellect of the white man, that gives this superiority to the white laborer. Menial services are not performed there by the white man.

Davis also accepted the divine retribution theory of slavery, which had by then been long interwoven into rhetoric.[56] Slavery was consciously exploited to avoid conflict. It was a safety valve for diffusing class tensions. It drew upon doctrines emotionally charged by years of use.

The English linguistic paradigm that formed the conceptual framework supporting slavery was highly evolved by the Civil War. Despite the utter incompatibility of slavery with the Constitution's protection of liberties, ideology denigrating blacks became so ingrained in popular Southern culture that it served as a catalyst for secession. The passion to retain that peculiar Southern institution at all cost was considered a noble sentiment since thereby the "equality" among whites could be maintained and a race war averted. Hate speech reenforced the belief in black inferiority and the rationalizations behind depriving blacks of their rights. As historian William L. Miller recently pointed out, studying the arguments for and against slavery in the years leading up to the American Civil War exposes the driving forces behind the ensuing combat.[57]

Racist classifications, repeated from the days of slave trading to the Civil War era, played a significant role in subordinating blacks. In fact, the longer and more often slavery's defenders repeated their messages, the more fanatical a following they drew, until people were ready to die to retain their legal right to reduce blacks to chattel. The model for slavery derived from ideology first disseminated during the colonial period. The framework for laws depriving blacks of their freedoms grew out of the biblical, religious, and pseudoscientific writings that blanketed the colonies. They fabricated black inferiority and raised the fear of violent uprisings to a frenzied pitch. This kept power in the hands of whites who were dependent on but unwilling to compensate their labor force.

A widening circle of scientists and anthropologists began lending their support to theories purporting that slavery was a natural institution, reflecting biological realities. In time, blackness became associated with slavery and slavery with blackness. The debate about slavery was based in large part on seventeenth- and eighteenth-century thought. Whites came to think of blacks as servile creatures, forgetting or refusing to recognize that it was inequitable treatment that had made them virtually incapable of rising from their degrading predicament.

No amount of abolitionist literature could move pro-slavery forces from their ideological positions. Even the eloquent and impassioned voices of public figures like Representative John Quincy Adams and Senator Francis Gillette were not enough. Gillette reminded his colleagues that they were to blame for the state of black abjectness:

> Ignorant! Who has doomed them to ignorance? Debased! Who has sunken them to debasement? They, be it understood, who have brought all the sanctions of law and custom to crush them; who have snatched from them the key of knowledge, and closed every avenue to their elevation and advancement. Put out the eyes of men, and then tell them scornfully that they are blind. Extinguish the Promethean fire in their souls, and then tell them tauntingly that they are darkened and debased.[58]

But his words were unheard for the din of propaganda. Instead, the racist ideology of hereditary servitude became a chief unifying force that gave vent to the Civil War.[59] It took the War, and not rational argument, to end the institution of slavery.

4

The Politics of Savagery and Indian Removal

Despite its self-image as a fair republican democracy, the U.S. has, at times, sanctioned the persecution of outgroups. Like derogatory ideologies about blacks, images depicting indigenous Americans as culturally inferior had their origins in early colonial society and left a deep imprint on the American worldview. The widespread acceptance of labels that denied the human dignity of Native Americans contributed to government-condoned injustices committed against them.

European misconceptions about Indians influenced their relations with the peoples they encountered. Even though it was Europeans who crossed the Atlantic to find new homes, they believed native tribes were more migratory than themselves. For the most part, colonists failed to investigate aboriginal ownership customs. They relied on inaccurate stereotypes to justify settling on aboriginal lands, claiming that native peoples possessed but did not own them. The reality of American life was far more complicated than they imagined. The concept of ownership differed substantially from tribe to tribe and from one geographic region to another. Aboriginal land tenure and ownership interests included improved and unimproved hunting sites, fishing areas, wild plant gathering fields, and agricultural tracts. Individuals, clans, communities, or tribes, made up of several communities, owned land and productive areas. As for inheritance, there were both matrilineal and patrilineal cultures. So, the colonists' categorization of Native Americans as nomads was far from accurate.[1]

John Winthrop, the first governor of Massachusetts Bay, and other arriving colonists presumed Indians were transient and unsettled. To them this meant colonists were welcome to take lands that were not then occupied, so long as enough remained for the natives. Winthrop defended this perspective against those who were opposed to entering lands owned by indigenous peoples. Natives, Winthrop wrote, "inclose noe Land, neither have any setled habytation, nor any tame Cattle to improve the Land by. . . . If we leave them sufficient for their use, we may lawfully take the rest. . . . God hath consumed the Natives with a great Plauge in those partes, so as there be few Inhabitantes lefte." Europeans formulated images of aborigines that were materially and morally self-serving. Whites believed the peoples among whom they settled lacked refinement and thus thought it their right to impose European ideas of land ownership, a puritanical work ethic, and the Christian religion on the Native Americans. Others presumed that natives would eventually abandon their traditions. Henry Knox, George Washington's Secretary of War, expressed the latter view, assuming that if the United States followed a just and humane policy toward the Indians, they would eventually adopt American customs and civilization.[2]

Rather than investigate the differences among the numerous tribes living on the North American continent, many colonists and explorers dubbed all native peoples "savages." This, we will see later in this chapter, helped establish widely accepted misrepresentations of native cultures and led to colonial and American policies consistent with defamatory images.

Early English writings depicted Native Americans as either having no religion or practicing satanism, having no ownership interest in lands, and disinterested in land cultivation. By 1609, Robert Johnson was helping spread the myth of the benevolent savage: Virginia, he wrote, "is inhabited with wild and savage people . . . they have no Arts nor Science, yet . . . they are generally very loving and gentle, and doe entertaine and relieve our people with great kindnesse."[3] The concept of the noble savage overgeneralized characteristics of peoples with varying cultures, languages, and traditions, depicting them as a childlike group in need of European guidance. This depiction gradually became firmly embedded in American culture.

Early seventeenth-century contacts between settlers and Native Americans were primarily predicated on commercial relations. The natives taught settlers reliable agricultural skills and pointed out effective hunting methods and abundant hunting grounds. Trade among them was common, and the settlers might not have survived in the new climate without guidance from their neighbors. Aborigines also profited from this exchange through the acquisition of products such as guns, which made hunting easier. As Professor Karen Kupperman has pointed out, based on these interactions, a few sixteenth and early seventeenth-century authors did write about the Native Americans' complex and organized social schemes.[4]

Competition for natural resources and fertile lands eventually altered the neighbors' attitudes toward each other. As the colonists became more settled and secure, they required less instruction. Negative depictions of Native Americans spurred the European drive for conquest. A linguistic framework developed side by side with the noble savage depictions that negatively stereotyped native inhabitants and eased European consciences about encroaching on aboriginal lands. Indian haters relied on dehumanizing images to encourage conflict. Samuel Purchas, an influential English compiler of travel books, in 1625 disparaged the Virginia Indians as being "so bad people, having little of Humanitie but shape, ignorant of Civilitie, of Arts, of Religion; more brutish than the beasts they hunt, more wild and unmanly than that unmanned wild Countrey, which they range rather than inhabite; captivated also to Satan's tyranny in foolish pieties, mad impieties, wicked idlenesse, busie and bloudy wickednesse."[5] Others similarly described Indian life-styles as little higher than those of wild animals. Writing about southeastern tribes, Henry Hawks stated, "They are soone drunke, and given to much beastlinesse, and void of all goodnesse."[6] Settlers regarded Native Americans as religiously and politically unrefined and decided to "humanize" them. Indian hatred aided in categorizing tribes and their members into a monolithic group and a common enemy. The images painted by these verbal sketches allowed colonists to dismiss the obvious distinctions between tribes they encountered.

To explorers and colonists, Indians represented their primitive past. Whether they were portrayed as noble or bloodthirsty savages, Indians were considered inferiors. The more positive depictions represented primitive peoples as being naturally moral but lacking in culture, while the negative ones represented them as cruel heathens whose actions had to be avenged. Colonists believed the Europeanization of America was a moral and benevolent way to save the Indians from their ignorance. Rather than helping Native Americans acquire contemporary metallurgical and pharmaceutical innovations that could have improved their lives, settlers preferred to wrest their lands. Demeaning images were invoked for self-serving ends. Stereotypes of Indians as ignorant about agronomy and as murderous wild men, intent on wreaking death and destruction, legitimized colonial violence and expropriation. Repeated frontier aggressions were excused by colonists as necessary antidotes against the savagism that resided in the popular mind. Thus arose the frontier saying, "They ain't no game like Injuns. Nossir, no game like Injuns!"[7]

Authors persistently represented Native Americans as deficient in European ways rather than as possessing their own positive customs and institutions. Multiple early writings spawned an oversimplified theoretical framework about aboriginal American cultures. Proliferating negative labels directly affected colonial interactions with them. Regardless of the many contacts between settlers and neighboring tribes, which made evident their diverse traditions and norms, colonists chose to homogenize them with broad brushstrokes. No matter how varied were their languages, tools, methods of transportation, and diets, they were all Indians as far as the settlers were concerned. "Indian" provided a definition pregnant with meaning. It suggested that aboriginal peoples were devoid of social sophistication and moral scruples.[8] It simplified what would have otherwise been a difficult task, distinguishing the many peoples living on the North American continent.

William Robertson's *History of America*, published in numerous editions, provided its many readers with a homogeneous impression of Indians. This highly influential work helped shape the image of Indians in the mind's eye of its readers. Robertson represented the Scottish historical school, which viewed human history as progressively developmental from the primitive to the complexly cultural. His depiction of Indians was intended to reveal humanity's upward progress. Indian communities, Robertson wrote, were a rich source of study on the rudimentary stages of human societies. They lived in a "state of primeval simplicity . . . strangers to industry and labour, ignorant of arts, and almost unacquainted with property, enjoying in common the blessings which flowed spontaneously from the bounty of nature."[9] This work was significant in disseminating an inaccurate portrayal of all tribes as an uncultured monolith and in rationalizing the United States' paternalistic treatment of them. It entirely failed to reflect on scientific advances, such as Mayan mathematics and astronomy. Neither did Robertson seem to be aware of property and inheritance rights, which existed among tribes in a variety of formulations. Advanced agricultural societies, like the Mississippian peoples, about whom the Spanish explorer Ferdinando De Soto wrote in the sixteenth century, were also ignored.

Missionary deprecations of Indian religious worship presented a more adamant line of attack. Colonists commonly considered Native Americans satanic and their medicine men witchcraft-practicing sorcerers. Early British settlers believed that civilizing and Christianizing Indians was part of their mission in the New World. They conceptualized themselves not merely as explorers out for fortune but also as propagators of the Good News abroad. The London Company's charter, authorizing the founding of Virginia, proclaimed as one of the colony's purposes: "[P]ropagating of Christian Religion to such people, as yet live in darkness and miserable ignorance of the true knowledge and worship of God."[10]

Indians became the colonists' supernatural enemies. Puritans saw themselves in a battle with Satan's children, victory over whom signaled their election to heaven. They interpreted the decimation of aboriginal tribes, during the contact period, through diseases as God's punishment visited on unbelievers. As John Winthrop saw it, "[the natives] are neere all dead of the small Poxe, so as the Lord hathe cleared our title to what we possess."[11] There is a shrill joy in Winthrop's tone vindicating the colonists' land acquisitions and the death of all those who might have possessed better title to it: God killed the Indians so that his birthright, the Elect, could have a little more room to do their farming and building. The death of Indians bolstered the Puritans' sense of self-righteousness, painting for them a picture of God's supposed retribution against infidels and indicating the impiety of religions different from their own. Indians became the mythologized adversaries of God, standing in the way of pious progress. Those who did not die from diseases could periodically be beaten in skirmishes, as Puritans had better weapons which, they presumed, God had granted them for mortal punishment. By the end of the seventeenth century, Puritans had destroyed almost all Native American groups living within their self-determined boundaries. It became easier to propagandize the savage Indian image with most of the southern New England tribes swept away through warfare, enslavement, plague, and religious conversion.[12]

The fraud and theft that were being committed against Native Americans were glaringly clear to some contemporaries. Robert Beverley's *History and Present State of Virginia* (1705) faulted both the colonists and natives for their violent relations and noted that "[t]he *English* have taken away great part of their Country, and consequently made everything less plenty amongst them."[13]

There were, of course, voices expressing admiration for Native American culture, but for the most part they were disregarded and unheeded. William Penn, a Quaker and founder of the Pennsylvania colony, wrote with interest about Native American languages, their family institutions, and governments.[14] The great American statesman Benjamin Franklin, himself a speculator in frontier lands across the Appalachian mountains, wrote about Native Americans with some admiration. He spoke well of their education system while recognizing that it differed from the European model. More importantly for race relations, Franklin represented Native Americans as friendly to their white neighbors rather than as bloodthirsty savages.[15] These ideas, however, did not filter into mainstream American culture.

The general trend among conquerors and explorers was to negatively depict Native Americans and thereby justify unlimited land grabs. Instead of realizing Native Americans were individuals with natural rights, colonists thought of them as an undifferentiated group of savages. This perspective made it psychologically and emotionally easier for settlers to snuff out Native Americans' property rights. Whites rationalized land expropriations by claiming that they, as farmers, had better title to lands than the primitive, hunter-gatherer natives. Agrarianism was considered more civilized than hunting, and white intrusion onto tribal lands was justified as a means of domesticating the Indians and leading them out of primitive darkness. Proponents of this theory viewed Indian culture as an impediment to human progress and thought Indians were obligated to cede lands for the sake of progress. Future president William Henry Harrison asked rhetorically, "Is one of the fairest portions of the globe to remain in a state of nature, the haunt of a few wretched savages, when it seems destined by the Creator to give support to a large population and to be the seat of civilization?"[16] Such sentiments allowed whites to overlook Native American horticulture even as they took over Native American farmlands. They desired the natives' clearings and crop lands because those were easier to cultivate for their own produce than to hew out fields from the thick forests that then covered the eastern United States. Thomas Jefferson, during his first presidential term, hit upon a scheme for keeping Native Americans dependent on the United States and acquiring more territory: "Establish . . . a factory . . . for furnishing them all the necessaries and comforts they may wish "spirituous liquors excepted," encouraging these and especially their leading men, to run into debt for these beyond their individual means of paying; and whenever in that situation, they will always cede lands to rid themselves of debt."[17] The ideology of western expansion coupled with the view that Indians were mere hunters combined to form a powerful cognitive construct that galvanized frontiersmen in driving many tribes out of existence and thereby acquiring their lands.

The colonists argued that as hunters Native Americans had no fixed ownership interests, but rather migrated with the game and merely occupied lands through which they passed. This often repeated characterization blinded the American social consciousness to the fact that some indigenous tribes had developed farming to such an extent that they helped pilgrims survive in the New World by teaching them how to grow maize and other crops. The precursors of the very tribes the settlers pushed off their lands had taught their ancestors many of the farming techniques still in use during the eighteenth century. The popular image of Indians as hunters made it easier to ignore that by the 1800s most eastern tribes, in whose midst much of U.S. population then lived, were predominantly agrarian and settled.[18]

Chief Justice John Marshall's opinion in *Johnson v. M'Intosh* acknowledged but nevertheless maintained the common disregard for Native American human and property rights.[19] The first in a series of cases Marshall drafted on Indian rights, known as the Marshall trilogy, *Johnson* interpreted and established an important precedent about Native American land rights. The Chief Justice maintained that Indians only had occupancy rights to their lands. European sovereigns, on the other hand, had the exclusive right to extinguish Indian title and, thereafter, to transfer property interests to grantees. Marshall decided that indigenous peoples had no right to title against the federal government. He thought European nations had "discovered" American territory and, therefore, became the land's exclusive sovereigns. Whatever rights Indians possessed were extinguished by the conquering states, which then suffered native inhabitants to live among them. He justified the conquests, stating that "the tribes of Indians inhabiting this country were fierce savages . . . whose subsistence was drawn chiefly from the forest."[20] Rather than leaving the land a wilderness and allowing indigenous people to retain their liberty, the Europeans enforced their "pompous claims . . . by the sword."[21] Although Marshall recognized that the United States expansionist policy was "opposed to natural right[s],"[22] he nevertheless held that Indians only had a possessory, but not fee simple, interest in the lands European nations occupied. The accepted "legitimizing narratives"[23] that were used by whites to justify their cruelties against the aboriginal peoples of North America influenced even great thinkers like Marshall to conclude that Native American claims to basic human rights were less legitimate than those of their white counterparts.

The U.S. government further justified taking lands from Native Americans based on an ethnocentrism that developed through prolonged propaganda. Luke Lea, the Commissioner of Indian Affairs from 1850 to 1853, typified this supremacist disposition:

> When civilization and barbarism are brought in such relation that they cannot coexist together . . . it is right that the superiority of the former should be asserted and the latter compelled to give way. It is, therefore, no matter of regret or reproach that so large a portion of our territory has been wrested from the aboriginal inhabitants and made the happy abodes of an enlightened and Christian people.[24]

This attitude stiffened the resolve of war parties and frontiersmen who expanded U.S. borders and private land holdings through bloody victories and strong-handed acts.

Indians became the bogeymen of U.S. society. They were specters sweeping up children and women in the middle of the night only to scalp them and then whoop it up around a fire afterwards. Proponents of these shrill overgeneralizations thought civilization itself was in danger from these supposed ghouls. Thomas L. McKenney, one-time superintendent of the Bureau of Indian Affairs and advocate of Native American rights, wrote how the Indian myth darkened American imagination from childhood: "Which of us has not listened with sensations of horror to nursery stories that are told of the Indian and his cruelties? . . . We have been lade to hear his yell . . . his eyes like fire, eager to find some new victim on which to fasten himself, and glut his appetite for blood."[25] Outright fabrications coupled with anecdotal accounts filled the American subconscious with fear about the deadly consequences of allowing Indians to live among whites. The fables were meant to caution settlers about the savage nature of Indians and to counsel them against too close a contact with their aboriginal neighbors.

Popular utterances about Native Americans shaped the views of English settlers. Using language that characterized Native Americans as barbarous, the settlers committed inhumane acts against America's indigenous peoples. Puritans hunted for Indians as they did animals:

[People] may be put into a way to Hunt the Indians with dogs . . . if dogs were trained to hunt Indians as they doe Bears; we should quickly be sensible of great advantage thereby. . . . If the Indians were as other people are, & did manage their warr fairly after the manner of other nations, it might be looked upon as inhumane to pursue them in such a manner. But they are to be looked upon as thieves & murderers, they doe acts of hostility, without proclaiming war . . . they act like wolves & are to be dealt withall as wolves.[26]

Negative images like this instigated violence.

The Pequot War of 1637 was an early example of the dangerous effect of the colonists' conception of white superiority over Native Americans. Animosities arose between the Connecticut settlers and the Pequots who possessed what is now central Connecticut. The war began as revenge for the murder of a white trader by Pequot tribal members. However, the revenge perpetrated by the white vigilantes was greatly disproportionate. At the Mystic River battle, the colonists set aflame wigwams, causing the death of several hundred Pequots, most of whom were noncombatants. The colonists' hatred was so vehement that they continued military operations until the Pequots were nearly exterminated. A day of thanksgiving was proclaimed on June 15 to commemorate the battle at Mystic River. Those who committed the massacre were greeted as heroes. Skirmishes spread to surrounding swampland, where most of the remaining Pequots were killed, sold into slavery, or drowned. After the Treaty of Hartford (1638), which ended the War, forbade the Pequots from returning to their villages or using their tribal name.

And in the war which we made against [the Pequots], God's hand from heaven was so manifested that a very few of our men in a short time pursued through the wilderness, slew, and took prisoners about 1,400 of them . . . so that the name of the Pequots (as of Amalech) is blotted out from under heaven, there being not one that is, or (at least) dare call himself, a Pequot.[27]

The aggression bordered on genocide, yet in the eyes of Connecticut colonists, the destruction of this entire people was a condoned religious act.

Brutal rampages continued throughout the colonial period and left their traces on the history of the new nation. One of the most infamous scars was inflicted during the Black Hawk War (1832). Troubles began in 1804, when Governor William Henry Harrison enticed lesser chiefs from the Sac and Fox tribes to sign away the rights to fifteen million acres of land for $1,000, "friendship" and "protection," and a blacksmith. The treaty, which was never ratified through mandatory tribal procedures and went largely unnoticed, only permitted the two tribes to hunt and remain on the land until it was "put up for public sale." Black Hawk, who had allied himself against the United States during the War of 1812, refused to honor the treaty. His group of Sacs and Foxes, desperate for food, returned across the Mississippi from Iowa Territory to grow corn on their old lands.

A bloody conflict ensued during which the U.S. Regular Army, commanded by Colonel Zachary Taylor, unmercifully expelled them. The behavior of Taylor's troops is telling of American attitudes toward Indians. While in pursuit, soldiers came upon several Native American corpses and scalped them for war trophies. The regulars pursued the fleeing tribes hoping, as one of them later explained, to "get a pop at the Indians." Arriving at Bad Axe River, Black Hawk attempted to surrender himself by raising a white flag. In reply, the Army shot its cannon at the surviving members of his cohorts. During the course of the next skirmish, one soldier was so angered when a bullet narrowly missed his head that he exclaimed, "See me kill that damn squaw!" while shooting at a mother with a child on her back. Another soldier resorted to long-prevalent stereotypes in describing the event: "We were by this time fast getting rid of those demons in human shape." At one point, the soldiers bayoneted women who had burrowed into the sand for safety, and shot others. One of the foremost historians of the event, Cecil Eby, explained the zeal with which the soldiers killed:

> The whites saw themselves as engaged in a holy war that exempted them from responsibility for the slaughter at Bad Axe. They were ridding the earth of hateful varmints, characterized by [Private] John Wakefield[, who chronicled the War,] as "wretched wanderers [who] are most like the wild beasts than man—wandering from forest to forest, and not making any improvement in the natural mind."[28]

The age-old depictions of Indians as inhuman savages resulted in deeply held beliefs, deadening any sense of remorse for the massacres.

The United States was clearing the land of Indians and Mexicans to make way for a "civilized man" who would till the ground and make it productive. The policy of removing aborigines to the West was predicated on the paternalistic idea that the United States was doing them a favor by protecting them from frontiersmen. The government preferred this policy to punishing settlers who encroached on Native American lands.

During the 1780s, U.S. relations with indigenous tribes closely resembled British policies. Tribes asserted their territorial rights and demanded prices for their lands. Treaties were often broken by squatters and prospectors ravenously searching for more land to expand their interests. They had little concern for the rights of those whom Hugh Henry Brackenridge, an author of that era, called "the animals, vulgarly called Indians."[29] Although power over Indian affairs was officially posited in the federal government in 1789, states and individuals continued intruding on aboriginal lands, where they could overpower tribal members with superior firepower. At the beginning of the nineteenth century, U.S. land acquisitions were furthered by intimidation and bribery, which were usually directed toward chiefs who favored land transfers.[30] President Jefferson was the first to propose Indian removal, but he never implemented it. In 1825, when John C. Calhoun, then Secretary of War, convinced President James Monroe to adopt a removal policy, the government began negotiating with various tribes. At this stage, the U.S. respected tribal rights to accept or refuse to sell their lands. But such a benign policy did not last long.

Andrew Jackson became President in 1829, winning the election in part because of his support for Indian removal. The aggressive attitude he brought to the project had developed through years of frontier living and Indian fighting. He considered it absurd and farcical to negotiate with tribes. To him, it was ridiculous that Native Americans asserted title over tracts "they have seen . . . from the mountains or passed . . . in the chase." His efforts to remove eastern tribes were couched in statements purporting a benevolent interest in their well-being. "The fate of the Mohegan, the Narragansett, and the Delaware is fast overtaking the Choctaw, the Cherokee, and the Creek. That this fate surely awaits them if they remain within the limits of the States does not admit of a doubt."[31] The Indians, as he saw them, were blocking the road of cultural progress.

Jackson's seemingly humanitarian pretense for removing indigenous populations made a positive impression nationwide.[32] It provided a perceptual framework for looking positively at women and children being dragged from their homes. Francis Scott Key, the author of "The Star-Spangled Banner," bought into Jackson's reasoning: "[S]peculators will harass the Indians with the State laws; & I am sure that the only effectual way of saving them will be to buy their lands & send them off."[33] Jackson also tapped into the expansionist ideology that had been in the national vocabulary since the late seventeenth century. Without westward Indian removal, the borders of the United States would remain static and the imperialistic drive would have to be halted. And Jackson, the unabashed Indian fighter, would not let that happen during his presidency. He sought to explain away violent expansion and expropriation as a necessary part of the nation's natural growth.

The imagery that portrayed Indians exclusively as hunters and gatherers also played a substantial role. The typical preconception of Indians denied they had strong attachments to their lands, representing them as wanderers who traveled with game, wreaking havoc wherever they passed. Jackson exemplified this spirit, and he held the reins of government.

> "And is it to be supposed that the wandering savage has a stronger attachment to his home than the settled, civilized Christian?" he asked rhetorically. "Is it more afflicting to him to leave the graves of his fathers than it is to our brothers and children? Rightly considered, the policy of the General Government toward the red man is not only liberal, but generous. He is unwilling to submit to the laws of the States and mingle with their population. To him from this alternative, or perhaps utter annihilation, the General Government kindly offers him a new home, and proposes to pay the whole expense of his removal and settlement."[34]

Widespread acceptance of the view that Indians were accustomed to "roaming from place to place" and had "the habit of invading without scruple the land of others"[35] eased the way for Jackson to push the Indian Removal Act through Congress. The Act authorized the President to initiate contact with indigenous tribes in order to remove them west of the Mississippi in exchange for their lands in the east. McKenney, then Superintendent of the Bureau of Indian Affairs, protested the terms of the Act as being "a mockery" and was promptly dismissed from his position.

Congress vociferously debated the Removal Act throughout the winter of 1830. Senator John Forsyth considered Cherokee assertions of sovereignty over their lands "intrusive" and wanted to occupy all Native American lands and compensate tribes through an annuity that, of course, the U.S. government would disburse.[36] The views articulated that winter, in support of removal and hostility toward Indians, had long been part of the accepted social dialogue and continued to be expressed for decades to come. Many speakers argued that tribes were dangerously encroaching on civilization and that for their own good they had to be removed west. One author argued that regardless of whether U.S. policy was "just or unjust," Indian resistance to it was "the very worst policy" because it would only "protract the" inevitable "catastrophe."[37] Another author argued that Indian relocation was "the removal of a sick bed from a place where death is certain, to one from which it is more remote. . . . One nation must perish to make room for another."[38] Indians stood in the way of this unbridled brand of civilization, which, in and of itself, was viewed as a positive good, regardless of how much dislocation was required to make it a reality.

Voices opposed to removal were audible through the din of mischaracterizations, but the truths they enunciated and the democratic themes they sounded were not triumphant in the marketplace of ideas. Congregationalist leader Jeremiah Evarts wrote that Indian removal sought "to *drive* the Indians, by *force*, from their country." Likewise, Pennsylvania Quaker Joseph Hemphill argued that whites should act toward Native Americans "with the strictest fairness" and to requite them for the destruction whites had caused.[39] Congressman Edward Everett realized in 1830 that the proposed Removal Act would legitimize the government's drive to divest Native Americans of their land. His statements in the House of Representatives evince an understanding of how the time-worn Indian savage image helped bring the conflict to a head:

> Ten or fifteen thousand families, to be rooted up, and carried a hundred, aye, a thousand miles into the wilderness! . . . To remove them against their will, by thousands, to a distant and different country . . . I never heard of such a thing! They are not barbarians; they are essentially a civilized people. . . . They are planters and farmers, they are tradespeople and mechanics, they have cornfields and orchards, looms and workshops, schools and churches, and orderly institutions![40]

The most vehement opposition to removal came from New Jersey Senator Theodore Frelinghuysen. He reminded his fellow senators that

American ancestors found "independent sovereigns" when they arrived in the New World. "They were not a wild and lawless horde of banditti, but lived under the restraints of government." The colonists dealt underhandedly with indigenous inhabitants: "The white men, the authors of all their wrongs, approached them as friends—they extended the olive branch; and, being then a feeble colony and at the mercy of the native tenants of the soil, by presents and professions, propitiated their good will." Out of trust and confidence, natives permitted settlers to live among them without claiming "elder title."

> By and by, conditions are changed. His people melt away; his lands are constantly coveted; millions after millions are ceded. The Indian bears it all meekly; he complains; indeed, as well he may; but suffers on: and now he finds that this neighbor, whom his kindness had nourished, has spread an adverse title over the last remains of his patrimony, barely adequate to his wants, and turns upon him, and says, "away! we cannot endure you so near us! These forests and rivers, these groves of your fathers, these firesides and hunting grounds, are ours by the right of power, and the force of numbers."[41]

So it was that might became the United States' chief claim to title, and even congressmen who spoke out against this course of action were powerless to stop it.

Jackson signed the Indian Removal Act into law on May 28, 1830, after Congress voted 102–97 in favor of its passage. Proof came quickly that it was meant to legitimize underhanded dealings with aboriginal tribes. The Chickasaws, Choctaws, and Creeks surrendered their lands by the end of 1830, and the Cherokees and Seminoles were the only southern tribes that remained defiant to governmental pressures to cede lands.

The story of the Cherokees is telling of the coercion and pressure that were brought to bear when they were needed. The Cherokee, unlike some western tribes, adopted many habits of the whites who lived around them. They set up grist mills and cultivated their fields, built schools, developed a Cherokee alphabet, and printed a tribal newspaper in the 1820s. A Cherokee constitution was ratified in 1827, signaling the stable course of self-government. While their constitution retained Southern racism against blacks, it signaled the existence of a sovereign and independent nation.[42]

Negative stereotypes abounded in Georgia during those years. Prevarication, as Governor Gilmer admitted, was part of state policy. "Treaties were expedients by which ignorant, intractable, and savage people were induced without bloodshed to yield up what civilized people had the right to possess."[43] Georgia acted against the Cherokee Nation for adopting its constitution, which it claimed violated Article 4 of the U.S. Constitution.[44] Shortly after passage of the Cherokee constitution, Georgia passed a law subjecting the Cherokee Nation to its own laws and abolishing all of the tribe's powers, except the power to cede land. The Resolution of 1828 resolved that all lands within Georgia's boundaries were under its absolute sovereignty, meaning the state could take possession *"at any time she pleases."*[45] Misethnicity against Indians was further inflamed by greed when in 1829 gold was discovered on Cherokee territory. To prevent wholesale encroachment onto Cherokee lands, the Indian agent called out federal troops, but, in the face of Georgian aggression and pressure, President Jackson abandoned the tribe to Georgian authorities. Instead of offering protection and asserting federal authority over Indian matters, Jackson advised the tribe to move west to avoid further hostilities against them. Thus, to accomplish his stated goal of civilizing the Indians, Jackson wished them to abandon their developed lands, their schools, and their newsprint for the western wilderness.

Understanding the desperation of its situation, the tribe took its case to federal court. In *Cherokee Nation v. Georgia*,[46] the second of Justice Marshall's trilogy of cases, the Cherokees challenged Georgia's attempt to expropriate their lands. The Court dismissed the case for want of jurisdiction, finding that the Cherokee Nation was not a foreign state capable of suing the state of Georgia. The Court's conclusion was based on Georgia's defined boundaries as shown "[i]n all our maps, geographical treatises, histories and laws." In dictum the Court found that tribes were "domestic dependent nations. They occupy a territory to which we assert a title independent of their will." Marshall, Jackson's avowed political adversary, nevertheless recognized the Cherokee Nation was "a distinct political society . . . capable of managing its own affairs and governing itself."[47] Privately, Marshall reflected "with indignation on our disreputable conduct . . . in the affairs of the Cherokees in Georgia."[48] In spite of his personal compassion, Marshall's decision elevated Georgia's title interests, which it gained by force, above Cherokee property rights.

The third of Marshall's trilogy came to a different conclusion. *Worcester v. Georgia*[49] arose when a Vermont minister was arrested for living on Cherokee land without a Georgia license. The Court held that Indian nations were distinct, self-governing political entities, affirming the Cherokee Nation's right to self-determination. Upon hearing the decisions, Cherokees were overjoyed: "It was trumpeted forth among the Indians . . . that the decision mentioned had forever settled the controversy about their lands; that their laws and country would be unconditionally restored to them again, and the Georgians expelled from their territory."[50] Their celebrations were premature; in the end Jackson refused to enforce the Supreme Court's decision. He countenanced the state's usurping federal authority and breached his fiduciary duty to the tribe, knowing that the greater the injustices to which Cherokees were subjected, the more leverage he would have to remove them without providing adequate compensation for their lands.

Marauding whites continued harassing Cherokees. Having nothing to fear from the state or federal governments, intruders violently seized farms owned by Cherokee chiefs like John Ross. They stole livestock, forced Cherokees to sign leases and sell their lands based on bogus claims. Hunting parties were attacked by the state militia, and Cherokees who protested were flogged. The Cherokees were powerless against these injustices because Georgian laws forbade them from testifying in courts against whites. Finally, broken by the lack of federal aid, Jackson's treaty commissioners were able to intrigue minority chiefs to usurp their authority and sign a treaty calling for the removal of the entire nation. The 15,000 Cherokees who refused to abandon their lands were hunted down and driven from their homes by General Winfield Scott's troops.[51] Soldiers forced people found in their homes to leave with few possessions, receiving no compensations for their lands. This project was part of the government's plan to "civilize" the "savages." The well-kept houses and plowed fields made clear the settled nature of the Cherokees. The visible reality was not enough to overcome the influence of long-believed myths about the American primitive who was supposedly so dangerous to civilized citizens. In the end, about 4,000 Cherokees died during the disease-ridden westward Trail of Tears.

Stereotypes of Indians guided U.S. policy toward indigenous peoples. Anger aroused by the recalcitrance of the Cherokee Nation and other tribes to sell and abandon their lands was driven by the assumption that Indians had no connection to any particular place. In the popular mind, they were mere wanderers moving with game but having no affinity to any particular place. When Native Americans did not conform to the savage hunter image that whites made up for them, they were livid that the Indians did not meet their negative expectations.

In the early days of colonization, images of Indians did little harm. Settlers did not have much power or desire to force their life-style on the "noble savages" who were their chief trading partners. But with time, they acquired the power to satiate their hunger for farmlands, animal pelts, and commercial latitude. Legends that were passed down through generations had a devastating effect on American aborigines. Imperialistic forces relied on paternalistic philosophy to justify their plans to destroy aboriginal cultures. Many whites believed Indians would replace their mores with American customs, comply in migrating west where there was plenty of game, or die off from diseases. Expansionists devalued the autonomy rights of indigenous peoples to live independently. "The red man," wrote George Bancroft in his seminal *History of the United States*, "is inferior in reason and the moral qualities. Nor is this inferiority simply attached to the individual; it is connected with organization, and is the characteristic of the race."[52] Thus, Bancroft thought it commonsense that the Indian who fought civilization was killed because he "could not change [his] habits."[53] The fault lay not in the colonial misethnicity but in the red man's stubbornness to acquiesce to a benevolent civilization that took away his lands for his own good. These beliefs were conducive to dislocation and expropriation. Their effectiveness grew through years of reiteration.

As with the pervasive, antagonistic stereotypes of Jews and blacks, derogatory images of Native Americans worked hand in hand with claims of superiority. Repeated messages about the inferiority of Jews, blacks, and indigenous Americans proved instrumental for carrying out misethnic policies. Hate propaganda regarding Jews in Germany and blacks and Native Americans in the United States provided a conceptual framework for systematic, widespread oppression. Although these groups experienced differing forms of persecution, in all three cases hate speech significantly contributed to discrimination and destruction. Misethnicity was harbored and nurtured by popular and intellectual dialogue, and then deployed by charismatic leaders.

5

A Glance at Contemporary Hate Speech

Hate speech and prejudice continue to plague the contemporary world. In central Africa, a long-standing animosity rages among the Tutsis, Hutus, and Batwa (plural for Twa) based in part on the differing physical characteristics of these three groups. The Tutsis are the tallest of the three and have dark skin but non-negroid features. The Hutus are shorter than the Tutsis and have negroid features, while the Batwa are lighter complexioned and of shorter stature. These subtle differences have contributed to inter-clan slaughter and legal discrimination. In India, where the caste system has officially been abolished, the lower castes continue to suffer discrimination based on race. Indeed, the word for the division of castes is *varna*, which means "color." The lighter-skinned Brahmin are considered religiously purer than the darker-skinned Kshatriya, Vaisya, and Sudra.

This chapter concentrates on two contemporary societies. I first discuss how hate speech perpetuates human rights violations against blacks in Mauritania. I then look into misethnicity in the contemporary United States.

Mauritanian Slavery

Americans tend to think the practice of slavery died out in 1865 with the end of America's Civil War and passage of the Thirteenth Amendment. The truth is much bleaker. Currently, approximately 27 million slaves around the world are beaten, exploited, and uncompensated for their labor.[1] More than 100,000 of them live in Mauritania, a country in Northwest Africa. Slavery has existed there since the twelfth century.

Individuals are born into slavery, as are the children they bear. Hereditary servitude passes to children through their mothers. Often, slaves are the biological offspring of their masters. Child slaves are put to work at an early age manning camels and doing other light work. The Mauritanian socioeconomic situation makes it virtually impossible for blacks to escape or survive outside their master's household. Having no money or professional equipment and fearing recapture, they usually see no viable alternative to staying with their masters.

The lives of slaves are bereft of any hope for freedom. They spend their days laboring from morning to dusk without compensation and, periodically, being punished for violating their owners' rules. In Mauritania, slavery continues to be based on racial and biological factors. All slaves are black Africans, and the slave owners are Arab/Berbers of various social classes. Names are used to retain clear hierarchical demarcations between them. Blacks usually have only one name, for instance Bilal. Arab/Berbers do not give their children slave names. Enslaved individuals cannot marry or associate with free blacks except with their master's consent. Routine punishments include whipping, food and drink deprivation, and prolonged exposure in the sun while bound hand and foot. More extreme traditional tortures, practiced against male slaves, involve joint dislocations and genital mutilations.[2]

Mauritanian President Mohamed Haidallah issued a decree purporting to abolish slavery in 1980. His decree was impotent, and in its stead Ordinance Number 81.234 was adopted on November 9, 1981. The first article of the ordinance abolished "[s]lavery in all its forms." The Second Article stated: "In keeping with the Shari'a [Islamic] law, this abolition will imply a payment of compensation to those entitled to such." The Third Article grants the Ulama, Islamic religious leaders, authority to decide what compensation is fair. What at first sight seemed like a positive development has turned out to be completely ineffective. The second and third articles have been the biggest stumbling blocks. Slave owners have successfully argued in the Mauritanian legal system that upon manumission, they, rather than freed slaves, should be compensated. Slaves usually lack enough possessions to pay the compensation demanded by their masters. Further, the required enabling legislation has never been passed, and there is no punishment for continuing to hold and exploit slaves.[3] The Human Rights Watch/Africa report of 2001 found that despite being outlawed, slavery persists in Mauritania.[4]

Ancient Islamic stereotypes of blacks purport that slavery is a religious institution. Bernard Lewis has surveyed Arab literature and folklore and found that many "early Islamic poets . . . suggest very strongly a feeling of hatred and contempt directed against persons of African birth or origin." The spread of Islam throughout Africa produced extensive Arabic written works about human interactions. Black slaves were distinguished by the title *abeds* while white slaves were called *mamlūks*. With time, *abed* became the appellation for any black man. Moreover, black slaves institutionally became used for more physically demanding labor than their white counterparts. The writings Lewis studied contain many derogatory assertions about blacks. They most frequently referred to Africans as stupid, "vicious, untruthful, and dishonest." They were also said to be lecherous, greedy, and ungrateful. Positive traits attributed to them were usually "piety and loyalty," denoting God's desire that slaves be obedient.[5] According to the 1994 Human Rights Watch/Africa report, Islam continues to be "an important instrument in perpetuating slavery."[6]

Misethnic language permeates Mauritanian culture. "*abed*" continues to be the Arabic word for both black man and male slave, thereby semantically wedding these two referents. Moreover, "*abed*" implies that black Africans are different than and subordinate to Arab/Berbers. Similarly, *khadem* means both black woman or female slave; no distinction is made between them, and the implication is clearly that black women are born slaves. Slavery continues in Mauritania partly because blacks are considered and spoken of as subhumans unworthy of civil rights.

Moctar Teyeb, the American Coordinator for El Hor, a Mauritanian anti-slavery organization led by former slaves like himself, greatly aided me in understanding some of the Mauritanian discourses underlying black slavery. Teyeb, who fled from his slave master in 1979, explained that the Moor (Arab/Berber) majority, known in Mauritania as *beydanes*, have been reared on ideology that characterizes blacks as not fully human. In their worldview, *abeds* live to satisfy the *beydanes'* needs and to perform manual labor, which the latter consider shamefully below them. Privileged status can never be achieved by *abeds* because their social standing is predicated on race. The very meaning of "freedom" is virtually incomprehensible to slaves because bondage is all they have known since childhood. They heard stories, songs, and poems in which the Arab/Berbers were portrayed as superior to blacks. Basic rights such as liberty, education, and compensation for labor are foreign to them because of the negative depictions they learned about themselves and other blacks. Yet there is something inside them, Teyeb said reflectively, that nevertheless rebels against the accepted order. That drive, however, rarely manifests itself because the destructive messages that are repeated throughout the course of slaves' lives represent them as inferior and psychologically prepare them for a life of enslavement. The degraded place they hold in Mauritanian society reinforces the message.

The images of subordinacy are endemic. Children's games and utterances are imbued with the culture of slavery. They use words, sayings, and singsongs that ingrain racism into their behaviors. Even as a child, Teyeb, like other slaves, experienced discrimination: "Children use the language every day. If they fight, they call their opponent an *abed*. They are obliged to use the vocabulary since they have no other." Even when the children play, the *beydanes* remind the *abeds* who they are socially, thereby inculcating distinctions from toddlerhood on.

Stereotypes used by adults are more sophisticated than mere name calling, but they also stem from a dehumanizing continuum. The chief obstacle to overcoming slavery in Mauritania, Teyeb—who is a religious Muslim—believes, is in surmounting the black self-hatred that is engendered by ubiquitous images depicting them as inferiors. Many of them believe that Allah requires their continued enslavement. Therefore, as in so many other countries including the Sudan, religion is manipulated to perpetuate privilege based on ethnicity. A common Mauritanian expression is, "Paradise is under your master's feet." Just as in the antebellum United States, blacks in Mauritania are taught that slavery is a religious institution and that obedience to their masters is a virtue. An elderly former slave explained why abolition signifies so little to slaves: "It is hard to ignore what they have been told all their lives, that without their master they cannot survive, that only he can ennoble them, give meaning to their life, and lead them to heaven. They believe this; so how can they also believe that they must escape the situation that promises to give them so much?"[7] Elderly people often tell younger slaves that to struggle for liberty is against Allah's divine order. Thus, the legitimizing paradigm has become so manifest in racial relationships that blacks themselves believe they are born slaves. Parents instill pride in their children for being slaves. They also teach offspring that they are dependent on light-skinned people because blacks are not completely human. Black slaves become so acculturated to this stratification that they grow to dislike other black Africans, calling them *erwakhy*, meaning people who are inferior and without dignity. Local legend has it that at night the *erwakhy* turn into wild animals.

The dichotomy between *abeds* and *beydanes* is sustained through manners of address reflecting power hierarchies. As long as blacks do not complain of their predicaments, their masters are somewhat benevolent, allowing them to marry whom they want to and often giving them lighter work; however, this minimal tolerance extends only so long as the rigid hierarchy is not questioned or otherwise challenged. Blacks who rebel are punished mercilessly. The cumulative effect of culturally sanctioned disparagements and religious customs helps maintain the status quo. The danger of this form of hate speech to social institutions is far greater than fighting words that threaten immediate but short-term harms.

Bigotry in Contemporary United States Society

The Internet and Hate Speech

Both the advocates of democracy and racist groups have realized the Internet's utility in spreading views and opinions. The Internet is filled by a multiplicity of variegated commercial and private users. It is a boon for all sorts of advocacy. Among the views available for consumption on the World Wide Web are those that degrade people based on their race, ethnicity, national origin, gender, and sexual preference. Hate groups take advantage of this relatively inexpensive medium for ideological distribution. They spread pamphlets, letters, and images to groups of users and individuals who can anonymously participate in racist meetings, think tanks, and planning committees. One of the Internet's down sides is that it provides a global forum for the advocates of intolerance and inequality.

A steadily increasing number of hate groups employ Internet forums. In 1995, the Simon Wiesenthal Center, a human rights organization, found that approximately fifty hate groups had their own electronic bulletin boards. Klan Watch and Militia Task Force, two agencies dedicated to monitoring racist hate groups, determined that in 1997, with the aid of the Internet, there were approximately 474 hate groups in the U.S., an increase of 20 percent from 1996. The number of Internet sites promoting hate and targeting "religious groups, visible minorities, women and homosexuals had grown to at least eight hundred by 1999."[8] In 2000, during unrest in the Middle East, hundreds of new Web sites and chatrooms that derided Jews bourgeoned. The Southern Poverty Law Center, which tracks hate group Internet sites, concluded that the Internet was a medium that was extensively used by hate groups calling for race war.

Groups using the Net to spread their messages include the Ku Klux Klan and White Aryan Resistance. Their messages are not, in many cases, new; rather, they rely on age-old prejudices that have proven to be effective vehicles for inciting oppressive conduct. For example, on its Web home page, Stormfront describes blacks as racially inferior to whites. Aryan Nation uses biblical passages to justify itself in characterizing blacks as "beasts." The National Observer Web site provides worldwide links to other hate-filled Internet sites and has a fairly broad range of anti-Semitic articles, T-shirts, and videos. Moreover, the National Observer advocates using "biological terrorism."[9] Such organizations embellish their propaganda through colorful, interactive Web pages where like-minded people can join their causes.

Many of these groups do not stop at discrimination and prejudice; they recruit Internet users to engage in violent acts against outgroups and propagandize white supremacy. Notorious among these is the World Church of the Creator, which calls for "Racial Holy War" against non-whites. The National Socialist movement sports a swastika logo and praises Adolf Hitler on its Web page. The cover of its magazine exclaims "Total War is Shortest War."[10] It solicits people to contact National Socialist headquarters and begin training, presumably to participate in their preparations for race war. Patrick Henry On-Line provides information for interested racists and anti-Semites who want to contact and join any of the numerous racist militias. The militias, in turn, prepare their members for a race war. Civil War Two sponsors a racist and anti-Semitic secessionist page. These Internet sites advocate and promulgate the violent aspirations and plans of hate groups seeking to increase their memberships. Some hate groups have even taken to recruiting children through catchy music and colorful games.

All these disseminated ideas are linked to specific sources. With the help of technology and Internet protocols, electromagnetic waves transmitting hate propaganda can be traced to their place and time of origin.[11]

Several commercially available filtering devices block Internet sites based on content. One way of limiting the audience to which bigots' messages are spread is for users to voluntarily install filters. Some persons have argued that the availability of these devices makes it unnecessary and undesirable for the government to become involved in censuring the Internet.[12] Instead, so the argument goes, individuals can purchase and activate any of the available filtering software to adequately comport with their individual moral or social perspectives. The filters are considered preferable to regulations and less likely to raise First Amendment issues because companies, groups, and individuals, rather than the government, maintain control over message transmissions and receptions. This view has become increasingly widespread.

Several relatively effective filters vie for market position, including CyberPatrol, NetNanny, SurfWatch, and HateFilter. These filters enable parents to block objectionable messages from being received by their browsing youngsters. They censor for particular words or contents indicating the undesirability of particular Internet messages or sites. For example, when it is activated, the HateFilter denies access to Internet sites "advocating hatred, bigotry or violence against Jews, minorities, and homosexuals."[13]

One problem with these filters is that they cast too wide a net and, inappropriately, block out nondiscriminatory Web sites. America Online learned this lesson when it prevented people from accessing sites with the word "breast"; unfortunately, the blocked areas included sites dealing with subjects like breast cancer. This was far afield from the intended outcome, which was to keep pornography out of children's hands. Likewise, using word-sensitive filters to block out hate propaganda is a good beginning, but it might also prevent researchers from reaching necessary historical and sociological information on the Web. Students would, for example, be blocked from accessing sites containing derogatory terms but posing no danger of inciting anyone to commit acts of violence.

The parameters of these filtering devices are drawn by organizations bound by mission statements, altruism, and marketing considerations. The filters are riddled with software bugs. CyberPatrol classifies the following useful and innocuous Web sites as FullNude SexActs: (1) MIT Project on Mathematics and Computation; (2) The National Academy of Clinical Biochemistry; (3) Department of Computer Science, Queen Mary and Westfield College; (4) Chiba Institute of Technology, and so forth.[14] The inaccuracy with which automatic tools filter out useful materials makes it impossible for those running the software on their computers to reach some helpful speech on important subjects. Furthermore, it is difficult for the purchasers of filtering devices to find out everything that is blocked and all the guidelines that went into the equation since that information is considered proprietary.

Beyond the technical problems of regulating hate speech with filters, there is the reality that bigotry remains accessible to everyone who does not have a filter. Even though some people choose to avoid Internet communications with hate groups, the many venomous Web sites, news groups, and emails continue disseminating violent messages to anyone interested in meeting other prejudiced, proactive people. Filtering devices are inadequate for repelling the socially destabilizing force of hate messages. The filters do not prevent unstable and destabilizing people from accessing hate-filled Internet sites to draw ideological sustenance and further inflame their bigotry. Laws preventing dangerous forms of hate speech, enforceable by state and federal legislation, not just voluntary purchases and installations of commercial products, are necessary to protect individual rights and to guarantee social welfare.

Other commercial arrangements also provide tenuous limits on hate speech. Internet service providers like America Online have policies against the use of hate speech. Offenders can have their accounts revoked. However, the vast number of messages that bombard search engines such as Yahoo make them unwilling breeding grounds for neo-Nazi groups. Nevertheless, a French court recently ordered Yahoo to block an auction of Nazi memorabilia from reaching browsers in France because such commercial activities are illegal there. This case is novel because it imposed French law on a Web site located outside the country. It is too early to determine whether this case will withstand the test of time in France or be followed in other countries that have enacted hate speech legislation.

The World Wide Web Consortium, an organization hosted by the Massachusetts Institute of Technology, originated yet another way of restricting access to Internet sites. It developed software for rating materials containing subjects like pornography and violence. The system does not actually filter materials, instead, it establishes rules for transmitting them. Organizations, governments, and agencies can develop Platform for Internet Content Selection (PICS) based systems, tailored to their particular agendas. But these systems are far from perfect. An extreme example of an undemocratic manipulation of PICS is how the Chinese government prevents Internet users from accessing U.S. government sites simply by blocking all Internet addresses ending in ".gov."

It would be a mistake to place in the hands of commercial interests the exclusive power of deciding whether hate speech should be blocked, and to what extent. When civil liberties are at stake, the power to preserve them rests squarely on democratically elected governments. Filters are a positive development for the maintenance of civil society; however, they fall short of the mark because they rely on private organizations to bear the torch of justice. For-profit companies are not beholden to humanistic principles, such as the advancement of equality, because their interests are private. Even not-for-profit companies have targeted interests. On the other hand, a representative democracy is obligated to increase overall well-being while preserving civil rights. Overreliance on the judgments of private powers relegates governmental duties to private prejudices, incentives, and priorities.

The social impact of derogatory Internet transmissions and the potential success of membership drives will partly depend on the historical significance of inciteful stereotypes. Portrayals of outgroups are most dangerous when they exploit images that have been extensively developed over long periods of time. Some examples of this are the depiction of Jews as ruthlessly power hungry, of blacks as uncontrollably sex depraved, of Native Americans as drunken savages, and of Gypsies as thieves. Web sites, which are designed to perpetuate these sorts of stereotypes and to induce others to act, have an impact on real people. They do not exist in a nonspatial world whose boundaries are separate from the world of actions and reactions. Hate crime is the end result of social paradigms about minorities, coupled with the promotion of actions against them. Orators calling for oppression and persecution against identifiable groups increase racial and ethnic tensions.

The Instigation of Hate Crimes

The Internet is only one vehicle used by bigots to spread their doctrines. Hate messages typically precede violent hate crimes. The World Church of the Creator is an organization that spreads hate propaganda through the Internet, pamphlets, and television interviews. It calls on its members to participate in a racial holy war. One of the World Church of the Creator's disciples, Benjamin Smith, recently acted on its doctrine, murdering a black man and an Asian man, as well as wounding nine Jews. Smith made his dangerous intent known in an interview given just weeks before the shooting. "To want to live in a world where blacks have power over whites, where Jews are in control, I think that's a sickness and I'd like to eradicate that sickness. In some ways it's inevitable—racial holy war."[15]

Under current U.S. First Amendment jurisprudence, the government could not have charged Smith with a crime for these words because they did not pose an imminent threat of harm. Had Smith's statement been actionable, based on his manifest intent to harm blacks and Jews, his lethal actions may have been deterred.

Just as Smith announced his deadly motives before committing the hate crimes, Dylan Klebold and Eric Harris also made their intents known before the bloody attack against their fellow students in Littleton, Colorado. Klebold and Harris planned their shooting spree to coincide with Adolf Hitler's birthday, rehearsing it on a video they showed to fellow students several months before the murders. The depictions on the video did not constitute an immediate threat of lawless action because they were recorded several months before the murders. Nevertheless, the danger was real. The video provided a warning sign of future violence, but its transmission was not punishable under U.S. laws.

The bombing of the Federal Building in Oklahoma City, on April 19, 1995, provides another example of a tragedy that might have been avoided by enforcement of a statute prohibiting hate speech. William Pierce's depiction of a bombing in his novel, *The Turner Diaries*, influenced the bomber, Timothy McVeigh. If Pierce intended his work to be a blueprint to that deadly action, he might have been prohibited by statute from distributing the menacing book, and the deaths of 168 people might have been avoided.

Hate speech also played a role in the murder of James Byrd Jr. John William King and two friends chained Byrd to a truck, dragged him for several hundred feet, and left him for dead. King, who was sentenced to death by lethal injection, and one of his codefendants, adopted white supremacist ideology while serving sentences for different crimes in a local jail. In prison, the two men joined a gang called the Confederate Knights of America, a chapter of the KKK. Hate developed gradually in these men, until the racism they heard ignited into a racially inspired, brutal murder.

Hate groups' dissemination of fallacies about the history and characteristics of identifiable outgroups has contributed to the rise of hate crimes in the United States. In the past, hate speech led to mob violence and the lynching of blacks, but more recently, hate speech inflamed racists into a spate of black church burnings. Before the conflagration of Macedonia Baptist Church, the KKK posted a paper on the doors of the church warning that the "KKK—is watching you."[16] A court subsequently ordered the KKK to pay $37.8 million to the church after a jury determined that the organization stirred up hatred "that led to the burning" of the "predominantly black church."[17]

Hate propaganda desensitizes people to the tragic consequences of bigotry. Although the Holocaust occurred just half a century ago, already a pseudo-intellectual movement denies that Jews were systematically murdered by Nazis. Nationally known figures, such as former presidential candidate Patrick Buchanan and Nation of Islam leader Louis Farrakhan, have expressed their disbelief that Nazis tried to commit genocide against the Jews. The dissemination of this view by influential figures has infected the thoughts of ordinary Americans. According to a 1993 Roper Starch Worldwide poll, 22 percent of the U.S. adult population thought that "it seemed possible the Holocaust never happened," and another 12 percent did not know if the Holocaust was possible.[18]

Hate Speech in Political Organizations

In recent years, white supremacists have lobbied politicians as well as pursued influential jobs in government to propagate their racist and anti-Semitic ideas. Even some current members of the U.S. Congress have supported an overtly racist organization. Representative Robert L. Barr Jr. of Georgia was the keynote speaker at a gathering of the Council of Conservative Citizens (CCC). The CCC rejects interracial marriages as a form of "white genocide," argues that blacks are mentally inferior, has close connections with David Duke, a former KKK Grand Dragon, and regularly engages in racist and anti-Semitic rhetoric. Barr has used his congressional power to oppose hate crimes legislation, additional funds for social programs, and the continuation of civil rights protections. In recent years, Senate Minority Leader Trent Lott also attended and spoke at many CCC dinners and rallies. Although Lott has recently tried to distance himself from the CCC's bigoted views, Arnie Watson, a member of the CCC's executive board and former Mississippi State Senator, has called "Trent . . . an honorary member." In 1998, Mississippi Governor Kirk Fordice was the keynote speaker at the CCC's semiannual national convention, where he and others stood to sing "Dixie," a Confederate war song, and then sat during the rendition of "My Country, 'Tis of Thee." The participation of high-ranking politicians lends the CCC's brand of bigotry an air of respectability and makes it more acceptable among their constituents.[19]

The present Attorney General of the United States, John Ashcroft, also has ties to the CCC. In September 2000, Ashcroft met CCC officials and expressed his sympathy for a jailed Council member. Ashcroft made his views clearer in an interview for the *Southern Partisan*:

> You've got a heritage of doing that, of defending Southern patriots like Robert E. Lee, Stonewall Jackson, and Jefferson Davis. Traditionalists must do more. I've got to do more. We've all got to stand up and speak in this respect, or else we'll be taught that these people were giving their lives, subscribing their sacred fortunes and their honor to some perverted agenda.

The Southern heritage Ashcroft referred to includes institutionalized slavery of blacks. All three people Ashcroft called "patriots" were American traitors. The praise he extended to the *Southern Partisan* might have referred to articles from previous issues which included views such as: "Negroes, Asians, and Orientals (is Japan the exception?), Hispanics, Latins, and Eastern Europeans have no temperament for democracy, never had, and probably never will," and "No one can doubt the effectiveness of the original Ku Klux Klan. Without it we might never have shaken off the curse of the carpetbag, scalawag governments that bound us hand and foot."[20]

Bigotry in the United States is not confined to white supremacists. Nation of Islam leader Louis Farrakhan, organizer of the Million Man March, has grown in popularity in the Black Muslim community. White supremacist ideology and Farrakhan's ideology exhibit striking similarities. The *Final Call*, the Nation of Islam's official newspaper, espouses separatist, nondemocratic ideology. At the end of each issue of the *Final Call* is a list of the Nation of Islam's demands and wishes. Among these is the following: "We want our people in America whose parents or grandparents were descendants from slaves, to be allowed to establish a separate state or territory of their own—either on this continent or elsewhere." Such ideas closely resemble those of David Duke and the KKK, which also advocate the view that whites and blacks should live separately because of their innate incompatibilities. Wanting to return to the days of "separate but equal" education, the *Final Call* argues for "equal education—but separate schools up to 16 for boys and 18 for girls. . . . We want all Black children educated, taught and trained by their own teachers."[21] Given the Nation of Islam's history, it is not surprising that its ideologies so closely resemble fascism. Malcolm X, one of its leading preachers, met with Ku Klux Klan leaders in the early sixties about formulating a joint approach to opposing the civil rights movement, and Elijah Muhammad, founder of the Nation of Islam, addressed his followers at an event featuring another speaker, George Lincoln Rockwell, leader of the American Nazi Party.

Jews are the main targets of the Nation of Islam's bigotry. Farrakhan has described Judaism as a "gutter religion" and has called Hitler "a great man." On a more dangerous note, Farrakhan "promised to 'grind' Jews and 'crush them into little bits.'"[22] During a meeting of neo-Nazi leaders in 1985, Thomas Metzger and Art Jones praised Farrakhan for his stand against Jews. Khalid Abdul Muhammad, one of Farrakhan's former aides, ranted that Jews are the "blood-suckers of the black nation." Kweisi Mfume, then president of the Congressional Black Caucus and later president of the National Association for the Advancement of Colored People (NAACP), said that Abdul Muhammad's speech had the same "'tone of intolerance' that allowed slavery and the Holocaust to happen."[23] While mainstream black leaders like Julian Bond, Chairman of the NAACP, and Martin Luther King III, President of the Southern Christian Leadership Conference, regularly speak out against anti-Semitism,[24] Farrakhan's hateful vitriol strengthens anti-Semitic attitudes festering in the black inner city.[25] University students have also been charmed by the charisma of Nation of Islam leaders.

Fascism and authoritarianism continue to sway opinions around the world. These ideologies have developed their bases of support through the manipulation of various economic and historical stereotypes. Propaganda remains a tool for repression and recruitment. Destructive messages aimed at creating a culture where discrimination and oppression are readily acceptable are dangerous not only at the time they are uttered. Sometimes active misethnicity is awakened after years of relative quiescence. Therefore, to wait until there is an immediate danger of violent actions is to ignore the empirical lessons of the past. My discussion of German anti-Semitism and American and Mauritanian racism indicates that the dissemination of bigotry has often been the springboard for ideologies that have catalyzed the abridgement of fundamental rights. This downward spiral is not, however, inevitable. Chapter 13 discusses how laws prohibiting hate speech can help prevent infringements on civil rights. Such laws can maintain domestic tranquility, while helping to prevent widespread, volatile racial and ethnic violence. First, however, I will turn to the social psychology of scapegoating.

PART II

Hate Propaganda's Socially Destructive Force

In chapter 1, I defined "misethnicity" to mean hatred toward groups because of their racial, historic, cultural, or linguistic characteristics. The historical survey in Part I of this book suggests a refined explication: misethnicity is the irrational, unsubstantiated, and unjustified antagonism toward an entire, identifiable ethnic or racial group. This attitude is rooted in socially legitimizing narratives promoting conduct consonant with aspersive beliefs.

I prefer "misethnicity" to "prejudice," "racism," or "ethnocentrism." "Prejudice" literally means a preconceived positive or negative opinion. "Racism" ordinarily only refers to malignant inclinations toward biological groups. "Ethnocentrism," which was first used by W. G. Sumner in his 1906 book, *Folkways*, is the most useful of these three. It denotes narrowness of thought about cultures and races. It has been used to refer to group aggrandizement at the expense of other groups' rights. While those three concepts are useful, "misethnicity" synthesizes them and more accurately describes the context of active racial and ethnic group animosity.

Misethnicity entails consistently disapproving, hypercritical, and oft-reiterated generalizations about groups and persons belonging to them. Members of outside groups emerge as malevolent, immutably evil, or base. Misethnicity assumes that despised groups are homogeneous, that stereotypes refer to their common and real attributes, that social and biological hierarchies naturally set certain people above or below others, or that derogatory descriptions of hated groups are grounded in their morally corrupt cultural backgrounds. Ethnic groups with customs and values differing from the mainstream are presumed to be inferior. These overgeneralizations become fixed in the popular imagination. Sweeping inferences about a whole group are based on misleading information. Even when faced with evidence against their assumptions, misethnists tend to maintain their vituperative sentiments.

These internalized mischaracterizations differ from other attitudes by their percipients' readiness to act to the detriment of a hated group. "Attitudes" refers to the combination of derogatory opinions with averse feelings. This results largely from the emotive response elicited by the repeated expression of disrespectful images about the ethical, political, sexual, religious, or familial qualities of targeted groups. Destructive messages further entrench established perceptions. They legitimize motivational predispositions that are committed to unjust social institutions.

Hate propagandists gather public support for their discriminatory and violent entreaties by evoking broadly accepted vilifications. The coupling of defamatory opinions about members of other racial and ethnic groups with provocative schemes of action is what I mean by "misethnic ideology." This conceptual framework provides a source of input about appropriate social practices and intra-and intergroup interactions. In this way, misethnicity establishes the cognitive foundation for actions directed at persons affiliated with particular groups. Such schemata diffuse into the social psyche through communications affirming the worth of one group and devaluing another.[1] Social outlooks about ethnicity inform individual mindsets and influence behaviors.

Misethnic attitudes are strongest when they occur within the context of an ideology that is supported by conventional mores and beliefs. For example, a society that countenances branding Latinos as lazy will probably also tolerate systematic job discrimination against them. Social consciousness about members of diverse human groups is saturated with cultural meanings about them. Misethnic attitudes that have long been tolerated and promoted have a tighter grip on the imagination than personal prejudices. Their frequent repetition in conversations, books, pamphlets, and newspapers increases popular credulity about the validity of dehumanizing representations. Surely, the anti-Semite believes, there must be something to the view that Jews are greedy, otherwise why would so many people believe it.

Social attitudes are abstract concepts that are applied to particular circumstances. Irrational inferences about the character of specific group members fail to take into account personal distinctions and the presence of traits unexplainable by stereotypes. Indoctrination takes place in schools, around family hearths, before televisions, through advertising, and over the Internet. The most effective propaganda and the least likely to be questioned is frequently proclaimed on various media by recognized and respected orators.

Misethnicity is an ideology that emerges in shared group predispositions that divide culture into ingroups and outgroups. "Ingroup" refers to the dominant social group that enjoys privileges on account of its mutual, salient features. "Outgroup" means a socially vulnerable group toward which many ingroup subjects feel hostility, aversion, or ill-will on account of the objects' race or ethnicity. Whether a group is especially susceptible to harsh treatment in a particular community depends on whether it has ever been systematically persecuted there. The extent of the group's continued susceptibility may be measured by assessing both the duration of previous institutional discriminations and the degree of cultural sympathy for perpetrators of ethnocentric acts.

Ingroups are considered better overall, more socially valuable, and having higher moral standards than outgroups, which are thought to maintain norms incongruous with and obstructive to ingroup aspirations. Outgroup qualities that are conceived as undesirable are distinguished from core ingroup priorities.

The sense of ingroup superiority functions side by side with the practical opinion that outgroups are less entitled to basic rights such as equal protection under the law. Outside groups are deemed politically, economically, and intellectually less important than ingroups. These negative dispositions entail disparate treatment, justified by the outgroups' presumably insignificant claim to fairness. Institutionalized misethnicity includes groupwide manipulation of power for the benefit of dominant groups at the expense of outgroups. The aim of structural favoritism is to protect ingroup interests. This does not mean that all ingroup members take advantage of the situation, but that conditions are more favorable to them because of supremacist ideology spread by popular discourse.

6

The Social Psychology of Scapegoating

Personality is a fairly stable self-conscious conglomeration of beliefs, practical opinions, emotions, biological factors, perceptions, cognitions, defense mechanisms, and judgments developed through a series of connected events. Personal experiences and third-hand reports stimulate thought and prompt conduct. The degree of preparedness to act on newly acquired information is a function of its consonance with previously developed attitudes. In this way, temperament underlies the readiness to receive freshly presented information.[1]

The psychology of misethnicity includes projection, displacement, and justification.[2] *Projection* is the casting of negative traits and faults from selves to others. In the case of misethnicity, powerful ingroups blame their shortcomings on weaker outgroups. A racist society may actually promote bigotry in order to unite ingroup members and distract them from real political and economic problems by sacrificing a historical scapegoat. Intragroup conflict is diffused by focusing anger on a common target. Thereby, misethnicity benefits ingroups and hurts outgroups. On individual levels, persons externalize malevolence and aggressive tendencies from themselves to outgroups. Bigots see outgroup members rather than themselves as inimical to society and equality. The conviction of group superiority is often driven by the sense of inadequacy and the desire for power.[3] *Displacement* is the delusional redirecting of grievances through a process of misassociation, linking unwanted social realities to persons having no hand in causing them. Imagination is critical to displacement because it links conflicts, disappointments, and failures to social pariahs instead of their real sources. Historical myths are instrumental to institutional, as opposed to individual, displacement. *Justification* is the process of purposefully or subconsciously rationalizing the commission of injustices.

Language plays a critical role in developing psychological mechanisms for engaging in racist conduct. As Richard Delgado and Jean Stefancic have pointed out, ethnic prejudice aims to detract from the humanity, dignity, self-respect, standing, and potential of individuals targeted by hate speech as well as the group to which they belong. Repetition of misethnic slurs perpetuates institutionalized discrimination.[4] Prejudice is transmitted through overt and subtle cultural processes. Hate speech expresses not merely personal animosity, but also manifests social attitudes that draw upon personal and communal experiences. The dominant group transmits stereotypes through utterances that are filled with derogatory connotations. Once individuals perceive members of identifiable groups as legitimate targets of aggression, their personal dislikes are reinforced by collective biases and rationalizations.[5] The semantics of destructive messages includes not only contemporary significations but also invokes historically unfair and intolerant power structures. Calling someone a "nigger," for instance, floods the imagination not merely with a personal affront but with insulting ideas that span a history of degradation from slavery to unequal access to education.

Culturally accepted images of the other reassure individuals who adopt them. They play out like a puppet show with clearly defined evil and good characters. Each succeeding generation receives its indoctrination into the cult of racial and ethnic superiority. Personal prejudices flourish in the context of cultural fabrications. Responses to outgroups are learned and conditioned much like other dispositions. Society's imprint on behavioral choice is expressed through popular media, jokes, education, and other modes of daily interactions that legitimize the deliberate maltreatment of minorities. Individuals rely on these for a sense of approval and belonging.[6] Cultural messages that are coupled with personal ambitions intrigue persons seeking either to retain existing power or relying on authoritarian structures as a means of self-aggrandizement. Disparaging speech encourages people willing to bring about ideological goals. The road to persecution is paved by communications confirming to prejudiced individuals that outgroup members are subordinate and unworthy of equal treatment. The cognitive foundations of bigotry are found in cultural discourse.

Destructive messages demean persons out of hand. Anyone in the minority with redeeming qualities is thought to be an exception to the otherwise accurate rule about "those people." "I have a Jewish friend who's honest, but most Jews are swindlers." "The Irish are drunks, but Pat's a'right by me." Misethnists reject some groups as irredeemably different from themselves. Their cognition is so clouded by belittling generalizations about minority attributes that any evidence tending to disprove provocative ideology is dismissed out of hand. Outgroups are viewed not only as alien but also as hostile to ingroup goals and as impediments to their likely continued success. People are classified based on their group's status. Appropriate reaction toward them is defined by legitimizing discourse. Each outgroup member is somehow thought to be connected with social banes. Aggression is displaced from specific causes to the universal culprits purportedly behind them all, whether they be black, Jewish, or a member of any other outgroup.

Stereotypes provide readily identifiable expressions that facilitate misethnic interlocutions. An esoteric quality pervades this lingo, a sense of being in the know about the natural human order and those who endanger it. In reality, the more widespread the dialect of hate, the more likely it is that orators will be successful at recruiting adherents and securing their services for carrying out plans to restrict outgroup rights. The vocabulary of hate speech dehumanizes its target and catalyzes its users to take action against the common enemy. It reduces tensions among ingroup members and increases their animosities against outgroups.

Stereotypes may be words specially formulated for disparaging a particular group or may simply be natural language expressions that channel hatred against an outgroup. These communications are geared toward representing the victims as objects of derision and designating a course of action against them—be it judicial unfairness or job discrimination.[7] In Kantian terms, stereotypes are schemas for memory, retrieval, evaluation, and understanding. Concepts assigned to outgroups, such as lasciviousness, greed, immorality, and infidelity, become integral parts of vernacular descriptions and imaginings about them. Stereotyping eases the processing of information because it furnishes an already established scheme for compartmentalizing sense stimuli.[8] After having been exposed to negative images of blacks, people are more likely to anticipate that blacks are dangerous. Completely innocuous events—for example, a black man approaching in the middle of the street at night—are often interpreted as perilous even when no factual reason for fear or added anxiety exists. The event may be recorded in the memory as having been a hazardous situation even though no evidence substantiates such a conclusion.

Stereotypes, then, are symbolic depictions transmitted through expressions that are filled with cultural meaning and sociohistorical significance. Orators synthesize semantic designations to create ideologies easily understandable to the audience because they appeal to their emotional impulse to find a vulnerable target on whom to vent frustrations. Effective ideology produces a worldview made up of various distinct fictions about outgroups, composing a unified doctrine that calls listeners to wreak havoc on their chimerical foes. This mutual cause unifies followers, especially during times of economic hardship, tapping into collective desires to shed responsibility for failure and seek a facile explanation for the downward turns in their lives. Misethnicity is an effectual means of positing blame where it does not belong because it strings together recognizable symbols into one systematic dogma whose familiar phrases captivate the masses. Support for active discrimination is usually based on existing, demeaning attitudes that spark organized actions, designed to retain privileges for ingroups. During times of high unemployment, a demagogue is more likely to find political backing by speaking against foreign workers than by giving speeches about the complex economic causes of the situation. The more engorged misethnic statements are in culturally accepted schemas of ingroup power and outgroup exclusion, the more likely it is that significant numbers of persons in the ingroup will lend a helping hand to accomplishing ideological objectives.[9]

Conventional character development in a society where misethnicity is the norm necessitates internalization of an irrational hatred for minorities. Social perceptions of ingroup and outgroup attributes are tied to the process of establishing and validating self-image and self-esteem. This proclivity begins in childhood. Children acquire and personalize racist and ethnocentric dispositions through a fourfold progression: (1) *indoctrination* through school, family, friends, media, and fables; (2) *questioning* why some people are treated differently than others; (3) *acceptance* of ethnic and racial stratification; and (4) *affectation* of inclinations, habits, and behaviors grounded in misethnic ideology.

Regardless of the predispositions of individual children, whether passive or aggressive, they are born with neutral ethnic mindsets. It is only through interaction with teachers and parents, whose examples young children implicitly follow, that views about various groups are transmitted.[10] Learned responses are, then, reinforced during children's play and by popular overt and subtle prejudices. Victors are children's heroes, and the victors usually happen to be ingroup members. Frantz Fanon, the great psychoanalyst of the racialist psyche, recalled how he and his black childhood friends identified with white conquerors, the bringers of "civilization," and thought of vanquished black Africans as savages, different from themselves. They acquired this attitude through indoctrination, through the language of colonization.[11] Although children go through a period of doubt, wondering whether the other really is as different from themselves as they have been told, the full weight of cultural meaning weighs heavily on concept formation and commonly sweeps doubt away, hopefully to be revisited when they grow up. By assimilating their group identities through the matrix of misethnic social attitudes, children incorporate prejudgments into their worldview about themselves and others. Finally, they are ready to act within the context of what they learned.

For those adults who do not recognize the inequity in all this, their sense of where they fit in the social hierarchy is correlative to what group they belong. The impressions people have about themselves are usually congruent with how they perceive both their ethnic group and its relation to others. Persons who harbor stereotypes and aversions against minorities retard their personal growth because they restrict their range of associates, develop an elitism that is impervious to contrary points of view, inflexibly maintain dogma in the face of reliable discrepant evidence, and deaden their ethnic senses.[12] The delusion of grandeur based on group membership saps constructive energy and replaces it with stagnant opinions that are based on false generalities instead of concrete facts. Rather than working through insecurities and inadequacies, shortcomings are posited on a bogeyman, existing only in the imagination. Fantasies displace reality and stifle personal potential by wasting productive hours with destructive apparitions. Psychological normalcy, therefore, should not be gauged by the degree to which a person adheres to popular culture. Instead, a psychologically stable person is one who integrates sentient data with theory to arrive at an accurate picture of the world and the social relations in it. Hatred directed at an abstract enemy, whose many-tentacled attributes are never confirmed by experience, denotes a personality disturbance. On the other hand, resentment of specific persons who have harmed someone is rational.[13]

Misethnic mental devices reduce an entire segment of the population into profligate, pernicious, and dastardly subhumans, quite different from ingroup members. They bolster bigots' egotism, making them seem a little more perfect in their own eyes, a little closer to the image of God.

They are above those base creatures. They know them from a schema, and need no contacts with outgroups to be impassioned in their convictions. It is for bigots a battle between good and evil, between civilization and savagism, between Christians and Christ killers, between light and darkness. Put in these terms, hate speech recruits followers willing to give their lives for the ideologies. Those people it attracts are generally (1) poorly adjusted or adverse to the ordinary political and socioeconomic interactions of a multicultural democracy; (2) ethnocentric, hating anyone outside their homogeneous group; and (3) prejudiced in numerous facets of their lives, including interpersonal bonds, educational interrelations, employment decisions, and political choices.[14] Misethnic declarations and membership in fascistic groups provide outlets for their paranoia, giving meaning to their lives by conceptually subordinating "the enemy" and presenting an object on whom to vent their aggressions.

Discourses that legitimize ethnic stratification stimulate emotional and motivational responses. These reactions are linked with cultural coping mechanisms and pervading paradigms. For conforming personalities, the prototypical rubrics of intergroup relations become their own; any deviation from accepted dealings become personal affronts.

The effectiveness of group animosity can be measured by the amount of mental associations elicited by relatively few characteristics. Stereotypes that have been communicated repeatedly in diverse social contexts require less information to evoke a whole series of negative connotations.[15] The longer a group defamation persists in a culture, the more readily it lends itself to justify violent action against targeted groups because of the degree of derogatory attitudes it enkindles.

Seeing outgroups behave in ways that contradict prejudices may be so divergent from conventional depictions of them that bigots will fail to internalize actuality. Discounting the ideological fallacy, they will explain the event as an aberration from an otherwise valid category. Walter Lippmann, who coined the term "stereotype," explained how those generalizations limit epistemology and values: "[T]he pattern of stereotypes at the center of our moral codes largely determine what group of facts we shall see, and in what light we shall see them. . . . And since my moral system rests on my accepted version of the facts, he who denies either my moral judgments or my version of the facts, is to me perverse, alien, dangerous."[16] The range of attitudes that stereotypes prompt indicates that they compose entrenched assumptions that are fundamental to personality makeup.

Prejudice serves as a convenient set of answers and self-defense mechanisms for persons wanting to deny their insecurities. The ideas of charismatic leaders figure prominently in these people's understanding of social reality. Reliance on predefined distinctions is a defense for masking painful truths about personal and group faults. Bigots may become angry when their ignorance of economic, historical, anthropological, religious, and linguistic presuppositions about hated minorities is tested and questioned. When the irrationality of misethnicity is pointed out to them, their emotional response is often intense because ethnocentrism is so wedded to core beliefs and dispositions.[17]

Stereotyping's invective not only wins over people's feelings but also enables them to rationalize committing injustices and treating designated peoples unequally. Hate speech creates targets for animus that might otherwise be directed against other ingroup members. Mass movements devoted to racist ideology create a pseudo-reality in which the most nonsensical accusations and fantastic confabulations about outgroups are unquestioningly taken for truths. Forever accusing Jews for the Crucifixion makes no sense as it blames countless individuals who have no connection to the event, yet this creed has drawn multitudes of adherents. This libel has repeatedly spurred rampages.

Prejudices are means for convincing oneself why it is appropriate to act in ways that contradict basic ethical standards against inflicting harm. They are instrumental for excusing behavior that undermines the underlying structure of well-ordered society. Supremacism has profound consequences both when opportunities to discriminate are present and in conditioning sentiments that can be conducive for later unfairness. Ethnocentric people recognize that oppressive acts are not humane. So, derogatory images portraying outgroups as inferiors help them dismiss the notion that the others are by nature worthy of compassionate treatment, too. A violation of ethical norms is easier to explain away if the victims belong to an outgroup and are widely portrayed as demonic adversaries who are purportedly menacing to the population.

For example, lynch mobs in the U.S. South typically accused victims of the perpetrators' pathological actions. They were persuaded, as they hanged people from trees, that it was blacks and not they who were violent. In the slaveholding South (and in modern-day Mauritania), while masters commonly raped their slaves, it was black men who were characterized as rapists and dangerous to women. "Many studies have shown, for example, that a ruling group which has exhibited violent aggression against a minority and has exploited it sexually is likely to be firmly convinced that members of the minority are uniformly violent and sexually unrestrained."[18] The depiction of blacks as inherently inimical has been essential in gaining support for attacks against them. Demagogues gather followers by eliciting age-old fears in them. Racist whites projected their violent sexual impulses on vulnerable blacks, all the time blind to their own perversity and cruelty, propelled by the many negative associations misethnicity imprinted over years of indoctrination. Whatever guilt racists experience is diluted by streams of racist propaganda.

Such rhetoric is internalized through moralistic rationalizations, taking sustenance from inflammatory cultural myths. Victims are blamed for their own sufferings.[19] Jews were defamed in pre–World War II Germany for allegedly being traitors, undermining Aryan purity, destroying the arts and sciences, and corrupting youths. Many Germans claimed that Jews caused circumstances requiring the Final Solution. Similarly, in imperial Russia, Jews were blamed for pogroms against their own shtetls. Protagonists of this view maintained that powerful Jews allowed mobs to decapitate, rape, and bludgeon their coreligionists to retain the facade that Jews were powerless. The consciences of people who took part in these rampages were numbed by shifting the blame for violence onto those whom they tormented. The Jews were Christ killers, filthy vermin, and diabolical financiers. The land had to be disinfected and cleared of them. Without this exonerating crutch, which gradually seeped into social semantics, the masses could not have been as easily stirred to action by anti-Semitic oratory. The intellectual community, too, zealously did its part in the Final Solution. Hitler's physician, Karl Brandt, spoke about the active participation of ordinary physicians in euthanizing the "socially unfit": "The individual doctor took full responsibility for his judgments as assessor. . . . In no circumstances is it to be understood that any doctor serving under this scheme was ever obliged to perform euthanasia in a case where he himself had not decided it was necessary."[20] The legitimizing discourses are like balm on the lacerated scruples of misethnists.

Likewise, in the United States, the mantra of pro-slavery advocates seeped into the marrow of society and sedated ethical sentiments until they were so dulled that slavery was considered beneficial to both whites and blacks. Somnolence was so deep that slavery flourished, even though it was contrary to all the principles for which this country stood. Blacks were seen as instrumental to whites and were not valued intrinsically. Supremacists hated blacks who tried to break the mold of social stratification, and they were condescending to those who groveled. The ideology was fraught with contradictions. Domineering individuals despised blacks for wanting their freedom, yet liberty was seen as one of the rights most to be honored and protected. They also worried about losing control over persons whose continued subservience was an integral part of their self-definitions: they were not like the others; they were better, smarter, more skilled. Emotionally they were puffed up by their imagined aristocracy in all human characteristics. Blacks fell short in their grandiose illusions. Self-image depended on who they were (white) and who they were not (black), and they were so committed to their worldview that they fought a Civil War to preserve those self-aggrandizements.

The supremacist struggle for self-identity comes at the expense of others' happiness. Any self-doubt about their preeminence is soothed with lingo that places blacks evolutionarily and theologically below whites.[21] Bigots feed on hatred to the point where their personal anxieties, their misplaced frustrations, and their self-justifications are directed at any outgroup they perceive as too weak to strike back. Fanon's insight highlights the generalizing nature of misethnicity:

> At first thought it may seem strange that the anti-Semite's outlook should be related to that of the Negrophobe. It was my philosophy professor . . . who recalled the fact to me one day: "Whenever you hear anyone abuse the Jews, pay attention, because he is talking about you." And I found that he was universally right—by which I meant that I was answerable in my body and in my heart for what was done to my brother. Later I realized that he meant, quite simply, an anti-Semite is inevitably anti-Negro.[22]

This passage brilliantly draws attention to the extensiveness of misethnicity. Hatred against one group presages danger to other minorities because misethnists do not stop at the sacrifice of one group but look to destroy all who stand in the way of their megalomaniacal ambitions.

Underlying stereotypes is the urge to oversimplify dilemmas and find designated scapegoats for complex predicaments. Approaching adversities from a biased perspective gives meaningful answers to inexplicable predicaments. Economic downturns are often difficult for experts and laymen to explain, so Jewish financiers make an easy target for those who are unwilling to search for market causes. It is easier to blame immigrants for unemployment than to enact politically risky laws designed to create jobs. Misethnicity provides an explanation that pits ingroups against outgroups. Individuals with disparate interests are united in the common objective, the weeding out of a shared enemy. Ingroup tensions are released through mutual or compatible beliefs, paranoias, attitudes, and aims.[23]

Persons with entrenched misethnic feelings are predisposed to obsess more about others' faults and to concentrate less on their own inadequacies. They are not adept at linking disputes and irascible emotions with real sources of conflict. Instead, they rely on universal stigmas rather than evidence and logical reasoning. Fixations and rigid assumptions tend to center around a small set of recurring targets.[24] Even when cultural institutions are in their favor, bigots ordinarily consider themselves victims and believe that depriving others of their rights is a proper means of obtaining their due. Retaining preeminent status for them goes hand in hand with lessening outgroup opportunities. Apprehensiveness about one's self-worth outside the context of a demarcated ingroup is channeled into animosity constructed on and guided by expressions of ethnic intolerance. The personality of such people, in large part, stands on the unsubstantial ground of what it is not, one of the hated ones with the big noses and dark skins. Failing to make rational self-evaluations, investigate valid causes, and ascertain adequate solutions makes contentment elusive for them.

Group-aggrandizing attitudes help avert attention from disparities in social standing that exist among ingroup members. They syphon discontent toward vulnerable minorities. Outgroup-ingroup frictions have profound psychological consequences on both groups. The general effect is one of embedded social stratifications.

The sustained impact of stereotypes on communities alters the perspectives of minorities. From childhood, they are exposed to a barrage of negative images about themselves, their parents, and their friends. Some stereotypes are designed to keep outgroups from gaining positions of authority and others are intended to remove minorities from the few footholds they enjoy.[25] Both of these methods of maintaining inequality make it more difficult for outgroups to find ways of fulfilling their potentials. Widespread disparagements cannot but burrow into their sense of self-potential. Minorities regularly encounter barriers against their advancement and expend energy in dissociating themselves from deceptive generalities about their group.

Prevailing paradigms, further, demand that outgroups efface themselves for the sake of ingroups, to commit hara-kiri so they do not stand in the way of dominant social forces. One of Franz Kafka's philosophical novels, *The Trial*, can be interpreted as an allegory about the plight of an insecure Jew living in an anti-Semitic culture. The protagonist, Joseph K., is charged with some wrongdoing, but he does not know what, if anything, he has done to deserve such an accusation. He is then subjected to a bureaucracy he does not comprehend, and no one working within it will help him make any sense of it. K. is hurled into a dilemma, seemingly not of his own making. The powers against him are overwhelming, and he has no way to change his circumstances. No one tells him who his accuser is, and the social and legal system is itself stacked against him. At the end, he is given a knife to kill himself, and when he refuses to do so, someone buries it in his chest. K. is butchered like an animal.

K.'s primary character flaw throughout his ordeal lies in a lack of self-reflection. He eventually accepts the faceless bureaucracy's charges without analyzing whether there is any substance to them. The court before which K. must offer his defense typifies bigots whose prejudices prevent them from reflecting on individual cases. Instead, they destroy lives based on interwoven misconceptions, fabrications, selfish motivations, insecurities, feelings of guilt, and irrational ideologies. K. lacks the strength of character needed to disregard the unfounded charges of an unyielding accuser, a Gentile world greater than himself, against which he can muster no advocates. His thoughts become confused and his emotional state becomes unstable because he belittles himself in succumbing to the empty allegations made against him by powerful social forces. K.'s ingrained sense of inferiority prevents him from rising to the spiritual heights of Sisyphus and Prometheus of Greek mythology, who transcended their punishments through introspection, self-knowledge, self-confidence, and the ability to discount the type of rationalizations that make misethnicity so seductive.

In similar terms, Fanon explained the black predicament of being characterized a social pariah. "A feeling of inferiority? No, a feeling of nonexistence. Sin is Negro as virtue is white. All those white men in a group, guns in their hands, cannot be wrong. I am guilty. I do not know of what, but I know that I am no good." Outgroups are made to feel that their very beings are in some way contemptible and their ethnic group is obstructive to progress.

Victims of misethnicity fear for their well-being. It is simplistic to quantify the harms of group hatred solely by the number of perpetrated hate crimes. Racism and ethnocentrism percolate into the sinews of virtually all facets of social life. They have direct and indirect consequences on victims' decision-making processes. The impediments they confront as a group are not placed in front of persons in the majority; therefore, minorities are more limited in career, education, and material options. The standards for climbing social ladders are set higher, so only stellar candidates can break into networks that for generations have been dominated by ingroups.

Experiences with misethnic customs and practices create a consciousness in historically persecuted groups of their precarious social position. Hate speech is integral to maintaining hierarchies by helping to legitimize degrading stereotypes and dangerous attitudes.[26] Biased speech engenders a sense of helplessness against established beliefs and behavioral patterns.

It also traumatizes children and sets them against relatives. Children learn negativism toward their own group from media, friends, and books. This can decrease their self-respect and impair their relationship with parents, who are children's chief role models and whose competence, potentialities, and moral rectitude are deprecated in a prejudiced culture. Children are confused by the difference between self-conscious awareness of parents' uprightness and the blistering attacks they hear upon all persons belonging to their group. It takes substantial mental effort and strength of character to remain confident in one's abilities in the face of widespread disparagements.[27] How does a parent answer a child when she asks why a flag so closely resembling the battle flag of traitors who sought to perpetuate the institution of slavery and import it into western territories of the United States flies over the state capitol? What should a parent do when the inferiority begins to swell in her heart? How does one prevent anger from informing her conduct toward whites? Children should not be subjected to the destructive messages of persons preying on their developing personalities, on their fragile self-esteem, and on their comprehension of reality.[28]

The pain of past oppressions affects an outgroup's posterity. Scars are left on succeeding generations even from injustices committed long before. The liturgy Jews use during Passover, the holiday celebrating their liberation from slavery in Egypt, brings this point home. It includes the injunction for each devotee to think of him- or herself as having been a slave there. Likewise, the suffering of the Holocaust has made an entire post–World War II generation of Jews leery that, given severe social strains, even civilized European nations might actively or complicitly attempt to liquidate them. Black encounters with slavery in the United States have residually affected people who see manifestations of state-approved racial stratifications on signs like flags that tout and extol the South's history of legal discrimination. Many Native Americans, too, are conscious that the United States' continued breach of its fiduciary duty to administer the Indian Trust Fund stems from a paternalistic undervaluation of Native American culture.

Vilified persons often internalize social stigmas and make them part of their self-identity. They may even display prejudices that are common in dominant society against their own group. This antipathy toward their own group, of course, accretes to a self-hatred and a sense of inability to rise out of socioeconomic inequalities.[29]

Books sometimes become classics even though they are tainted by racism. Outgroups swallow their anger and ethnic pride, recognizing misethnicity while acknowledging and learning from works written and performed by ethnocentrists. Here Fyodor Dostoevsky comes to mind with his penetrating existential novels that are spotted by xenophobic and anti-Semitic Russian nationalism. Thomas Jefferson, who wrote so eloquently and wisely of liberty, owned slaves; and Andrew Jackson, who asserted federal power against South Carolina's nullificationists, abandoned indigenous tribes to the mercy of the states and then removed them from their native lands. Fanon describes how racist culture seeps into minorities' personalities:

I read white books and little by little I take into myself the prejudices, the myths, the folklore that have come to me from Europe. . . . [T]he Negro selects himself as an object capable of carrying the burden of original sin. The white man chooses the black man for this function, and the black man who is white also chooses the black man. . . . After having been the slave of the white man he enslaves himself.[30]

Victims are surrounded by images of their people as malignant and their ways as regressive. Unless they are aware of their individual capacities for thought and constructive conduct, they flow with whatever conception society has of them.

Hate speech, then, has long-term psychological ramifications. It establishes the definitional parameters within which minorities are dehumanized into throwaway objects, unworthy of respect and compassion.

7

Spreading Group Hatred

The psychic health of a society can be measured by the extent to which its policies and laws exclude and constrain prejudices. One sign of social stability is the degree to which a community and the individuals who compose it are willing to acknowledge the humanity and learn from the cultures of other peoples. Many cultures have resorted to discrimination and prejudice despite their self-destructive consequences. Dehumanizing representations of minorities disseminated through social discourse are integral to the formation of movements bent on harming outgroups. I now turn to the social linguistics of misethnicity.

Semantics is based on a broad variety of diverse and interdependent societal factors. Language does not exist in a vacuum; it is not merely a group of syntactic rules with universal application. Prevalent linguistic practices evolve from historical circumstances often involving intergroup power struggles and various religious and cultural conflicts.[1]

Success in a society requires mastery of its language to some lesser or greater extent. The better persons understand how to exploit formal grammar and idiomatic nuances, the greater is their potential for success. Speakers incorporate phrases loaded with cultural baggage to get their meaning across. A well-placed word adds to the symbolism of remarks, thereby increasing their breadth of meaning.

Ethnocentric linguistic paradigms are comprehended within the context of social history, literature, religion, and political philosophy. Some terms and expressions are steeped in meanings reaching into the pulsating heart of misethnicity.[2] Blackness, for instance, often signifies evil in European cultures. It is no coincidence that "black" came to describe dark-skinned persons of African descent. A breadth of subject areas express adverse and repugnant attributes about anything that is figuratively black. Sixteenth- and seventeenth-century explorers, who first called them blacks, considered Africans to be morally reprobate and dirty. The devil is the prince of darkness, and one of the derogatory titles for blacks is "darkies." On the other hand, the Book of Revelations teaches that God's chosen shall be clothed in white, and Jesus is equated with light in whom there is no darkness. Black magic invokes images about the use of mystical power for evil intents, while white magic is the harnessing of such power for good. The use of blackness in many contexts as a bad and wicked quality lends cognitive content to cultural definitions not only of abstractions but of people, too. On the other hand, whiteness denotes an air of innocence and godly, clean living.

Manipulation of the syntax of ordinary language makes traditional stereotypes more believable because it vests them with a semantic framework that brings the persuasive power of culture to bear on their validity. Ethnic innuendoes, therefore, are broadly persuasive. Stereotyping feeds into the divide between ethnic groups, diminishing potential cultural benefits of ethnic diversity. The process of conferring arbitrarily distributed entitlements on dominant groups draws upon a lexicology filled with symbolism. One group is consecrated by language and practice as superior and it is contrasted with the other ones, who fail to make the grade.

Widely propagated names and labels create an artificial picture of reality. The symbolic power of language generates impressions that, when unquestioned, come to be presumed indications about actuality. "Naming" a group means assigning a qualitative concept to it. The epistemic purpose of names is to refer directly to the concept. They substitute for elaborate descriptions. There is also a semantic element to naming that incorporates the cultural conscience. Epithets, therefore, not only evoke the idea of the object itself but of the cultural meanings attached to it. "Knowledge of a language" refers not only to understanding its lexicon and grammatical rules but also the contextual use of appellations.[3] Contextualization through sentence structure and word choice adds color to declarations.

Ethnic and racial insults are defamatory statements against individuals based on their membership in identifiable groups. Disparaging labels can represent a whole group as socially undesirable. How effective such labels are in delivering desired blows to outgroup dignities partly depends on the prevalence of the insult and the institutional credentials of the speaker. Demagogues who have a broad following communicate the misethnicity of a politically and religiously powerful group. The entire group assigns them the authority to state and embellish its views. The victims of hate speech are at greater risk from groupwide threats than from personal attacks. Counterspeech is less effective against a group with deeply held beliefs, which feels the power of its numbers and the passions of its hateful convictions, than against an individual expressing only his or her biased ideas.[4] Labels reify prejudices through stories that exaggerate and falsify outgroup traits and extol the presumed advantages of excluding minorities from ingroup privileges. The broad, dark strokes that are then applied to scapegoats make for an auspiciously hostile environment filled with slights and vilifications. Aspersive names schematize the world into groups of good guys and bad guys.

As stereotyping becomes more and more respectable, perceptions of outgroups become increasingly associated with belittling social definitions. Bigoted ideology, then, energizes shared cultural and political beliefs, attitudes, and behavioral rationalizations into a cauldron of volatile formative constructs.[5] In the mouths of charismatic orators, sweeping generalizations and outright fabrications can be combined with cultural injunctions about how to deal with the hated others. Interactions with members of other races and ethnic groups are strained by deep-seated, often subconscious, social ideologies.[6] Traditional, easily recognizable images of outgroups shape cultural presuppositions. They can then be applied to specific contemporary social situations in order to galvanize mass movements. Persons who internalize an ideology are deeply influenced by its conceptions of virtue and evil. They adhere to its dictates both in personal and public life. Misethnic ideologies are so inciteful that even when they serve no direct economic aspirations, they nevertheless facilitate the functioning of hate movements. As Gunnar Myrdal wrote in his classic study about the social and economic problems of American blacks, "We must not forget the influence of ideological forces. And we must guard against the common mistake of reducing them solely to secondary expressions of economic interests."[7] The antebellum South's retention of slavery, even though the institution was economically regressive, illustrates this point. The power of ideology is also evident from the inefficient manner in which Nazis maintained labor camps. They literally worked Jews to death there, losing valuable wartime resources in the process.

Destructive messages are the main vehicles for spreading ideology. Hate speech is an essential means for popularizing hate groups. Physical persecutions of outgroups are commonly preceded by institutional inequalities resulting in part from the popularization of misethnic ideology.

Gordon Allport, one of the foremost authorities on the psychology of prejudice, detailed this sequence of events in *The Nature of Prejudice*: "Although most barking (antilocution) does not lead to biting, yet there is never a bite without previous barking. Fully seventy years of political anti-Semitism of the verbal order antedated the discriminatory Nürnberg Laws passed by the Hitler regime. Soon after these laws were passed the violent program of extermination began. Here we see the not infrequent progression: antilocution → discrimination → . . . violence."[8] Slurs are disseminated by many media, including newsprint, schools, music, and movies. Communications among dominant group members are also important. Pejorative and malicious intragroup conversations develop into a vocabulary and grammar depicting a common enemy, affording a mutual interest in trying to rid society of the designated pest. Prejudices can become galvanized into a cultural conscience about hated outsiders.[9]

Often, preconceived animosities are coupled with spurious accusations that spread like wildfire through communities harboring misethnic attitudes. Jews have, since medieval times, periodically been accused of kidnaping Christian children, crucifying them, and using their blood as an ingredient in Passover matzah. All American Indians were reputed to be brutal savages who killed frontier people. Lynch mobs were often riled up by unwarranted charges alleging that a black man had raped a white woman. These accusations were unquestioned by riotous crowds that had been reared on the common assumption that blacks could not control their sexual urges, especially in respect to white women. Japanese Americans living on the West Coast during World War II were interned after being branded spies who were inimical to the United States' war efforts. Accusations are most noxious when they import traditional stereotypes into specific insinuations and false charges. Stating that Jews kill Christian children increases anti-Semitism but will probably not be enough to start a riot. However, in a culture already inundated with anti-Semitic literature and where intergroup tensions are high, saying "Massacre Rabinovich and all his Jew neighbors for killing Christianson and baking matzo with his blood!" is probably enough to instigate violence. Scurrilities produce illogical ingroup paranoias, displace grievances from their causes to scapegoats, and rationalize oppression.[10]

Not all intolerant utterances are so blatant. Jokes targeting ethnic and racial groups seem innocuous enough, but many of them subtly transmit harmful stereotypes. They draw on existing offensive characterizations of outgroups: in the United States, Poles and blacks are usually portrayed as stupid, Irish as drunk, Jews as greedy. Jokes evoke acculturated attitudes that are often so common that even children can identify the object of derision. Persons having little or no contact with outgroups formulate opinions about them from humorous anecdotes that exploit common stereotypes. The shared mentality and mirth at the humor of degradation confirms to bigots that the overgeneralizations must have some merit to them, why else would so many people understand the ideology on which they are based? Defamatory jokes also implicitly or explicitly proclaim the superiority of the dominant group; they distance themselves from the alleged attributes of outgroups.

These rhetorical maneuvers, like many other linguistic forms that convey prejudices, use juxtapositions, distinctions, and hyperboles. Ingroup definitions derive partially from the comparison between themselves and outsiders. Juxtapositions glorify ingroup character, morality, fidelity, intelligence, beauty, and devalue the intrinsic dignity of outgroups. They render the world into distinct camps with impenetrable boundaries. Negative stereotypes, therefore, elicit illusions of grandeur. Ingroups describe themselves in positive terms. Outgroups, on the other hand, are perceived as dangerous to civilized institutions. Hate speech divides the world into good and evil forces that are embodied in the differing races and ethnic groups. Outgroups are sometimes viewed as belonging to altogether separate species than ingroups. Their humanity is denied, making it easier to treat them unequally and to persecute them with equanimity.[11] Reducing society to black and white forces, embodied in dark- and light-skinned peoples, maintains emotionally charged conflicts. American slave owners saw themselves as God's Elect and compared blacks to monkeys. Germans thought they were Aryan supermen while relegating Jews to the status of vermin.

Hyperboles, too, make minorities look absurdly comical. Their physical attributes are exaggerated, faults of individuals are imputed to the entire group, and they are mockingly depicted with thick lips, big noses, and childlike behaviors.

Derogatory generalizations about minorities direct cultural thought about them. They are like blinders that restrict the range of public perceptions of outgroups to a narrow set of defamations, charged with cultural meanings, that misrepresent outgroup characteristics. Stereotypes help sustain the status of minorities as outsiders who are indelibly inferior and downright evil. The language of racism comes to define outgroups in the public mind, particularly when there is little interaction between ethnic groups.

Eventually, stereotypes become clichés and supposed truisms. Judgments of an outgroup become part and parcel of its social definition, whence come expressions like "He jewed me down" and "He gypped me." The disparaging images apply to the entire group.[12]

Roughly speaking,[13] perceptions are interpreted through short- and long-term memories. Short-term memory (STM) refers to cognizance of external stimuli and usually involves processing a limited amount of information from immediate or just-past empirical input. Long-term memory (LTM) is an abstraction relating to the storage of information that arose out of STM. LTM tends to be composed of social and individual judgments coupled with previous experiences and present sensations. Recollections are not solely factual accounts of prior occurrences since they include structural schemas attached to earlier impressions. Further, the mental blueprints that individuals possess about their social environments play an integral role in gathering information through STM and then storing it in LTM. Data are arranged through predefined categories. It is easier to understand new situations in terms of existing opinions. Communications require structure to make sense of otherwise novel information, and semantics functions as a lexicon for categorizing incidental circumstances.[14] Ingroup-outgroup interactions occur within the framework of social semantics. Individuals approach events with established beliefs and ideologies. Episodic encounters are understood through schemas for interpretation that often relegate minorities lower in the social hierarchy. Thus, slurs are most detrimental when directed at historically persecuted groups because they contain more sinister significations than animosities expressed toward individuals. The victims of hate speech are not just the objects of a specific vituperation; rather, the entire group is implicated by the syntax.

Persons who have internalized misethnic linguistic constructs have faith not only in their validity but also believe in the solutions they offer. Misethnicity, therefore, has a compelling effect on persons, especially on those who have low self-esteem and are predisposed to following authoritarian figures. With a bit of prompting from charismatic leaders who harp on popular discontents, racists are prone to act violently against hated minorities. Whether disdain, workplace and educational discrimination, battery, murder, enslavement, or genocide is the modus operandi of such persons depends, in part, on how widespread are the mischaracterizations and how deeply misethnic sentiments run in individuals.

The oratorical power of hate group leaders comes from their ability to harness the verbal paradigms of the cultures from which they spring. On the one hand, speakers influence listeners' emotions through the social content in their vitriol; on the other, their adherents infuse demagogues with the potency of groupwide sentiments about the source of social ills. By drawing on age-old fictions about outgroup culpability, expressing extreme and uncompromising aims, and putting them into stark terms, demagogues unite devotees loyal both to them personally and to the ideas they advocate.

Dehumanizing the targeted outgroup legitimizes efforts to harm them. On the conceptual level, effective stereotypes strip minority groups of their individuality and of their personal worth. They subject minorities to the will of the dominant group and expect outgroups to participate in their own demise: Nazis expected Jews to help round up their brethren for deportation to concentration camps; American slaves were told by owners and preachers that God decreed that they be obedient to white masters; Americans demanded that Native American tribes sell their lands for a pittance and vacate themselves to a place most of them had never seen; and today, in Mauritania, Arab/Berbers demand unquestioned dedication and loyalty from their black slaves.

Bigots frequently become livid when minorities refuse to comply with traditional ingroup expectations because they believe their insistencies are part of the unalterable social and moral order. In Mauritania, when slaves unsuccessfully flee from bondage, they inevitably receive even harsher punishments than usual. An outgroups' urge for liberty is not recognized as valid because slaves are not considered their owners' equals. *Beydanes* deem it an affront for slaves to even speak of autonomy because it so contradicts their imagined docile black African. Tortures for defiant actions include joint dislocation and genital mutilation. In the ante-bellum South, masters flogged and amputated the limbs of any captured fugitive slaves.

The denial of outgroup humanity is a thread that runs through such cases. Not only are legal and political rights withheld from outgroups, supremacists also deny that despised minorities have any fundamental rights because they do not regard them as fully human.[15] They are thought of as subspecies or, worse yet, as diseases on humankind which must be eradicated. Mass persecution requires collectively understood derogatory labels, mutual understandings, and a ruthless leader to stoke the embers of destruction. The process paving the way to outrageous acts of injustice is, of course, gradual. It begins by indoctrinating children with the culture of racial and ethnic stratification.

Acquisition of misethnic attitudes begins early in life through childhood observation, language development, formal education, and behavioral and verbal imitation. During their formative years, children begin conceptualizing and applying generalizations.[16] Subtle and not so subtle cues transmit historical stereotypes. Children hear expressions that connect blackness with evil and whiteness with goodness. They see movies with good frontier people being chased by and fending off barbaric Indians.

Children become cognizant of themselves as members of a group and distance themselves from persons not possessing certain salient qualities. Besides self-realization, children develop group awareness and identity. They grow conscious of both their distinct personalities and their membership in identifiable groups. Coupled with these notions is the apprehension of what identity cognitions entail socially. Minority children discover that multiple negative insinuations are regularly made publicly against their ethnic group. They soon perceive that their social standing is partly based on group membership.[17] Misethnic cultures and households juxtapose races and ethnic groups the same way they might distinguish between "white" and "black" or "good" and "evil." This leads to the categorization of human groups into divergent, morally stratified groups: "Christians" and "heathens," "Muslims" and "infidels," "Jews" and "*Goyim*," "Brahmin" and "Sudra," "*Beydane*" and "*Abed*." The characterization of one group includes distinguishing it from another group. Thus, people become members not only of diverse but also of adverse groups whose conflicts are often predefined by previous generations. These types of group differentiations sow seeds for future hostility and animosity.

Cultural imagery is strengthened by overtly racist speech that young children might hear from adults, learn at school, or discover through the Internet. Insidious innuendos integrate themselves into concept formations. Comprehending the contexts in which stereotypes are used and events in which they are applicable initiates children into the cognitive acceptance and emotional internalization of discrimination.[18] Long-standing social orientations toward minorities influence children's acculturation. Learning the prevailing, majority attitudes is part of ordinary social indoctrination. Children's acquisition of cultural dislikes and antagonisms results from complex perceptions of multiple external stimuli: defamations about minorities, experiences with how persons of other races are treated, parental cues about who are appropriate companions, and the extent of interracial intercourse. Thereby, children learn the place society assigns to various ethnic groups.

Childhood instruction influences attitudes and personality. Repetition in a variety of social settings instills stereotypes, altering them from mere opinions to ardent convictions. Inculcated beliefs about outgroups ("avoid the black kids," "don't hang out with Jews," and "those Indians will teach you no good") elicit long-term consequences by engendering aggressive affects and generating intolerant practices. Often, generalities about outgroups are formed before children have any contact with other groups. They develop background information, anxieties, and prejudices which then are imported to future interpersonal interactions.

Eventually, children's relatedness to their social group can culminate in averse ideas and destructive conduct toward outgroups. Minorities then become the outlets of aggression. Children, thereby, develop a personal, hedonistic interest in misethnicity: hatred of an outgroup focuses feelings of discontent, exasperation, and vexation on a countenanced pariah and reduces conflict with parents, playmates, and other ingroup members. As children grow into their social roles, they formulate psychic representations of outgroups that are picked up from fables, anecdotes, jokes, misinformation, and overt misethnicity. Their reasons for hating minorities become cultural ones.[19]

The attitudes people acquire as children often galvanize into passionately embraced but nevertheless irrational creeds in adulthood. The existence of persistent animosities eases the acceptance and orchestration of virulent misethnicity. Further, deeply held contemptuous presumptions assuage guilt about acting violently toward targeted outgroups.

Positive social institutions such as the tolerance of diversity and fairness under the law, and negative ones such as racism and discrimination are imbedded in grammar. Derogatory connotations that are implied in phrases and words are fertile grounds for nurturing ethnocentric proclivities into fully grown nefarious movements. It is easier to harness hate for the purpose of maintaining power when grammar and lexicon identify certain groups as the enemies of everything that is good. Propaganda takes advantage of people's inclinations to conform and respond to linguistic paradigms. It draws from mutual attitudes and dogma to meld destructive factions into unified movements. The lingo of misethnicity soaks up the dominant tradition from which it arose and creates outlets that are driven by herd mentality.[20]

Stereotypes are endemic to prejudiced societies. Where misethnicity has become part of culture, it pervades virtually all facets of life, including language and social dealings. Institutional racism and ethnocentrism are transmitted from one generation to another by the descriptions of and customary actions toward other groups. On the sociocultural level, the personalities of bigots pour themselves into the mold of common opinion as sources of support, justification, and meaning. Like many other misethnic societies, Nazi Germany claimed that it was the exclusive repository of culture. "[It] estimated which races were capable of cultural development and pronounced the apparent culture of the Jew to be nothing but a sham."[21] Jewish life-styles, religion, musical forms, literatures, and historical backgrounds were considered countercultural. Jews were reduced to a group of outcasts. This doctrine infested German society. Anyone who dared to defend Jews was "abnormal" and spoke an alien tongue. Likewise, in South Africa racism permeated the Afrikaners' lives. Black inferiority was imprinted through many forms of expression. Novels were filled with degrading images. Misethnic educators, relatives, sermonizers, and associates assured listeners that there were objective bases for degrading blacks and forcing them to live in squalor.[22]

Narratives about the insignificance of minorities are part of society's lore, and the depth of prejudice often varies not only between countries but also between communities. Idioms qualify stereotypes that are accepted for particular regions. The supposed danger from an outgroup will vary, for example, depending on whether the myth about it is circulated among an agricultural or urban community. Ultimately, however, prejudice preys on weaker social elements.

The demagogic use of stereotypes is practically arbitrary. That is, which groups are singled out for persecution and what generalizations are used to discount their humanity are not based on impartial estimations and rational judgments. Historical elements are inserted into ideology to elicit greater emotional response from the audience. Stereotypes that are effective are later elaborated, becoming ever more believable through repetition and popular identification. The fewer words needed to evoke violent attitudes against an outgroup, the more effective is misethnic propaganda. Moreover, potent hate speech bolsters the ingroup's sense of importance. By alleging that the devil was on the side of Africans and Indians, colonists inferred a religious and moral superiority for themselves. Surely their conquests and rapines could not be questioned since they had God on their side: it was God, not they, who was exacting punishment against the heathens. This anthropomorphic conceptualization of God was a smoke screen for violent materialism and ethnocentrism. The justifications given and the symbols used for aggression correspond with the need of the oppressing groups. When the Nazis needed an enemy, they claimed Jews were communists; when the Soviet communists required one, Jews were capitalists; and tsarist Russia claimed Jews were the financiers and revolutionaries of the world, trying to destroy imperialism. Blacks have been variously described as lazy by those with little job security, as sexually uncontrollable by those opposed to miscegenation, or as less evolved by those harboring a sense of inferiority.

Traits ascribed to outgroups are contrived through erroneous reasoning and connivance. They are designed to stigmatize minorities and make unjust treatment of them more palatable. Stereotypes often fixate on a number of characteristics and exaggerate their prevalence in the population. Fabrications are enmeshed in unsubstantiated allegations. Historical-sounding information may also be used to pass off libels as truths. Positive information is tactically excluded or proclaimed anomalous. The majority group is believed to exemplify and embody superior human attributes.[23] Besides stroking the group ego, stereotypes encourage a sense of ingroup belongingness and encourage common aims.

These attitudes translate into discriminatory conduct against despised groups. The oft-repeated aspersions become internalized and integral to a bigot's self-definition, self-esteem, and all-around worldview.[24] Stereotyping rationalizes emotionally charged attitudes of contempt, aversion, and disrespect. The outlets for these attitudes are actions that range from eschewal to oppression. Violent misethnicity sparks a conflagration fueled by prejudice. Culturally embedded stereotypes perpetuate derogatory attitudes. In times of crisis, traditional prejudices facilitate picking scapegoats on whose head social ills can be placed to expiate society of its faults. Having remained relatively dormant during times of stability, the continued popularity of stereotypes makes it easier to gather adherents to misethnic causes.

While persecution is not the inevitable outcome of hate speech, vitriol calling for the oppression of an identifiable group encourages the efforts of organized hate groups and racist political organizations. As Allport explained, "While many people would never move from antilocution to avoidance; or from avoidance to active discrimination, or higher on the scale, still it is true that activity on one level makes transition to a more intense level easier." During times of tranquility, hatred toward an out-group may only figure prominently in the lives of a few individuals; meanwhile, it continues to linger in the mind of the majority. But during economic downturns, armed conflicts, or other social upheavals, familiar hatreds can increase the power of ingroups, divest outgroups of their rights, and distract the public from real causes. Such a process is counterproductive because it does not solve actual problems but focuses on concocted enemies.

In late nineteenth-century Germany, anti-Semitic political parties enjoyed little support. However, the catastrophe of losing World War I and the hyperinflation that followed brought age-old hatreds to the surface, enabling Hitler and his henchmen to win broad-based, sustained support. Preparatory destructive messages "made it easier to enact the Nürenberg discriminatory laws which, in turn, made the subsequent burning of synagogues and street attacks on Jews seem natural."[25] Likewise, years of negrophobia strengthened Southerners' conviction that black slavery was such a worthwhile cause that it, along with states' rights, was important enough to risk their lives during the Civil War. Sustained ethnocentrism directed against indigenous American tribes was harnessed to pass an Indian Removal Act, taking ancestral lands from the tribes and then repaying them primarily with illnesses and abject poverty. Empirical evidence makes it abundantly clear: hateful voices have long and resonant effects on the real world. Denigrating labels about historically persecuted groups are not cathartic for ingroups; however, they are devastating for outgroups.

Bigots propagate prejudices for popular consumption through everyday discourses, news items, movies, fables, and books. In Frantz Fanon's passionate denunciation of racism, *Black Skin, White Masks*, he described how popular images in magazines and comics spread bigotry among the children of the French Antilles. The heroes of folktales, legends, and illustrations were inevitably white. Children, white and black, identified with the heroes of these stories and developed antipathy toward vanquished Africans. Based on cultural images, children wanted to be grandly clad conquerors, not cannibals.[26] Derogatory images of outgroups are not only confined to pop fiction and comics. Even great works of fiction often evince their authors' immersion in ethnocentric culture. Jews have commonly been depicted as social outcasts and pests. These depictions are found in medieval writings that portray Jews as Christ killers, and in Geoffrey Chaucer's *Canterbury Tales*. The "Prioress' Tale" tells how the "cursed Jews" kidnapped and killed a Christian child. The Prioress makes clear that the Jews are collectively responsible for the murder:

> Ther was in Asye, in a greet citee,
> Amonges Cristene folk a Jewerye,
> Sustened by a lord of that contree
> For foule usure and lucre of vileynye,
> Hateful to Crist and to his compaignye
> . . . .
> . . . the Jues han conspired
> This innocent out of this world to chace.
> An homycide therto han they hyred,
> That in an aleye hadde a privee place;
> And as the child gan forby for to pace,
> This cursed Jew hym hente, and heeld hym faste,
> And kitte his throte, and in a pit hym caste.
>
> I seye that in a wardrobe they hym threwe
> Where as thise Jewes purgen hire entraille.
> O cursed folk of Herodes al newe,
> What may youre yvel entente yow availle?
> Mordre wol out, certeyn, it wol nat faille,
> And namely ther th'onour of God shal sprede;
> The blood out crieth on youre cursed dede.

William Shakespeare's *Merchant of Venice* also buttressed the materialistic and ruthless stereotype of Jews. Another equally important story, *Oliver Twist* by Charles Dickens, drove home the view that Jews are low, mean creatures by showing Fagin the Jew as a Satanlike creature, gradually corrupting boys and turning them into heartless thieves. Dickens made his point by repeatedly reminding the reader that Fagin was a red-headed Jew. Not until *Our Mutual Friend*, which was written almost thirty years after *Oliver Twist*, did he make amends with the Jewish community. But the harm was already done. These sorts of representations, in the hands of eloquent writers, make ethnocentrism respectable in the eyes of the lay public. Dissemination through printed media makes it easier for hate groups and demagogues to gather broad-based support for hate movements.[27]

Negative images are especially effective in cultures where there is little interaction between majority groups and outsiders. Prejudices become the norm, and persons fighting for racial equality face social censure. People with little firsthand knowledge of outgroups are more likely to base their ideological views on social images than on facts. Without some investigation into the cultural background of a group and its particular sensitivity, popular defamations guide notions about persons with salient features. Persons indoctrinated in misethnic dogma are unlikely to internalize the individual traits of outgroup members. Instead, they typically view ostracized persons as the embodiments of stereotypical attributes.[28]

Where citizens lack familiarity with minorities, they tend to perceive them through the prism of broad, entrenched categories. They interpret experiences with minorities that deviate from expectations as outliers rather than indications that their ideology is flawed. The inferiority of outgroups lies in their theoretical ideation rather than in concrete examples. They are all theoretical constructs rather than sentient people. That mindframe makes it easier to commit violence against outgroups with little remorse.

Even in a society where contact does occur, if various groups do not interact as equals they probably will not shake off traditional stereotypes. The circumstances under which ingroup-outgroup contacts take place is a significant variable in calculating the probability that attitudes will change or remain fixed. Having few acquaintances and communications with outgroups decreases the likelihood that persons steeped in a misethnic culture will change their thoughts and practices. One study concluded that superficial contacts with outgroups did not reduce the incidence of prejudice "as does intimate 'equal-status' contact. Only a fairly close knowledge of a minority group reduces one's susceptibility to secondhand stereotypes and epithets concerning it."[29] Brief encounters between interlocutors, arising only in structured settings or during chance meetings, limit the extent to which they are exposed to details about one another's family lives, hobbies, and career ambitions. The narrowly defined purposes for these meetings discourage people from communicating in ways that are favorable for altering internalized mischaracterizations. On the other hand, less structured forums are more conducive for individualized behavior and, therefore, tend to personalize contacts. Intimate camaraderie reduces racist attitudes by bringing out the common humanity of interactants.[30] In a society where the workplace is integrated, coworkers will see that whether a person is laborious or lazy is not predicated on race. Where people meet as friends, they are more likely to share joys and dispel notions about any innate incompatibility.

Persons who stir up racial discord often do so for self-interested motives. Destructive messages are critical for a dominant group seeking to consolidate its power. They help organize frenzied movements dedicated to harming outgroups. Propaganda builds on contemporary anxieties by combining them with traditional stereotypes and engendering the fear that society's treasures will be destroyed by vilified outgroups. For centuries, in the United States racism remained crucial for Southern cohesion. It stabilized the culture by defining natural inferiors and superiors. This social order alleviated aggression among Southern whites by focusing it on a common adversary. Institutionalized discrimination was conducive to a self-serving ideology and joint social aspirations. The white establishment maintained its power through an oft-repeated value system that placed it at the top of the racial totem pole.[31]

Likewise, Germanic ideologues looked at Jews as a danger to their Teutonic culture. The nation was bound together by the mutual eagerness to rid itself of the Jewish presence. All economic levels in society that tacitly or actively supported Hitler's chancellorship in 1933 subscribed to the belief that Jewish competition had to be eliminated. Years before, in his autobiography, *Mein Kampf*, Hitler had announced his intent in traditional anti-Semitic terms. Decades of anti-Semitic literature had deluded common Germans into believing that Jews manipulated the world economy. The ideology was so deeply entrenched that it seemed logical to them to round up Jews, put them in concentration camps, and eventually try to exterminate them. Political propaganda was a necessary part of that cycle. Furthermore, the historical record of German and European anti-Jewish sentiments indicates that the prejudice was not strictly based on economic ambitions. The animosity goes back to the Christian portrayal of Jews as continuing to perpetuate their ancestors' alleged sins. Religious zealots conveniently forgot that Jesus and his apostles were Jews teaching an unorthodox brand of Judaism, and they accused all Jews for failing to heed his words and then crucifying him to boot. From the gospel of John, which proclaimed that all Jews were from their father the devil,[32] to the myth of the Wandering Jew, and to the European pulpits, the message that the Jews were God's enemies became the devotees' adamant conviction. Although the Enlightenment heralded a significant step away from this anti-Jewishness and toward the universal human fraternity, when German orators rejected cosmopolitanism and humanism, traditional stereotypes reemerged, tailored for their own political climate.[33]

Perceived conflicting goals often contribute to intergroup animosity. The rhetoric of hate is a tool for exclusionary aims in the quest for scarce resources. By depicting outsiders as inimical to ingroup interests, virulent orators gather a diverse following from the ranks of intellectuals, professionals, and laborers. They develop a divisive rhetoric for systematically spreading views and hoarding power.

Demagogues invoke familiar social images that elicit stereotypes. Their messages represent not only the speakers' sense of superiority, but also the dominant ingroup's perception of itself. This adds weight and gravity to orators' messages. Hate speech should be understood as a form of communication among dominant group members intended to intimidate outgroups and galvanize ingroups. The targets of the messages are ethnic minorities, not just individuals. The goal is not only to inflict dignitary harms, but also to influence listeners to follow various courses of action. By mixing false facts about contemporary social crises with long-standing stereotypes, demagogues sharpen ethnic attitudes, making them better directed and focused. Immersion in ideology is a group endeavor. When the message is disseminated widely and given time to bury its roots into the ingroup psyche, popular discontent and organized discrimination follow. This can only be accomplished by agitators who adequately penetrate the inner workings of cultural linguistics.

Ideology is a bond that solidifies relationships between people who, while being members of the same ethnic, religious, or racial group, otherwise have very little in common. The sense of ingroup identification and belongingness unifies rich and poor. It is a means of subduing intragroup socioeconomic conflicts by horizontal identification. Racism and anti-Semitism give indigent members of a dominant group a sense of superiority; they share with the affluent common interests in discriminating against minorities.

Resolution of real personal and social problems can be avoided so long as evaluating and solving them can be replaced by sacrificing a conveniently weak scapegoat. This is what happened in post–World War I Germany. The economic crisis, arising from the legacy of Versailles and the worldwide depression, was blamed on Jews, who were said to be purposefully causing Germany's decline. In the United States, proslavery ideologues allayed discontent about economic disparities by an ideology that claimed there was equality between whites because they were all potential slave owners. Whiteness was considered a status that could not be attained by blacks. The title "black" (and worse pejoratives like "nigger") brought to mind a creed that assigned intellectual and biological inferiority to persons with African ancestry. Politicians conjured supremacist dogma in order to reduce class tensions among whites by elevating them above an entire class of persons. No matter how criminal or immoral their white brothers were, racists considered them innately and morally superior to the most venerable of blacks. The culture of inferiority was built into the semantics of American English. The social construct "Indian" also functioned as an excuse for grave injustices. Frontier people stole Native lands while the U.S. government turned a blind eye. The lore that Indians were roaming hunters who had no ties to specific territories and did not own any real property made land theft easier. The ideology united many American speculators, rationalized their actions, and persuaded them to try their hand at stealing from Native Americans. With an abundance of aboriginal lands to expropriate, many intra-white conflicts over land were avoided.

Misethnicity flies in the face of egalitarian ideals. It violates the principal that all persons' rights are of equal importance and should be protected with the same zeal. Within a society where the human rights of an entire segment of the population are not respected and, even more, trodden under foot, lie the seeds of noxious ideologies that threaten to destroy democracy and its legal institutions. Where outgroups are often subjected to racial or ethnic indignities, it is more likely that their lives will be considered of smaller value, and persecution or injustice toward them will be considered the norm.[34] Treating a whole group of people inhumanely through discriminatory laws and social customs diminishes the potential of the whole society because intolerance limits the ability for all its members to fully express their talents. Once a malignant social ill begins festering, it often goes undiagnosed until it has consumed much healthy tissue. Hate speech gradually wheedles away at democratic norms until it grows into a chronic disease that undermines representative government and turns a state toward an autocratic path. Harming racial and ethnic minorities by excluding them from privileges, emoluments, and benefits decreases a society's well-being.

Not only does prejudice lessen outgroup happiness, it also erodes ingroup contentment by raising the level of anxiety and paranoia about outgroup retaliation for its mistreatment. Ingroups begin to fear the social pariah they have imagined into existence, and then justify brutal acts by characterizing them as defensive measures. In the South, the Ku Klux Klan was organized after the emancipation of slaves as a "defensive" organization to supposedly protect the white population. Particularly, it asserted that women had to be guarded from blacks who would otherwise rape them. Forgotten was the fact that whites had been raping black women for centuries, fathering their children and perpetuating their slavery. Also, while the KKK spread its campaign of terror against innocent men and women, it claimed to be arming itself for future race riots.[35] Racist ideology places bigots into a labyrinth from which they can only escape if they cease following irrational generalizations and direct their ways through rational ideas. Until such an awakening, they continue promulgating misethnic propaganda, become engrossed by it, and act on its tenets.

Established stereotypes are the most easily imprintable of derogatory symbols. Rather than invent new images, speakers who borrow old defamations, coupling them with more recent ones, are likelier to convince a broad audience to actively discriminate. Demagogues entrance listeners by appealing to their common interests, calling for unity, and finding a readily identifiable outgroup on which to assign blame for social problems. The Jews have been a convenient scapegoat for millennia because they have been the perennial outsiders, tossed out of one country after another, establishing life anew, only again to find inequitable restrictions placed on them elsewhere. This recurrent process has been perpetuated by the persistent entrenchment and dissemination of anti-Semitism. Whatever the misethnic ideology, that it remains subdued during tranquil times is no assurance that it will not spew to the surface during social cataclysms. Then, history teaches, racism and ethnocentrism often become rallying cries in the mouths of plunderers and murderers.

Misethnic ideology refuses to acknowledge the humanity of outgroups and offers them no compassion. The intellectual, psychological, cultural, emotional, and physical reality of a group is denied, and this ideological gymnastics is critical to desensitizing oppressors about the plights of their victims. Outgroups become the cause of every social bane; in fact, they become the very blight of society, the adder that must be contained or killed before it poisons the whole culture. The implication of this line of thought is that the pests must be reckoned with through drastic measures. When an outgroup becomes labeled as the problem, its members are objectified and viewed no longer as individuals but rather as so many infestations into an otherwise healthy body politic.[36] Ingroup anger and aggression find an easy outlet in a traditionally shunned minority.

Solutions recommended by the perpetrators of misethnic injustices include genocide, unfair and inequitable subordination, and separation. Nazi Germany used all three of these methods in its persecution of Jews, while the United States employed the latter two methods of oppression in dealing with blacks and Native Americans. Ideologues rely on dehumanizing imagery to develop broad-based followings devoted to injustice. Beliefs about the purported irremediable evil or insignificance of outgroups drives negative attitudes to a frenzy that can blow up into cataclysmic consequences.[37] In the deep-seated hatred of racists and ethnocentrists lies the hope of repressing outgroups and rendering them virtually powerless, or, even more, of exterminating them altogether. The impulse to lash out at outgroups is part and parcel of ardent misethnicity. The firm commitment to the ideology of hate commends destructive messages to hate groups. Exclusionary institutions are easier to proselytize in a society permeated with long-standing narratives of outgroup inferiority.

Hate speech is not a harmless release for misethnic attitudes. It does not mitigate threats to minorities. To the contrary, during opportune times, it inflames and recruits persons who can be catalyzed to wreak havoc on outgroups. Discriminatory oratory functions to unify ingroups through a mutually captivating ideology. It distinguishes ingroups from minorities, expresses the superiority of the dominant group, and organizes for collective actions against outgroups.[38] Cultural preparation for perpetrating crimes against humanity takes time and is vastly more dangerous than fighting words that lead to fisticuffs. With the aid of charismatic orators, bigots exploit social unrest to consolidate power by blaming outgroups for social ills. Misethnists then go beyond talk and back up their self-perceived superiority by brute force.

PART III

Legal Response to Hate Speech

Two classes of laws in the United States aim at eradicating misethnic crimes: (1) "penalty-enhancing" criminal statutes that increase the penalty for nonassertive acts committed with biased motives, and (2) "pure bias" criminal statutes that penalize the expression of bigoted messages.[1] The Supreme Court upheld the constitutionality of a penalty-enhancement statute in *Wisconsin v. Mitchell*,[2] while in *R.A.V. v. St. Paul* the Court found a statute that prohibited biased expressions such as cross burning unconstitutional.[3] It is time to address the latter issue; that is, what parameters, if any, can be established to prohibit biased speech that threatens outgroups. Is hate speech antithetical to the principles underlying representative democracy? Several democracies' laws restrict hate speech, suggesting avenues for passing legislation prohibiting expressions that elicit violence and have a substantial probability of harming identifiable groups. At the end, I offer two alternative causes of action.

8

United States Jurisprudence

The Roots of First Amendment Jurisprudence

First Amendment jurisprudence was not significantly developed until the beginning of the twentieth century, when the Supreme Court of the United States decided three major cases—*Schenck v. United States*,[1] *Frohlwerk v. United States*,[2] and *Debs v. United States*[3]—under the Espionage Act of 1917. Justice Oliver Wendell Holmes wrote the Court's opinion in all three cases. In the first of these to come before the Court, Schenck was accused of printing and circulating a pamphlet declaring that forced conscription violated the Thirteenth Amendment's prohibition against involuntary servitude. Convicted for violating the Espionage Act of 1917 and sentenced to six months in jail, Schenck appealed, first to the federal Court of Appeals, then to the Supreme Court. The trial court had found that Schenck intentionally mailed the leaflet to obstruct the draft effort. The Supreme Court agreed that he intended to influence men eligible for the draft not to participate in it; therefore, it upheld Schenck's conviction. Justice Holmes, writing for the Court, based his decision on what came to be known as the "clear and present danger" test: "The question in every case is whether the words used are used in such circumstances and are of such a nature as to create a clear and present danger that they will bring about the substantive evils that Congress has a right to prevent. It is a question of proximity and degree." As an example of what speech the government may censure, Holmes provided the following oft-quoted example: "The most stringent protection of free speech would not protect a man in falsely shouting fire in a theater and causing a panic."[4]

Holmes also wrote the opinions for a unanimous court in both *Frohwerk* and *Debs*, which were decided just a week after *Schenck*. These decisions expand Holmes's view about the constitutionality of proscriptions against words that could trigger unlawful actions. Frohwerk, like Schenck, was convicted under the Espionage Act of 1917 for intending to publish newspaper articles opposing the draft and praising Germany. Writing for the Court, Holmes noted that his decision to uphold the conviction was not solely based on the message but on the surrounding circumstances as well:

> It may be that all this might be said or written even in time of war in circumstances that would not make it a crime. We do not lose our right to condemn either measures or men because the Country is at war. . . . But we must take the case on the record as it is, and on that record it is impossible to say that it might not have been found that the circulation of the paper was in quarters where a little breath would be enough to kindle a flame and that the fact was known and relied upon by those who sent the paper out.[5]

Holmes further acknowledged that freedom of speech was not an absolute right:

> [T]he First Amendment while prohibiting legislation against free speech as such cannot have been, and obviously was not, intended to give immunity for every possible use of language. We venture to believe that neither Hamilton nor Madison, nor any other competent person then or later, ever supposed that to make criminal the counselling of a murder within the jurisdiction of Congress would be an unconstitutional interference with free speech.[6]

Holmes then wrote *Debs*, upholding socialist Eugene Debs's conviction for protesting the World War I draft and for attempting to cause insubordination among soldiers. His rationale was very much the same. Observing that Debs intended to impede recruitment, Holmes upheld his conviction, concluding that it was reasonably probable that Debs's efforts would have in fact obstructed recruitment.

Justice Holmes played a further role in establishing doctrine concerning inflammatory speech in his dissent to *Abrams v. United States*.[7] Abrams was a member of a group of anarchists who supported the Russian Revolution. The group drafted a pamphlet speaking out against President Woodrow Wilson and opposing the United States' decision to send troops to Russia. The pamphlet called on workers to engage in a general strike opposing "the barbaric intervention." The leaflet was published before the end of World War I. Five members of the anarchist group were sentenced to twenty years in prison for printing the leaflet.[8] This case signaled Holmes's departure from the view, which he expressed in the *Schenck* trilogy, that speech could be curtailed upon a showing that it was reasonably probable that the expression would cause a clear and present danger.[9]

In his dissent, which opposed Abrams's conviction, Holmes asserted that "[i]t is only the present danger of immediate evil or an intent to bring it about that warrants Congress in setting a limit to the expression of opinion where private rights are not concerned."[10] For Holmes, the crucial factor was that while Abrams supported the sovereignty of the Russian government, he did not advocate overthrowing the U.S. government. Abrams was prosecuted and convicted only because he advocated communism, not because his words posed an immediate danger to the safety of the United States.[11] Holmes's dissent, then, represents his opposition to the suppression of political ideas.

It was in *Abrams* that Holmes adopted the famous "marketplace of ideas" doctrine, which has become a dominant First Amendment metaphor:

> [M]en . . . may come to believe even more than they believe the very foundations of their own conduct that the ultimate good desired is better reached by free trade in ideas—that the best test of truth is the power of the thought to get itself accepted in the competition of the market, and that truth is the only ground upon which their wishes safely can be carried out. That at any rate is the theory of our Constitution.[12]

As we will see, Holmes based this doctrine on relativistic premises that he espoused throughout his writings. He clarified the sort of truth he envisioned emerging from the marketplace of ideas in his dissent to *Gitlow v. New York*.[13] The case arose when Gitlow, who was a member of the Left Wing of the Socialist Party, was convicted for violating New York's Criminal Anarchy Act of 1902. That statute, which Congress enacted in response to the assassination of President William McKinley by an anarchist, defined criminal anarchy as "the doctrine that organized government should be overthrown by force or violence, or by assassination [*sic*] of the executive head or of any of the executive officials of government, or by any unlawful means."[14] Gitlow published the Left Wing Manifesto, which argued that "[t]he mass struggle of the proletariat is coming into being."[15]

While Holmes's dissent in Gitlow is usually cited as indicative of the Supreme Court's later First Amendment jurisprudence, the majority opinion in that case has never been explicitly overturned. However, under the Court's current content-neutral stance in *R.A.V. v. St. Paul*[16] (the St. Paul, Minnesota, cross-burning case), *Gitlow*'s reasoning would probably not withstand judicial review. Nevertheless, the premises enunciated in that case are instructive. Writing for the majority, Justice Sanford recognized that the future effects of violent rhetoric "cannot be accurately foreseen." Therefore, the state may enact laws to protect "public peace and safety" without having to "defer the adoption of measures for its own peace and safety until the revolutionary utterances lead to actual disturbances of the public peace or imminent and immediate danger of its own destruction; but it may, in the exercise of its judgment, suppress the threatened danger in its incipiency."[17] The *Gitlow* majority, then, clearly recognized the potentially long-term inflammatory effects of speech and understood the dangers of not immediately curbing instigative words.

Holmes's dissent to *Gitlow* was primarily based on his disbelief that Gitlow's manifesto posed a clear and present danger. As he put it, the manifesto "had no chance of starting a present conflagration." Holmes contended that all ideas, especially eloquent ones, are incitements in that they move people to action or inaction. Most revealing of Holmes's radical form of populism was his statement that "[i]f in the long run the beliefs expressed in proletarian dictatorship are destined to be accepted by the dominant forces of the community, the only meaning of free speech is that they should be given their chance and have their way."[18] Holmes thereby implicitly condoned the doctrine that allows a dominant majority to manipulate free speech to further dictatorial ends. In fact, it has historically been the case that bigotry has often undermined egalitarian democracy. Socially accepted racialism brought the Nazis to power through the German elections of 1932, and federal laws, such as the Fugitive Slave Act of 1850, embedded slavery in antebellum American culture.

Justice Holmes adhered to a vision about the desirable consequences of speech that was different than that of Justice Louis Brandeis, who often joined Holmes in dissent. While the results of their free speech decisions were often the same, they significantly differed in their reasoning. For example, Brandeis's concurrence in *Whitney v. California* left no room for Holmes's relativistic rationale. Holmes's ideology, in fact, was contrary to Brandeis's. Far from acknowledging that it was permissible for ingroups to exploit the First Amendment of the Constitution to establish proletarian autocracies, Brandeis thought that the institution of free speech was a safeguard against, not a facilitator for, "tyrannies of governing majorities."[19] Brandeis held the optimistic view that the dissemination of "more speech" would expose falsehoods and fallacies and, thereby, avert evils.[20] Abstract fears about future harms, Brandeis argued, do not justify restricting free speech. The framers of the U.S. Constitution, he went on to say, believed that liberties, such as the freedom to think and speak one's mind, are essential for the elucidation of political truths and the maintenance of happiness.[21] "Recognizing the occasional tyrannies of governing majorities, [the founding fathers] amended the Constitution so that free speech and assembly should be guaranteed."[22] Brandeis noted further that

> [f]ear of serious injury cannot alone justify suppression of free speech and assembly. Men feared witches and burnt women. It is the function of speech to free men from the bondage of irrational fears. To justify suppression of free speech there must be reasonable ground to fear that serious evil will result if free speech is practiced. There must be reasonable ground to believe that the danger apprehended is imminent. There must be reasonable ground to believe that the evil to be prevented is a serious one.[23]

Moreover, he said, open forums are more secure: "It is hazardous to discourage thought, hope and imagination; that fear breeds repression; repression breeds hate; that hate menaces stable government; that the path of safety lies in the opportunity to discuss freely supposed grievances and proposed remedies."[24] More recent cases dealing with the freedom of expression have built on the foundations that Holmes and Brandeis established.

Contemporary Formulations of First Amendment Doctrine

If the clear and present danger cases introduced the public to modern First Amendment jurisprudence, the Supreme Court's "fighting words" doctrine in *Chaplinsky v. New Hampshire* advanced things even more.[25] The Court upheld Chaplinsky's conviction for violating a statute forbidding persons from using "offensive, derisive, and annoying" words and "derisive" names against persons in public places. Writing for the majority, Justice Murphy concluded that certain types of speech, such as "fighting words," are not, and have never been, protected by the Constitution. Fighting words are epithets reasonably expected to provoke a violent reaction if addressed toward an "ordinary citizen."[26] "[S]uch utterances are no essential part of any exposition of ideas, and are of such slight social value as a step to truth that any benefit that may be derived from them is clearly outweighed by the social interest in order and morality."[27]

In *Brandenburg v. Ohio*,[28] the Court revisited the issue of how to determine whether statutes aimed at limiting inciteful speech are constitutional. Decided in 1969, the case remains the ruling authority on this subject. The Court protected the advocacy of illegal conduct and tightened up the "clear and present danger" test in a context it found devoid of any true danger.[29] At issue was a film showing the defendant, who was the leader of an Ohio Ku Klux Klan chapter, asserting that revenge might be taken against the U.S. government if it "continues to suppress the white . . . race." Reversing the defendant's conviction, the Court held that the First Amendment guarantee of free speech prohibits government from proscribing the "advocacy of the use of force or of law violation except where such advocacy is directed to inciting or producing imminent lawless action and is likely to incite or produce such action." Further, the Court found that the Ohio statute violated the First and Fourteenth Amendments because it did not distinguish between persons who called for the immediate use of violence and those teaching an abstract doctrine about the use of force.[30] However, in explaining and analyzing its decision, the Court failed to evaluate whether there were historical reasons to think that a Ku Klux Klan rally might spark racist conflict. Thus, its opinion that the speech would not incite listeners to lawless action was not grounded in an empirical foundation.

The most recent Supreme Court decision on the legality of "pure bias" laws—*R.A.V. v. St. Paul*—imposed a near-blanket prohibition against legislation regulating speech based on its misethnic content.[31] The majority opinion, which represented the views of five Supreme Court members, differed substantially from three concurring opinions. The case arose when several teenagers made a cross and then burned it on a black family's front yard. The juveniles were charged under a St. Paul ordinance that made it a misdemeanor to display, in public or private places, symbols such as Nazi swastikas or burning crosses that are known to arouse "anger, alarm, or resentment on the basis of race, color, creed, religion or gender."[32]

Writing for the majority, Justice Scalia found that the St. Paul ordinance violated the First Amendment because it was a form of "content discrimination."[33] Only those "fighting words" that were enumerated by the ordinance were prohibited, while other forms of potentially inflammatory utterances, such as those about persons' political affiliations, were not so proscribed. Scalia acknowledged that St. Paul had a compelling interest in protecting the human rights of the "members of groups that have historically been subjected to discrimination." The majority, nevertheless, held that this legislative aim could only be constitutionally effectuated by a total ban of "all fighting words, rather than focusing on hate speech."[34] Scalia made clear his belief that it is unconstitutional for legislators to adopt laws specifically intended to prohibit inflammatory racist and anti-Semitic utterances.

Justice White, who wrote one of the concurring opinions to *R.A.V.*, criticized the majority reasoning as being contrary to Supreme Court precedents. He argued that the Court had long allowed the regulation of low-level speech based on its content. It was disingenuous, in his view, to require the government to proscribe an entire class of utterances (i.e., fighting words) but forbid regulation of a subset of that class which "by definition [is] worthless and undeserving of constitutional protection."[35] According to Justice White, banning all or some fighting words would help eliminate social harms while not limiting the potential for ideas to compete in the marketplace of ideas. The majority's approach "invites" persons to utilize racist expressions, which, in terms of the First Amendment, are worthless.

Further, Justice White warned that the majority's decision would influence future First Amendment case law for the worse. The majority's opinion signaled to the disseminators of racial and ethnic animus that their expressions are more worthy of governmental protections than the peace and tranquility of the targeted groups. By calling the use of fighting words a "debate," the majority placed hate speech on the level of political and cultural discourse. Nevertheless, Justice White found that while the ordinance forbade certain speech that was unprotected by the First

Amendment, it was nevertheless unconstitutional because of its "over-breadth" in prohibiting expressions that hurt feelings, caused offense, or produced resentment in others.[36]

Justice Blackmun, in a separate concurrence, agreed with Justice White that the St. Paul ordinance was unconstitutionally overbroad. However, Blackmun declared that it was generally constitutional for cities to enact laws aimed at preventing hooligans from burning crosses intended to drive minority residents from their homes.[37]

In yet another concurrence, Justice Stevens pointed out that there are many constitutional, governmental regulations that target utterances based on their content: for example, a city can "prohibit political adver-tisements in its buses while allowing other advertisements."[38] Therefore, the majority's contention that all content-based regulations are unconsti-tutional is insupportable by First Amendment jurisprudence. Further-more, Justice Stevens believed that just as a governmental entity could constitutionally restrict only certain forms of commercial speech, so too could St. Paul regulate only certain types of fighting words and not oth-ers. According to Justice Stevens, a city can regulate certain fighting words more stringently than others based on the greater social harms they caused. However, like other justices, Justice Stevens found that the St. Paul ordinance violated the First Amendment because it was overbroad.[39]

The Supreme Court has long held that government cannot suppress ideas it finds "offensive or disagreeable."[40] But why not place some re-strictions on certain forms of hate speech that have low or zero social value?[41] The next chapter critically reflects on this issue in light of the Court's doctrine.

9

Reconsidering Supreme Court Precedents

Freedom of expression is of primary importance in a representative democracy devoted to individual rights and social stability. Yet, it is not an absolute right. When speech is used to disparage others and spread falsehoods about them, it can be restricted because "the law of defamation is rooted in our experience that the truth rarely catches up with a lie."[1] Constitutional premises, including those of the First Amendment, are not like mathematical postulates. Instead, they are vital words, the social justice of which is derived from their applicability to novel situations for the establishment of equitable laws and rules. The literal translation of the words contained there does not exhaust the depth of the principles in which they are found.[2]

> The language of the First Amendment is to be read not as barren words found in a dictionary but as symbols of historic experience illumined by the presuppositions of those who employed them. Not what words did Madison and Hamilton use, but what was it in their minds which they conveyed? Free speech is subject to prohibition of those abuses of expression which a civilized society may forbid.[3]

These issues can only be resolved by assessing and balancing the various constitutional premises. Absolutist dogmas about speech often mislead because they cast aside relevant concerns about the democratic process. The Supreme Court has established a balancing test that permits the state to restrict speech only when it is necessary to further a compelling governmental interest.[4] Furthermore, there must be no less restrictive alternative that could effectively achieve the state's legitimate goals.[5] While the Court typically applies this test in content-neutral cases, it would likewise be relevant when hate speech poses a substantial and realistic probability, based on the context within which it is uttered, of inciting injustices against historically oppressed minorities.

Current Supreme Court hate speech doctrine fails to take into account the long-term social dangers of hate propaganda. The need for reconsidering that doctrine emerges after our sociohistorical survey of how, at various times, utterances and ideology gradually raised the pitch of hatred until they instigated grand-scale tragedies such as the Holocaust, Native American dislocation, and black slavery. Historic facts indicate that hate speech has, in recent and ancient times, in both European and non-European cultures, created fertile preconditions for oppressing outgroups. Even John Stuart Mill, the philosophical founder of the "marketplace of ideas" doctrine, recognized that "the dictum that truth always triumphs over persecution is one of those pleasant falsehoods which men repeat after one another till they pass into commonplaces, but which all experience refutes. History teems with instances of truth put down by persecution."[6] The validity of Mill's observation is borne out by U.S. colonial history. The free flow of abolitionist ideas did not peacefully overcome slavery through logical arguments about its evils; instead, it took a civil war to end that cruel practice. The long-term effects of racism in America have been devastating to human rights and social welfare.

"Marketplace of Ideas" Doctrine

At first, Holmes appears to be an advocate of objective truth, being tested in the embers of dialogue and alighting like the Phoenix from the historical ash heap of false ideas. His "marketplace of ideas" analogy, which today continues to dominate First Amendment jurisprudence, speaks of truth being examined through the free and competitive exchange of ideas.[7] However, upon close scrutiny, Holmes's writings reveal that "truth" for him is not the absence of fallacy; instead, it is whatever ideology is accepted by the strongest segment of majoritarian society. Holmes rejected "inalienable human rights . . . [and] absolute principles of law." For him, the concepts of truth and common good are empty, while "desire and power are everything."[8] "I am so skeptical as to our knowledge about the goodness or badness of laws that I have no practical criticism except what the crowd wants."[9] The marketplace of ideas is, then, a forum for herd mentality to direct the flow of law and to force others to follow it, regardless of whether the product is conducive to overall social well-being or only increases the happiness of those who are in power. Thus, "the best test of truth is the power of the thought to get itself accepted" is not referring to the establishment of legal truths that will improve society for everyone. As John Dewey pointed out, "At times, [Holmes's] realism seems almost to amount to a belief that whatever wins out in fair combat, in the struggle for existence, is therefore the fit, the good, and the true."[10]

Holmes's legal relativism and skepticism were the philosophical vertebrae of his "marketplace of ideas" doctrine. According to Holmes, freedom of speech is a transitory right that the dominant group in society (i.e., the majority) can withdraw at its discretion. Holmes maintained a relativistic philosophy of law and morals throughout his writings. Conceptions of truth, which according to Holmes are always subjective, are not derived through rational argument but rather imposed by the dominant forces of society.[11] Powerful persons determine what is true and what is good. His view that the "free trade of ideas" is "the best test of truth," therefore, represents the position that the marketplace of ideas is a means of creating "truth" rather than of discovering it.

Speech is of such importance to Holmes that he thought it justifiable for "the dominant forces of the community" to impose a "proletarian dictatorship."[12] It is irrelevant to Holmes whether public discourse will lead to a society striving for equal treatment of its subjects. The principal force behind laws is the will of those who are in power: "All that can be expected from modern improvements is that legislation should easily and quickly, yet not too quickly, modify itself in accordance with the will of the *de facto* supreme power in the community." When the will of the powerful interest conflicts with the desires of those who "competed unsuccessfully," it is only natural that legislation should reflect interests of "fittest."[13] We can expect that dominant forces will sway public opinion to believe their doctrine(s), whether secular or religious, and when it is to their benefit, they may enforce their desires and sacrifice the welfare of outgroups.

Holmes was not merely stating the fact that governments are often formed by subordinating the weaker members of society. For him, the value of government lies in its ability to carry out the desires of the powerful:

> What proximate test of excellence can be found except correspondence to the actual equilibrium of force in the community—that is, conformity to the wishes of the dominant power? Of course, such conformity may lead to the destruction, and it is desirable that the dominant power should be wise. But wise or not, the proximate test of good government is that the dominant power has its way.[14]

The guiding precepts of the rule of law and public policy should be based on the desires of the strongest.[15] The object of all legislation is "the greatest good of the greatest number," and the question of whether in the long run it is more beneficial to respect the highest good of minorities is as irrelevant as it is unpredictable.[16]

Holmes believed that law is grounded in the will of the sovereign to exert its "power to compel or punish."[17] A legal right, according to him, is an "empty substratum" that is useful for predicting how courts will decide cases, but it is not reflective of an objective reality.[18] Holmes's view supports the notion that legal rights are created concepts representing a sovereign's ability to enforce its resolutions by force.[19]

Even the right to live an unmolested life is not an unconditional good that society must protect; rather, the right to life is a discretionary "privilege granted . . . by the state."[20] As Holmes put it, "The sacredness of human life is a purely municipal ideal of no validity outside the jurisdiction."[21] The state, according to this scheme, determines whether human lives should be preserved and, if so, whose lives deserve governmental protections. By virtue of its public power to legislate, the state has the right to so discriminate since human life is not intrinsically valuable. Laws are malleable but enforceable customs that are posited on society by the will of the dominating (i.e., ruling) group. Legal protections are available to outgroups at the behest of those who are then in power. Humans, *qua* individual members of society, have an innate concern for their lives, but they have no natural right to life that the sovereign must imperatively honor:

> I don't believe that it is an absolute principle or even a human ultimate that man always is an end in himself—that his dignity must be respected,

etc. We march up a conscript with bayonets behind to die for a cause he doesn't believe in.[22]

In order to further its purposes and cosmology, the sovereign may unscrupulously sacrifice whosoever's life it views as expendable for its aims:

> The most fundamental of the supposed preexisting rights—the right to life—is sacrificed without a scruple not only in war, but whenever the interest of society, that is, of the predominant power in the community, is thought to demand it. Whether that interest is the interest of mankind in the long run no one can tell.[23]

Holmes's strand of thought on the relative value of life leads to the premise that the crowd (*hoi polloi*), armed with the full power of the state, may improve its lot by withholding or harming the lives, liberties, and properties of outgroups.

What then of minorities? Did Holmes think the government has any formal duty toward them? Yes, it must enact legislation that will keep minority losses to a minimum through the inculcation of "an educated sympathy."[24] However, Holmes had no sympathy for the passion of equality in commercial interactions nor, probably, in intellectual ones. On the other hand, in his personal life, he was an abolitionist and despised demeaning depictions of blacks.[25] Nevertheless, there is an opposite, highly disturbing train of thought that runs throughout Holmes's writings. For example, Holmes was of the opinion that the powerful had the right to use sterilization[26] in order to rid society of the "unfit."[27]

Outgroups can expect that their rights will be honored only if they gain power and rewrite laws currently discriminatory against them. And then they might become the perpetrators of injustices. Force is the remedy between two groups with divergent worldviews.[28] "If the welfare of the living majority is paramount, it can only be on the ground that the majority have the power in their hands."[29] In the model of the state Holmes envisioned, class and racial conflicts are inevitable.

This is not to posit that Holmes's judicial opinions were anticonstitutional or opposed to democratic ideals.[30] In fact, his doctrine on the right of dominant powers required that as a judge he follow the supreme law of the land, the Constitution. My argument is against Holmes's brand of populism and his theory of power, which legitimizes any political typhoon supported by the power of dominant social forces. The place of inalienable rights is filled by a subjective set of laws, enacted and pursued at the discretion of the "dominant forces of the community. . . . [T]he ultimate question is what do the dominant forces of the community want and do they want it hard enough to disregard whatever inhibitions may stay in the way."[31] In Holmes's governmental scheme, the ultimate judge of which laws are good and which are bad is the crowd whose system of morality is based on emotional whims. The dominant group's conduct toward minorities may be propelled by its adverse feelings and prejudices toward them. Taken to its logical conclusion, the argument that the predominant social powers should be given the opportunity to forcefully replace democracy with a proletarian dictatorship has horrifying implications: (1) Jews should be exterminated if Nazi ideology wins over the majority of people; (2) blacks should be enslaved for life if that is the will of the dominant majority; (3) Native American lands should be violently wrenched from them if those holding political power so decree.

His philosophical writings indicate that Holmes accepted with equanimity the right of groups to throw off democratic order and replace it with a state that uses its authority arbitrarily and does not respect the individual rights of any but the most powerful. In *Gitlow*, Holmes acknowledged and accepted that the consequences of unlimited speech might be the disintegration of fair and equitable government, and the establishment of a repressive state. Holmes's view on the subjugation and elimination of the weak might lead at least to authoritarianism, and at worst totalitarianism, and the denial of basic rights to vulnerable peoples. As Holmes's writings make clear, he thought it irrelevant that the free trade of ideas would not necessarily establish or maintain a just society.[32] His formulation of the "marketplace of ideas" doctrine in *Abrams v. United States* provided no objective mechanism for distinguishing what is right from what is wrong, nor for evaluating what is true and what is false.[33]

His relativism loses track of the overarching goals of representative democracy: social well-being, fairness, justice, and equal representation. Holmes's model of speech, which has been adapted by the Court in pure speech cases, stands in sharp contrast to the Madisonian tradition of speech as a facilitator for civil liberties, political representation, and exchange of ideas.[34] Under the latter model, the government has an interest in maintaining open dialogue. Holmes's market of ideas, on the other hand, is a virtually unregulated arena in which dominant groups are given license to indoctrinate and impose any political order, regardless of its selfish and intolerant practices. It acknowledges that a well-functioning democracy can be destroyed from within, and does nothing to curtail that possibility.

Although Justice Louis Brandeis was a great admirer of Holmes, his notions on the role of speech in U.S. democracy diverged from Holmes's. Brandeis was more inclined to "social and economic equality," while Holmes's perspective was closely allied to Social Darwinism.[35] Although Brandeis believed that increased speech is beneficial for society, he observed that the role of discussion is to expose falsehoods and avert social evils like "tyrannies of governing majorities." This is in direct contrast to Holmes, who contended that the crowd could harness speech to promulgate and maintain any political system, including a dictatorship. Brandeis's concern for repressing speech was that it could destabilize the United States: "It is hazardous to discourage thought, hope and imagination; that fear breeds repression; repression breeds hate; that hate menaces stable government; that the path of safety lies in the opportunity to discuss freely supposed grievances and proposed remedies."[36] Thus, Brandeis's view of free speech follows the Madisonian tradition, while Holmes's does not.

In fact, hate speech does not further the interests of democracy because it advocates that certain social elements should be denied fundamental rights. Furthermore, passing legislation prohibiting powerful incitement, much like existing laws abridging other forms of discrimination, would probably reduce hate and facilitate mutual understanding. Inciteful and false statements about outgroups or individuals do not advance "uninhibited, robust, and wide open"[37] dialogue about social improvement. Like fighting words, hate speech plays "no essential part of any exposition of ideas and [is] of such slight social value as a step to truth that any benefit that may be derived from [it] is clearly outweighed by the social interest in order and morality."[38] Purveyors of hate speech aim at spreading degrading falsities and proposing intolerant solutions, which, like defamation, can be limited without violating the First Amendment.

The Internet poses new risks to egalitarianism. Hate groups commonly use it for the worldwide circulation of messages intended to recruit and consolidate forces bent on discriminating, degrading, and destroying outgroups. Information sent through cyberspace threatens real people, entrenches racist attitudes, and, therefore, undermines social, political, and economic equality. It is not a separate social community, but one that impacts and is impacted by others in the real world.

Beyond the philosophical incongruities of Holmes's marketplace of ideas with respect to democratic ideals, it is simply untrue that the dissemination of vitriol defuses misethnicity. Experience disproves the notion that falsehood is always vanquished by truth. To the contrary, history is riddled with examples when distorted propaganda empowered groups like the Nazis to repress speech and perpetrate mass persecutions. Years of anti-Semitic speech in Germany preceded the rise of national socialism and the perpetration of the Holocaust. The foundations of death camps like Auschwitz were established on years of rhetoric dehumanizing and condemning Jews for German misfortunes. Even when both true and false beliefs are available, persons often cling to the false in order to retain power. Although abolitionist literature was readily available in the United States, slavery did not end through rational discourse.

Society derives no benefit from deliberately falsified scientific data, fabricated fallacies about the intellectual and economic attributes of people, and other concocted facts. The use of public forums by Holocaust deniers and groups demeaning blacks does not strengthen democracy. Hate propaganda injures targeted groups because, instead of informing and edifying through dialogue and deliberation, it debases and foments insensitivity and brutality. Propagandists are interested in control, not truth, so, when it is opportune for them, they resort to violence rather than discussion to settle their disagreements and differences. Bigotry has helped establish and bolster tyrannical, demagogic, and arbitrary regimes. It has shown itself, time and time again, to be essential in instigating violence against identifiable groups. Even if, after many injustices, truth eventually wins out, that does not right the wrongs committed against past victims. Their sufferings are irreversible, in spite of future rectifications.[39]

Close examination of the "marketplace of ideas" metaphor reveals that its theoretical foundations are antidemocratic and antiegalitarian. Speech is more analogous to a bright flame, similar to the Promethean fire that can warm and bring to light knowledge, understanding, and wisdom; on the other hand, like the conflagration that burned down Troy, it can raze society by consuming it in a blaze of oppressive ideology. The First Amendment value of messages is significantly greater when they further justice, equality, and social contentment than when their triumph in the marketplace is solely based on the dominant power of proponents, no matter how unethical they may be. Holmes's relativistic metaphor is ambivalent as to whether the winners support beneficent or malevolent laws and social conventions.

The "marketplace of ideas" doctrine is based on a relativistic social theory that has imbedded itself into American jurisprudence. Its premises support the powerful, even when their aspirations endanger democracy. Discrimination and intolerance should not be given the opportunity to win in the power market. Even if tolerance will eventually rise to the top, the harms victims experience while waiting for justice to burgeon are too heavy a price to pay for Holmes's social experiment. The potential long-term dangers of bigotry can be measured from numerous historical examples of gradually inculcated linguistic paradigms that justified and fomented injustices. Hate propaganda should be checked because it threatens to popularize group hatred and catapult the forces of inequality.

Imminent Threat of Harm

The Supreme Court doctrine that anti-incitement laws are constitutional only when their scope is limited to preventing imminent lawless action is based on the false assumption that the advocacy of future violence cannot have devastating effects.[40] Sometimes, incitements for long-term preparations are not solely ideological but are also realistic about the current and future prospects of success. The planning stages of crimes against humanity, like the Nazi Holocaust and American slavery, were fomented by years of inflammatory literature and education. Charismatic leaders were able to harness misethnicity to kill and enslave only after decades of anti-Semitic and racist dogma had done their damage. Given the historical documentation showing the gradual development of group hatred through propaganda, it is simplistic, disingenuous, and cynical for the Court to argue that only immediately inflammatory oratory is socially dangerous. "It is apparent . . . that under certain circumstances there will be stepwise progression from verbal aggression to violence, from rumor to riot, from gossip to genocide."[41] The longer destructive messages about minorities are given free rein, the more likely it becomes that the hated group will be considered unworthy of essential human rights. Eventually, they come to be depicted and treated as subordinates. Verbally, symbolically, or pictorially evoking charged and loaded vitriol, then, is part and parcel of hate crimes.

Racism, when tolerated, is not an innocuous part of political discourse. Violence against outgroups is perpetrated in the context of sociohistorical background. The gradual development of group characterizations and the promotion of demeaning treatment is generated over a long period of time. Prejudicial speech initiates, perpetuates, and aggravates socially accepted misrepresentation about outgroups. It increases the risk that extremists will act on proffered solutions, instigating human rights violations against racial and ethnic minorities. The greater the barrage of misethnic and subordinating stereotypes, the more likely it is that persons with intense hatreds will release their pent-up frustrations and angers on vulnerable minorities. There is a close and, virtually, necessary connection between advocacy, preparation, coordination, infrastructure development, training, indoctrination, desensitization, discrimination, singular violent acts, and systematic oppression. Those things take time and have more impact than spontaneous acts of violence instigated by phrases uttered in the heat of the moment.

The point of the imminent threat of harm test, on the other hand, is that dangerous, bigoted instigation is in all circumstances analogous to fist fights in which one party draws another into a spontaneous confrontation through verbal taunting.[42] Hate speech is part of a spiraling downward cycle in which aggressive talk turns into avoidance, physical attacks, and systematic injustices.[43] Empirical evidence on how nefarious social movements exploit hate speech demonstrate that the "clear and present danger" test is too narrow. For example, as previously mentioned, it was decades before the image of the Indian savage developed a strong enough following in America to legitimize expropriating tribal lands and removing the inhabitants, and centuries of dehumanizing Arabic discourse about blacks has contributed to the perpetuation of black slavery in contemporary Mauritania and Sudan. The extensive long-term effects on society reach far beyond the immediate circumstances when the denigrations are uttered; these can reduce the social standing and opportunities available to the victims.

Intolerant diatribe not only causes dignitary harms to targeted groups, it also decreases overall social well-being. The government need not wait for an uprising to act against violence-fomenting organizations.[44] The state should act against bigoted organizations before they manifest an immediate danger of social destructiveness. Hate propagandists appeal to images that are already in the popular mind. They use existing stereotypes for greater effect on attitudes and habits. Racist and ethnocentric behavior is part of an intricate web of cultural meanings that function within existing social constructs and etiquette.[45] The Nazis effectively utilized nineteenth-century anti-Semitic slogans, originated by popular authors like Heinrich von Treitschke and Paul de Lagarde, to gain political power, pass the Nuremberg laws, and attempt to exterminate Jews. President Andrew Jackson employed widely disseminated paternalistic images of Indians in order to unite political forces critical to his program of dislocating tribes into the Western states. The existence and popularity of age-old images and enmities enable charismatic leaders to organize movements far before oppression against outgroups is imminent.

Hate speech seeks to undermine the egalitarian ideals of representative democracy because it adjures followers to intolerantly and inhumanely treat groups of people purportedly unworthy of human rights and dignities. Discriminatory acts are more likely to be perpetrated in a society where minorities are commonly derided as intrinsically inferior. Destructive oratory works in concert with readily recognizable images to create intolerant and volatile conditions. It is not always predictable where and when a spark of prejudice will ignite harmful social movements to commit brutal acts. As the majority of the Supreme Court stated in *Gitlow v. New York*, "It cannot be said that the State is acting arbitrarily or unreasonably when, in the exercise of its judgment as to the measures necessary to protect the public peace and safety, it seeks to extinguish the spark without waiting until it has enkindled the flame or blazed into the conflagration."[46] However, the Court has not followed the *Gitlow* line of reasoning; instead, it has sided with a narrower view about the types of inciteful speech that poses a threat to society.

It is unduly facile to discount all but the most imminently dangerous calls to repressive actions as benign. A balancing of social concerns would better get at the value of various expressions. Courts must look at whether the speech furthers democratic ideals or fascist ones; they must consider the extent to which it furthers tranquility or causes instability; whether less restrictive alternatives to prohibiting speech are available; the identity of the speaker and targets; the probability of harm; and the intent of the speaker.[47] Speech can incite persons to contemplation, debate, and action. It can direct people to act altruistically, self-interestedly, or destructively. Given the historical information about the long-term power of hate speech and about its lack of constructive social value, it is too dangerous to wait until there is an emergent threat to democracy.

Content Regulations

As we saw in the previous chapter, while *R.A.V. v. St. Paul* was a unanimous decision, the concurring justices questioned much of the majority's reasoning. Prior to that case, fighting words were considered unprotected forms of expression. St. Paul's ordinance, which singled out certain verbal attacks such as those made on the basis of race, religion, and gender, reflected a decision on the part of a city government that certain fighting words are more dangerous than others. In finding that law unconstitutional, the majority in *R.A.V.* held that government can prohibit the use of all fighting words or none at all.[48] It cannot impose special penalties for fighting words that may pose a greater social harm to the common good than others.

All three concurrences complained that the majority deviated from precedents permitting some content-based restrictions on speech. Justice Blackmun considered it illogical to argue that the state "cannot regulate speech that causes great harm unless it also regulates speech that does not." Blackmun thought *R.A.V.* was so wrongheaded that he believed it would be an anomaly, which would "not significantly alter First Amendment jurisprudence." He maintained that the majority arrived at its reasoning because it disagreed with St. Paul's position that race-based fighting words were more harmful than others. No First Amendment principles were jeopardized by a law preventing "hoodlums from driving minorities out of their homes by burning crosses on their lawns." In fact, Blackmun deemed it a "great harm" to prohibit St. Paul from penalizing racist fighting words "that so prejudice their community."[49]

Scalia's reasoning against content-based speech restrictions was arbitrarily selective. Justice Stevens brought attention to the contradiction in the majority's analysis. He pointed out that Scalia accepted that the state could criminalize threats against the president because such use of language was outside First Amendment protections because it put persons in "fear of violence" and threatened to bring about violence. Thus, while Scalia was averse to having St. Paul single out racist speech for higher punishment, he contradicted himself, writing that the state was allowed to "choose from the set of unprotected speech (all threats) to proscribe only a subset (threats against the President) because those threats are particularly likely to cause 'fear of violence,' 'disruption,' and actual 'violence.'"[50] Elsewhere, Stevens pointed out, the majority conceded the state could regulate advertising in one commercial industry but not another because of a higher risk of fraud in one industry than in another. This same rationale, Stevens wrote, would uphold the constitutionality of a narrowly drafted law prohibiting biased speech: "Certainly a legislature that may determine that the risk of fraud is greater in the legal trade than in the medical trade may determine that the risk of injury or breach of peace created by race-based threats is greater than that created by other threats."[51]

In a law review article published in 1993, Justice Stevens pointed out that "freedom of speech" is a legal term of art that does not comprehend all verbal intercourse that is included by the lay definition of "speech." "For it is obvious that the Framers did not intend to provide constitutional protection for false testimony under oath, or for oral contracts that are made against public policy." The First Amendment, he concluded, does not protect all verbal communication "no matter how unlawful threatening or vulgar it may be."[52]

Justice Scalia's opinion is committed to a government that is wholly neutral to the varying points of view in competing messages. It discounts the numerous instances of restrictions on speech that discriminate based on the substance of communications. Content-based limitations have been found constitutional for the following forms of speech: operating adult theaters, threatening the president, electioneering within 100 feet of a polling place on election day, using trade names, burning draft cards, and distributing obscene materials.[53] It should be noted that these constitutionally permissible content-specific restrictions involve both political and nonpolitical expressions. Electioneering is a form of dialogue about the merits of various political candidates. Draft-card burning also involves political statement, speaking against government involvement in military action or affirming the validity of pacifism. Speech that is not political, such as practicing medicine without a license, is also subject to regulations that are intended to preserve and enhance social welfare and achieve political equality. It is arguable that, similar to obscenity or threats made against the president, hate speech has little or no social and political value.[54] Furthermore, like fighting words, hate speech, whether it aims at long- or short-term harms, is "of such slight social value as a step to truth that any benefit that may be derived from them is clearly outweighed by the social interest in order and morality."[55]

It is incongruous for the Court to uphold content-specific speech laws in some cases while refusing to do so with hate speech legislation. This dichotomy does nothing to alleviate misethnic stratifications. While significant exceptions have been carved out of the First Amendment, vulnerable outgroups continue to be exposed to dangerous calumnies. On the one hand, wealthy individuals can hire expensive lawyers to file libel or slander suits for harms to their reputations. Corporations and inventors can sue for copyright or trademark infringements. On the other hand, according to Scalia, burning a cross on a black family's lawn, signifying that its members are unwelcome in the neighborhood and that they must live there at their peril, is not actionable.[56]

The *R.A.V.* majority failed to consider whether St. Paul had a compelling reason for targeting hate speech. The tremendous danger posed to individuals and to society by expressions of misethnic animus would for most persons outweigh bigots' private interests of venting their hatred and of inciting others to commit hate crimes. The Court revealed an insensitivity for reasonable minority worries concerning the effect symbols of oppression have in energizing misethnic movements. The Court even acknowledged that the City had a compelling interest in passing legislation securing the rights of groups that had historically been victims of discrimination.[57] Nevertheless, it did not ponder the rationale behind St. Paul's decision to direct its efforts against words driven by antagonistic stereotypes. Instead, Scalia articulated a novel and unsubstantiated premise to support his conclusion.

One of *R.A.V.*'s greatest shortcomings is that Scalia failed to reflect on whether cross burning and other destructive messages infringe on constitutional values other than free speech. He only considered First Amendment rights to the exclusion of other civil rights amendments. For instance, the Fourteenth Amendment, which affirms the right to equal protection and due process, was entirely overlooked. The tension that sometimes exists between the values of free speech, equality, and fairness was unexamined. Scalia should have addressed the issue of whether the state ever has the authority to restrict expressions that significantly undermine the common good. Such a discussion would have been pertinent since it was the Fourteenth Amendment that made the First applicable to the states and municipalities. Therefore, at least in issues involving state and city hate speech legislation, attention to Fourteenth Amendment values is integral to constitutional interpretation. In large part, the First Amendment was ratified to protect political speech about issues such as undesirable governmental policies, and the Fourteenth Amendment was meant to secure racial equality. The Fourteenth Amendment effectively incorporated egalitarian ideals into free speech standards.[58]

The *R.A.V.* majority fixated on the First Amendment without considering how that bulwark of freedom fits into the grand scheme of U.S. constitutional democracy. The opinion is based on a paradigm that places free speech in a nebulous realm, impervious to concerns for social, political, economic, and substantive equality. Its absolutist treatment of expression guards against depriving speakers of their autonomous right to communicate defamatory views but fails to address the diminished freedom targets of hate speech experience. Neither does Scalia's opinion deliberate on the violent racist history associated with burning crosses or about the psychological effect on the immediate victims and other black families living nearby.[59] His holding focuses on the value of speech while giving short shrift to the social harms associated with hate speech.

Courts, then, must study whether principles of equality and free speech conflict in given cases. If they do, courts must balance the principles against each other rather than cavalierly asserting one to the exclusion of the other. "Allowing the broadest scope to the language and purpose of the Fourteenth Amendment, it is well understood that the right of free speech is not absolute at all times and under all circumstances."[60] The Fourteenth Amendment, then, is a safeguard against expressions of misethnic propaganda calling for the persecution of identifiable groups of people. In this constitutional scheme, which contains principles both of the First and Fourteenth Amendments, the speech of demagogues who call others to commit misethnic violence is not protected from narrowly tailored hate speech laws.[61] Representative democracies have an interest in safeguarding the equal distribution of privileges and immunities, which unregulated hate speech undermines. The state has a social contract mandate to guard fair institutions and not give way to authoritarian political movements; after all, "the Constitution is not a suicide pact."[62]

Justice Scalia failed to consider that speech is a powerful tool for infringing against constitutional liberties as well as for upholding them. The majority did not balance the right of bigots to express their views with the right of targeted outgroups to be protected against the realistic effects of misethnic propaganda. For example, Scalia did not reflect upon readily available historical examples of cross burnings, the purpose of which has often been to establish a racist base of support. In the past, this inflammatory symbol has led to lynchings of blacks. Burning a cross on a black family's lawn raises autonomy issues other than just those about the free speech of the culprit.[63] Hate speech engenders personal safety concerns in outgroup members, thereby inhibiting them from freely traveling in their own communities. Sometimes, fearing for their safety, minorities are forced to move from their homes. After a cross has been burned on their lawn, blacks are likely to be leery of approaching their own house. The spread of bigotry signals a diminution of egalitarian ideals.

It is simplistic to regard the phrase "Congress shall make no law abridging freedom of speech" as a prohibition against any law whatsoever. The underlying idea is far more complicated. It involves an extensive analysis of the proposed restrictions and their congruity (or lack thereof) with an integrated and civil society. This process requires at least deliberation on the purposes of free speech protections, the threats those guarantees are meant to guard against, and the institutions they are meant to advance.[64] First Amendment issues are decided by considering the competing public and private concerns involved in a particular case.[65] Justice Felix Frankfurter explained that "[t]he demands of free speech in a democratic society as well as the interest in national security are better served by candid and informed weighing of the competing interests, within the confines of the judicial process, than by announcing dogmas too inflexible for the non-Euclidian problems to be solved."[66]

Using this balancing approach, the state can conclude that hate speech is in a class of words posing greater social danger than other fighting words. Legislators may properly find that some verbal threats are more malignant than others. The interest of a bigot spouting off hateful and provocative oratory is far less than is the interest of a family forced to cower at home, fearing for their well-being because symbols of oppression and exclusion were placed on their lawn.[67] After all, the United States is not a society that only tolerates the value of dialogue, it is also committed to the principles of racial and ethnic equality.

Hate speech, then, is one of those classes of utterances that should not be protected under the First Amendment because its value is so low to the orderly functioning of a representative democracy. It communicates fallacies, condescending attitudes, and combustible instructions that are averse to the Constitution. Destructive messages have repeatedly, in many different cultures, shown themselves instrumental to perpetrating some of the greatest crimes in history. The propagation of misethnicity simply does not soothe irrational hatreds. It imbeds them deeper into the social psyche, making their eradication all the more difficult. Hateful speech is designed to impinge on the civil rights of targeted outgroups. Traditional civil remedies, such as the imposition of monetary damages against hate groups for burning black churches or painting swastikas on synagogues, are not enough to show society's disapprobation for racist and ethnocentric harms.[68] Moreover, they are after-the-fact solutions that are likely to prove insufficient for preventing massive injustices. It is better to nip them in the bud.

R.A.V. creates the illusion that cross burning and other bigoted forms of expression are legitimate types of political debate. To the contrary, hateful expressions, especially when they are advanced before the private residence of a victimized outgroup, have time and time again destabilized the multifaceted ethnic fabric of the United States. The cross burned on the lawn of the family in *R.A.V.* was a real and deliberate threat to their right to live and travel in peace.

Courts hearing challenges to legislation that forbids the dissemination of hate propaganda should evaluate the historical realities of persecuted minorities rather than just enunciating abstract theories that do not empathize with the plight of persecuted peoples. The aspirations of an entire racial group can be compromised by false aspersions about the character of its members.

Beauharnais v. Illinois, decided in 1952, came to a conclusion about the power of words very different from *R.A.V.* The Court, in *Beauharnais*, upheld the constitutionality of a group libel statute that made it unlawful to "portray depravity, criminality . . . or lack of virtue of a class of citizens, of any race, color, creed, or religion" and to expose those citizens to "contempt, derision, or obloquy." The majority found that based on Illinois' history of racial conflict, the legislature had the power to punish group libel when it threatened "the peace and well-being of the State."[69] The Court found the statute constitutional and upheld the defendant's conviction for distributing lithographs urging white homeowners to resist neighborhood integration.[70] Justice Felix Frankfurter, writing for the majority, relied on historical evidence indicating that bigotry had caused damages to the inhabitants of Illinois.[71]

The Court declared group libels damaging to society and not integral to the exposition of truth. Since libel laws protect individuals from being harmed and preserve social tranquility, the Court was "precluded from saying that speech . . . cannot be outlawed if directed at groups with whose position and esteem . . . the affiliated individual may be inextricably involved."[72] Important, too, is that Frankfurter held that since Beauharnais's utterances were libelous, his speech was punishable and could be prohibited even though it did not pose a "clear and present danger."[73] While the Court acknowledged that the statute could be abused, it noted that all laws can be abused, and such a possibility was too remote to find the law unconstitutional. *Beauharnais* considered historical facts rather than simply abstract theory. Therefore, it represents a more discerning opinion than *R.A.V.* about the potential harms of hate speech.

Beauharnais was decided by a 5–4 majority, and most of the dissenting justices supported, in principle, the constitutionality of group libel legislation but found the Illinois statute at issue unconstitutional. Only Justice Hugo Black held the absolutist view that group defamations were a form of public discussion on issues about segregation.[74] Justice Joseph Reed found the ordinance vague, but otherwise thought the state had the power to pass group libel laws to protect public peace.[75] Justice Douglas pointed out that "Hitler and his Nazis showed how evil a conspiracy could be which was aimed at destroying a race by exposing it to contempt, derision, and obloquy." He therefore believed such group defamation was an indictable offense but thought it could only be curtailed in cases when there was a clear and present danger.[76] Finally, Justice Robert Jackson agreed that the state could pass group libel laws, but dissented because the trial judge did not give Beauharnais the opportunity to offer up a defense.[77]

One of the peculiarities with *R.A.V.* is the majority's reliance on *Beauharnais* to illustrate that some words, like group libels, have so little value to social order and morality that they can be constitutionally prohibited. Even though Scalia thought fighting word regulations must be neutral, he considered group defamations to be outside the scope of First Amendment protections.[78] Thus, *Beauharnais* seems to have survived *R.A.V.* intact even though its scope has been limited by decisions like *New York Times v. Sullivan*.[79] The latter case established an actual malice requirement for defamations against public figures, so its effect on *Beauharnais* extends only to cases where group libels are directed against public personalities. The Supreme Court made this point in *Ferber v. New York*, stating that except in those special cases dealing with public officials, *Beauharnais* continues to be precedential authority on the publication of group libels.[80] Consequently, it appears that even when misethnic group defamations are directed against public officials, they can nevertheless be prohibited so long as they are expressed with actual malice, meaning that they are uttered with the actual knowledge that the statements are false or with the reckless disregard for their truth value.[81] Nevertheless, keeping in mind the *New York Times*'s limitations on defamation laws, it is still constitutional for the state to place prohibitions on expressions that "portray depravity, criminality . . . or lack of virtue of a class of citizens, of any race, color, creed, or religion" and make that group subject to "contempt, derision, or obloquy."

Cross burnings pose an even greater threat of harm to social order than group libels. The intimidating messages signified by symbols of oppression are clear, and they are neither a step to truth nor social justice. The continued vitality of *Beauharnais* is irreconcilable with *R.A.V.*'s content neutral requirement on hate speech. Scalia's use of the case is one of the more contradictory aspects of his opinion, but not the only one.

Of course, laws designed to suppress communications based on their content are ordinarily deemed unconstitutional; however, there is a qualified set of conditions under which such legislation has been found valid. These conditions are met when the government has an interest in ensuring the free enjoyment of individual rights and overall well-being. The regulation must not, however, inhibit democratic or egalitarian debate, which aims to achieve equitable social justice. Given this framework, it is legitimate for the state to prevent persons from persuading others to commit acts that have consequences more deleterious than personal harms. Therefore, the legislature may find that given minorities' special vulnerabilities, hate speech poses a greater likelihood of harm to both individuals and society than do other types of fighting words. Such a conclusion can rationally be drawn from empirical examples of the power of hate propaganda.

Supreme Court precedents leave ample pathways for hate speech to become part of accepted discourse in the United States. Hate speech does not contribute to dialogue on social and political justice; instead, it detracts from it by spreading rumors, innuendos, and outright falsehoods. The "marketplace of ideas" doctrine is based on relativistic principles that remain imbedded in American First Amendment jurisprudence. The "imminent threat of harm" test is based on a disregard for the potentially long-lasting dangers of hate propaganda. And *R.A.V.* is riddled with contradictions that fly in the face of other Supreme Court precedents.

10

Out of the Quagmire

The social harms of hate speech are extensive. Dominant majorities have time and again used propaganda to promulgate a vision of society that excluded minorities from full political participation. Destructive messages have often causally preceded grave human rights violations committed against outgroups. It seems evident, therefore, that nations and communities, particularly those dedicated to the equal protection of rights, must determine how best to grapple with the threats posed by the dissemination of hate propaganda. Before reflecting on whether it is appropriate to restrict hate speech in a democracy, it is essential to consider the extent to which governments must protect persons against infringements of their rights. I now turn to the political institutions grounding republican democracy and making it precious and worthy of preservation. The principles presented here are important predicates for formulating a cause of action restricting hate speech.

The conclusion I draw from this discussion is that in order to decrease intergroup tension and increase public contentment, society has a duty to reduce misethnic conduct through fair legislation. This social obligation requires the prohibiting of intentionally harmful hate speech because that brand of communication flies in the face of principles at the foundation of representative democracies and decreases social well-being. Destructive messages that advocate augmenting the rights of the majority at the expense of the minority are antithetical to justice and equality.

The Reciprocal Duty of Humanity

Persons singly and collectively have a *reciprocal duty to humanity* that relates to the interpersonal obligations owed by and to all humans regardless of their standing or place in society.[1] The reciprocal duty attaches to a subject's actions without regard to the social group to which the objects belong. It makes requisite that actors respect the universal yearning for fair treatment. The capacity to contemplate on and to behave justly is part of each person's sense of empathy. A person must act fairly toward another regardless of the recipient's racial or ethnic group. The implication here is that persons can and should be regarded as ends, as Immanuel Kant, following the wisdom of generations of philosophers before him, wrote in *Metaphysics of Morals*. Each individual's aspirations, feelings, and thoughts have intrinsic value; therefore, no one should be degraded to merely a utility function for someone else's success. People's value is in their very being, not just in their usefulness. It is critical, therefore, to be sensible to other people's aims and, as much as is practicably possible, to help them achieve them. I am, therefore, only one factor in assessing the means and outcomes of my actions: I am a social actor. It is irrelevant whether I think a particular person is worthy of empathy. The reciprocal duty to respect others is socially obligatory and not a matter of personal preference.

The broad valuation of what each of us has accomplished as a member of society is discernible from the social good connected either immediately or residually from our actions. Society functions collectively, and each person's set of goods is realized and advanced in the good of the whole. No action can be just unless it takes into account this panoramic picture and tries to promote the public good. Of course, given our limited understanding, knowledge, and capacity to foresee the consequences of words and conduct, the best that we can do is to choose rules that will result in optimal internal and external improvements. Therefore, the normative factors that are best are those that maximize the overall good.

Persons join organized communities to protect their *fundamental rights*. By "fundamental" or "essential rights" I mean those prerogatives that all persons have naturally by virtue of their humanity. They include the rights to a good life, liberty, personal integrity, freedom of movement, and self-preservation.[2] States are created to protect those rights and to augment them. Persons living in social entities also have *basic rights*. The latter are prerogatives members of a society owe each other. Each citizen abiding by state laws can expect to enjoy fair and equitable legal treatment, freedom of association, protection from vigilante violence, the right to accumulate wealth fairly, and the right to run for political office.

Rules and laws that are reasonably calculated to protect these rights take each individual's equal worth into account. Rational persons freely agree to follow the regulations because they see that adherence both benefits them and furthers the purposes of their communities. The pertinent question to ask in establishing rules and laws is, What principles are designed to protect the fundamental and basic rights of all social players? The question presupposes the existence of a certain degree of empirical knowledge about the outcome of actions. The conception of practical justice can be ascertained by comprehending it as a set of reasonable principles for the governance of daily life. These principles must be public and amenable to debate.

Reason alone, however, could just as easily rationalize selfishness as altruism. Rationalized injustices can be avoided by integrating fair policies and statutes. Overall well-being can then be achieved through mutual respect, which involves consideration for one's own and others' interests. It is important, along this line of thinking, to consider whether the recipient might have a reasonable objection to a particular course of conduct or to specific legal restrictions.

Human dignity is due to each person because the individual is preeminent to the state and has fundamental rights prior to the enactment of its laws and institutions. People have a right to be treated with respect on account of their humanity. Fundamental rights arise from life itself because they are integral to personal existence. Defense of these essential interests is the primary objective of the social contract, which is the free association of individuals with ethical and civic obligations to one another. Persons join or remain in such societies consensually. Justice is one of the social contract's chief cornerstones, demanding that all individuals be treated fairly and humanely. A social contract is an ideal set of principles whose parameters are applicable to all civil constitutions. The legitimacy of legislation is based on the consistent respect its precepts afford all persons regardless of their physical appearances or ethnic backgrounds. Thus, a social contract is normative. It draws attention to interpersonal and public obligations.

On the other hand, the political and cooperative compacts are secondary. The political compact creates states through legal acts, such as the Declaration of Independence. And the cooperative compact, which is composed of a constitution or basic laws, provides the rubrics or terms for beneficial intercommunion. It draws from general principles and contains laws specific to the particular needs of a people. A cooperative compact is a series of ratified laws setting forth obligations among individuals, groups, and governmental entities, while the social contract is the explicit or implicit agreement, or, more accurately, an accepted ethos, to respect everyone's personhood.

Legal restrictions are enacted because humans do not always act benevolently. Punishments are designed to deter persons from violating the reciprocal duty of humanity and thereby harming the community. People's actions can be restricted to the extent that they threaten the rights of direct or residual objects. One fairly obvious example is that people can express their aggression so long as they do not put others into imminent fear of harm by their words and actions. Anyone who violates this principle can be charged with assault, and, if the person is convicted, the state can curtail his or her freedom of movement. Uncontrolled aggression is harmful to a community and, therefore, justifies laws designed to prevent and punish it.

Sometimes the diminution in welfare is immediately felt by the objects of injustice, but, at other times, an antisocial action is part of a chain of behaviors that much later culminate in the commission of crimes. Law sometimes seeks to cut the links of that chain before a crime is committed. Conspiracy and attempt statutes are types of preventative laws.

Constraints recognize that persons are often led by self-interest and the desire for power even when those drives are averse to reason. Societies are established primarily for safeguarding fundamental rights and establishing a set of protected basic rights designed to improve subjects' lives. Alone, humans would face impossible odds in guarding against abuse and infringement by more powerful individuals and factions. Humans, who are social animals, are driven by their instinct of self-preservation to live in association with others. They abide in communities, subject to restraints devised to improve the overall well-being of individuals, families, neighbors, and nations. Persons form social units, such as states, because of their meager capabilities to live alone. However, a conglomeration of existentially separate beings can only function if an organizational structure is established demarcating certain actions as antisocial. This arrangement is initially based on commonsense morality, prohibiting obvious infractions like murder. With time, a more complex system of regulations, such as those dealing with inheritance, is needed for persons to feel safe about their personal and property rights. Predictable rules are conducive to successful social and commercial dealings. They facilitate governmental administration and accountability. A person will probably agree to limit his or her actions toward others as long as it is realistic to expect that others will likewise abide by the same terms of behavior.

Determining what conduct is reasonable is introspective: it involves evaluating how in a given situation people should act toward me, and then behaving accordingly toward them. Empathy, then, is an essential component of just dealings.

The process of placing oneself in the circumstances of another (through imagination) and recognizing their humanity is known as *empathizing*. Persons empathize when they, first, reflect on how dignitary affronts affect others' temperaments, expectations, and emotions and, then, behave in ways that respect those people's rational desires. The proclivity toward empathy may be developed by learning about the backgrounds, hopes, welfare, sense of serenity, and sufferings of others. It does not mean that one must take on the joys and suffering of others but "rather requires possible openness to meaningful, contextualized encounters."[3] This process is not identical with *faux* compassion, which, as Andrew E. Taslitz has pointed out, falls short of internalizing other people's life experiences.[4] A person with false empathy takes on the sufferings of those whom he or she cannot help, thereby decreasing overall happiness without doing anything helpful. Pity also makes others look pathetic instead of making them equals whose hardships can be comprehended, understood, and allayed. The adoption of empathy and the avoidance of pity are compatible and productive. Other people's human rights should be systematically guarded as if they were one's own. The highest social ideal is to maximize each person's happiness and thereby augment the public good.

As long as the ability of people to live freely is dependent on the enforcement of mutual obligations, some entity with a well-crafted legal system that reflects the general will of its inhabitants must be formed. That construct, the state, must protect its citizens' tranquility and improve people's lives better than they could if they lived in a state of nature. The degree to which citizens can express their freedom extends only so far as they do not infringe on other people's rights.

Those who abide by civil order need not all have directly agreed to current institutions and mandates. Persons not born in a community may later choose to immigrate there, and those born there may decide to leave. Nevertheless, persons are bound by the cooperative compact of the place in which they have voluntarily chosen to live, so long as the culture methodically protects rights, alleviates existing injustices, and increases well-being. Institutions not established on the reciprocal duty of humanity can be rewritten from scratch, making all social members or their elected representatives bargainers to the cooperative compact, or existing laws can be amended through predetermined, organized, and abiding methods.

Where prejudice was a factor in drafting any constitutional provisions, succeeding generations need not follow those dictates. A society with a solid foundation of social justice can rectify institutional wrongs. Witness, for example, the United States: many of its founders were slave owners. The Constitution itself contained provisions protective of slavery, such as the Three-Fifths Clause and the Fugitive Slave Clause.[5] Despite the legacy of misethnicity, the Constitution was amended and laws were enacted enabling the country to shed the worst elements of its racist past and to continue cleansing itself of those that yet remain through an abiding commitment to due process and equal treatment under the law. The rights of blacks and Native Americans, who did not originally have any say in framing the social contract, were acknowledged by later amendments.

Establishing the parameters of an ideal political system, beholden to the rights of individuals, is critical to the formation of beneficent states. Existing laws should be tested against principles, and their effect on society must be scrutinized. The goal is to formulate a conceptual framework for a constitutionally established, democratic state not beholden to any particular religion, ideology, race, or ethnic group. The cooperative contract should be grounded in a commonsense understanding of empathic behavior. It is intuitively ascertainable from public expectations that citizens have the following reciprocal, public expectations: that their fundamental rights will be protected and that they will be respected as inherently important to the social structure.[6] At the heart of orderly and just governmental systems lie primary principles for enjoining persons' actions toward others. Those imperatives are based on commonsense morality about institutions that are essential to the mutual cooperation of people with differing interests.[7] Correspondingly, principles should be rejected if rational persons would find them repulsive to a representative form of government and if there is no potential for improving human lives.

Persons give up some freedoms when they join political entities. Yet communities, while restrictive, also protect precious rights and guard them from infringement by other people. Social contractees never forfeit their essential, natural human qualities, such as dignity and autonomy; otherwise, joining a society would be counterproductive. People consent to abide by laws drafted and passed by governmental representatives for the public good. Overall, societies make it possible for people to express their identity better than they could in a state of nature. The natural urges to protect one's life, to live peaceably, and to make critical decisions about substantive issues, such as where to live or what profession to pursue, call for a pooling of intellectual and material resources into a state. When people live in circumstances where mutual obligations are explicit and basic rights are parsed, their material possessions too are more secure.

The primary purpose of a political society is the protection of people's fundamental rights, not, as John Locke contended, the preservation of their estates. Property rights never come before the right to self-preservation, autonomy, or a good life. A person cannot kill someone for stealing property because a thief's right to life is preeminent over the right to retain property. However, the right to self-preservation allows persons with at least a reasonable apprehension of an imminent threat to their lives to justifiably kill another in self-defense. The fundamental rights of individuals are correlative, and basic rights vary based on rational rules and are subordinate to them. Legally, essential rights always trump derivative ones. The former are integral to individuals, while the latter arise in relation to others. I have a right to a good life regardless of whether I live alone in the woods or among many others in a metropolis. However, my right to own a particular object is relative to the right of other people to own it. Laws are unbiased sets of rules for resolving conflicts of interests.[8]

Even though all who join and live in societies agree to certain restrictions on their autonomy rights, they do not merge into the whole. Each person is a distinct member of society whose human essence must be honored and respected. The members of society transcend the collective political body. Society, after all, is nothing but a conglomeration of persons whose unique and collective interests it exists to protect. Each person has a distinct dignity and essence, independent of any others, while society exists to augment human potentials and is nothing without its members. Strictures on essential rights and proscriptions on basic rights can only be justified for the purpose of extending collective tranquility and contentment. Public policies must take into account and recognize each person's distinct being. Laws must balance between public and private interests, with individuals being the more significant of the two.

A system of governance that is based on the reciprocal duty of humanity encourages persons to follow the rational guidelines of social morality. Reasonable persuasion to behave fairly is preferable to coercive force. Each person is expected to treat others as integrally valuable. Justice requires regard for everyone's contentedness and for his or her right to personal autonomy.[9] It is only when persons deviate from social justice, as for example by acting against minorities or inducing others to do so, that it is appropriate to enforce coercive laws. Misethnic institutions such as slavery, segregation, racist violence, and discrimination are a denial of human dignity. They subsume individuals into a hated group unworthy of rationally governing their own lives. This is not only disruptive to the happiness of targeted groups but to society as a whole because it arbitrarily singles out persons and prohibits them from using their talents, knowledge, and abilities for the social well-being.

Thus far, I have argued that the principles of justice arise from an intuitive, rational, and interpersonal ethic, and that it is binding on persons who freely choose to live in a community of equally precious individuals. Each of them has a mutual obligation to treat others fairly. Involuntary socialization, through civil and criminal laws, is necessary to prohibit antisocial behavior that infringes on others' rights. Just legislation is grounded in principles that reasonable people would agree are empathic, conducive to a good life, and respect social members as intrinsically valuable beings. So long as persons reside in representative democracies they must abide by established rules and the reciprocal duty of humanity on which they are established.[10]

Principles and rules are indispensable to achieving the best empirical results, but there is also another part of the story. The contractarian view is too limiting. The complexities of human life, with the multiple unexpected circumstances we encounter daily, indicate that in choosing which rules to follow there is a farsighted aim of just actions. How else can equity, which sides with fairness rather than strict construction of rules, be explained? Deontological consequentialism posits that contractees to the social contract should agree to specific obligations that would best increase contentment, decrease suffering, and alleviate other harms. The basis of this judgment should be partly rooted in inductive reasoning gained from other political systems and historical information. A political theory could then be developed by analyzing the moral, political, and social complexities of a community. Consequentialism explains the goals and contractarianism the rules of social morality. On that account, persons' rights should be protected because adhering to the reciprocal duty of humanity promotes the common good.

Assessing whether persons are well off in a particular society is an important factor in deciding whether one set of political principles is better than another. A just legal system protects fundamental rights and improves people's lives. Considering whether people's lives are better than they would have been in a state of nature should not be done solely by quantifying overall social goods because such an analytical method might regard the reduction of welfare for some minorities legitimate so long as the overall common good is elevated. Instead, the evaluation must reflect on how individuals, regardless of race or ethnic group, are treated, counting each person as equally valuable. Factions, although amalgams of individuals, are not in and of themselves more valuable by virtue of their ability to dominate political discourse. Since society is a composite of individuals, an evaluation of social well-being should take the broadest possible perspective of the population's level of contempt. The results should then be applied to improving current laws, making them more sensitive to human needs, and thereby magnifying public welfare.

General social welfare can be measured only by the degree to which society respects and protects the rights of all inhabitants. Wherever groups of people are singled out for persecution, the common good is diminished. A group that seeks to improve its well-being might do so fairly, but it will achieve an even greater good if it also seeks to benefit others. Furthermore, there are circumstances that might fairly benefit others even though an actor's group receives no immediate gratification beyond the sense of altruistic accomplishment.

In an interwoven society, where persons rely on the responsible behavior of others, the diminution of substantive happiness of even one individual reduces overall welfare. Civilized societies are interconnected through personal, business, and entertainment relationships. Therefore, where harm comes to one person, others who are reliant on that person's love, friendship, work, or play are affected. General happiness is intrinsically tied to the happiness of individuals. It is, of course, possible to imagine cases in which the loss of happiness to an individual or to a group is negligible and goes almost unnoticed by anyone else. However, any major reduction in their mental or material goods will reverberate into society at large. Unfair and irrational strictures on fundamental and basic rights decrease people's contentment in the most significant and basic ways. They impede persons from fulfilling their potential and deny them common human advantages. Increasing the common good, then, necessarily implicates protecting individual rights.

Interpersonal relations flourish when free actions and decisions operate in conformity with the principles of justice. The formula of deontological consequentialism recognizes that each person's happiness is just one factor of social well-being. Interactions thrive when they are not solely predicated on self-interested aims. Each individual benefits from being benevolent toward others.

Social harmony is not, however, achieved through personal effacement. Instead, it results from the acknowledgment that other people's rights are as legitimate as one's own, regardless of their social group or class. It matters not, then, to which racial or ethnic group I belong because my actions will be the same regardless of whether they are aimed at my group or another. Recognizing other individuals' interests and passing laws to protect them is the best way to achieving a tranquil social existence. The opposite course of action—holding biases against others, especially those not belonging to one's group—creates friction and is a path to unconscionable stratification and, in extreme circumstances, violence and destruction.

These injustices can be avoided only through the preservation of fundamental rights. Laws fortify those rights and put the weight of society behind prohibiting unjust institutions like slavery and segregation. The reason for promulgating laws and the social mores that fortify them is that people are happier living in a culture that prohibits violations of their rights. In societies where groups of people can be abused and their humanity is disregarded, even those who are not persecuted come to fear for their safety, live from day to day in terror and uncertainty, and are, therefore, unhappy. One need only recall the Stalinist Soviet Union, where culprits could never be certain that they would not become the next victims. Terrorizing an outgroup might pay short-term dividends for the dominant group, but the resulting loss of welfare to society as a whole is enormous and lasting.[11] Anti-Semitism has reverberated through the ages causing an enormous trail of destruction. Racism in Mauritania has hurt countless numbers of people. So too with gender discrimination, which has for centuries repressed women from realizing their aspirations.

Legal rules based on just principles should be adhered to, but they are not the ultimate end at which the social contract aims. Fair laws are enacted to create a society where everyone can pursue a rewarding and meaningful life. Any laws that turn out to be counterproductive to that end are discarded. They are not absolute, and when they do not help citizens enjoy a happier life they must be either amended or revoked. The principles of justice are refined concepts, worked out as a means to increasing human happiness.[12]

Even the finest principles can be twisted to commit cold-hearted crimes under legalistic guises. For instance, fairness and equality have been claimed as exclusively applicable to ingroup intra-action. So it was with pro-slavery advocates in the antebellum South, who explained away the recognition of human equality and unalienable rights as asserted in the Declaration of Independence. Slavery's defenders, like Henry Wise, Congressman from Virginia, during the ill-fated attempt to censure Congressman John Quincy Adams in 1842, claimed that human rights protections applied only to whites, making it psychologically easier and socially more acceptable for them to enslave fellow humans.

Reason dictates that personal and public ethical imperatives be followed to promote beneficence. These will increase benevolence and decrease friction between individuals and groups. Each of us can discern how we would like people to act toward us, given the range of known possibilities and limitations, and can internalize the reasonable expectations of others for a contented and unmolested life. In a word, we can all empathize. From this I derive the following imperative:

> *Act so that if you were the object of your actions you would consider them fair, making sure to increase contentment within the range of alternatives available to you.*

Each action has a ripple effect on the universe. In a social context, human behaviors not only affect immediate object(s) but have ramifications on a broader community. Thus, conduct can increase or decrease happiness not only among the small number of persons at whom it is directed but, on a limited scale, among other people as well. The further individuals are from the action, physically and intellectually, the less likely it is they will be affected. This further contemplation augments the previous imperative into what I call the *private imperative of reciprocal beneficence*:

> *Behave according to principles that you would consider just and fair if you were the recipient of the action, keeping in mind that the intended*

end of your conduct should be the general welfare of society insofar as you can affect it.[13]

Both imperatives are based on deontological concerns for individuals' fundamental rights and the consequentialist appreciation for social welfare.

I derive the duty that nations owe their residents from the personal imperative. The *public maxim of reciprocal beneficence* requires the following:

Laws should be based on principles that are intended to maximize social benefits and which reasonable legislators would consider just and fair if they were affected by the legislation.

Lawmakers should evaluate whether to enact proposed legislation from the perspective of those who will be affected by it. They should empathize with the groups whom the law will impact. The legislative branch should consider the short- and long-term social implications of their enactments. Deliberations upon the social consequences of laws must, at a minimum, take into account whether they are based on rational principles, respect fundamental rights, and are designed to improve the common good. Laws should be based on the public maxim of reciprocal beneficence.

Misethnicity flies in the face of these maxims. Hate speech creates the background conditions necessary to denigrate minorities and exclude them from participation in civic life. Decreasing the well-being of people based on their racial or ethnic status more profoundly diminishes overall social happiness than would individual affronts. Hate propaganda directs persons to disrupt social harmony by inflicting arbitrary harms against outgroups. As such, it is contrary to good social order because it deviates from respectful rules for interpersonal transactions and increases strain among peoples. Furthermore, hate speech reduces social contentment because it recruits persons to commit destructive acts. I elaborate on these points in chapter 11.

Equality of Right

I now turn my attention to what may be called the *basic right to equal treatment*. This right is not fundamental because it involves issues that arise in the context of social interactions, including political participation, the allotment of power, and access to valuable resources. An inclusive society can best increase the wealth of its human capital and augment well-being by promoting the rights of equal opportunity and reciprocal respect. Misethnic stereotypes, to the contrary, catalyze exclusionary social constructions and degrade vulnerable minorities, creating oppressive strata of access to the good life and decreasing the common welfare.

The private imperative of reciprocal beneficence is a key concern in a diverse society because it requires that we accord the same degree of import to all its members. The relevant gauge of equality in a community is whether rights are protected through a legal system that affords everyone, regardless of whether they are powerful or uninfluential, the same constitutional or basic powers and protections. There are, of course, allowable differences: persons who hold government positions in representative democracies have more say in policy and decision-making processes than other citizens, parents have an unequal relationship with their youngsters, and employers have the upper hand over their employees. These differences do not in and of themselves violate the principle of equal treatment. What is relevant is whether individuals' fundamental and basic rights are equally safeguarded. Equality under the law means that each individual must be treated consistently with rational and non-prejudicial laws designed to improve social contentment and protect individual rights. It requires that ethical principles, policy concerns, and legislation be the key factors in determining whether any offense has been committed. Government must treat persons with equal respect without arbitrarily favoring any identifiable group.

Persons *qua* humans are interchangeable insofar as their worthiness to social justice is concerned. The principle of equality acknowledges individual differences but does not regard them as pertinent to the application of those political and legal rules which are critical to social inclusion. Any deviation from this principle can be justified only if it leads to the common good, and exploiting any person or group can never satisfy that end. Egalitarianism maintains that political equality is due each person simply because of his or her humanity, not based on any merit, accomplishment, or social status. Humanity does not admit to degrees. All people have an equally legitimate claim to bettering their lives, protecting their properties, and expressing their personhoods.

The principle that all humans are equal implies that certain substantive rights are intrinsic to everyone. Each person is born with the same fundamental rights, and, as members of political entities, each enjoys the same basic rights and is limited by the same legal strictures. Each person can recognize his or her own humanity in others: all of us strive for happy and fulfilling lives. Thus, empathy is a natural attitude that becomes psychologically tainted by misethnic projections, displacements, and rationalizations. All people are existentially alone—self-conscious of their individual strengths and weaknesses, with their own pleasures and sufferings, possessing a free will, holding to a sense of self-dignity—they are ends in and of themselves, not merely exploitable objects.[14] The principle of equality affirms that each person is worthy of respect, and that no degree of stereotyping can take that away.

Personal and social interests coincide in the concept of equality. Each is furthered when persons are coequally valued for their unique talents and abilities. Each person's intrinsic importance demands that in return for abiding by fair laws, society treat everyone impartially and with "equal concern."[15] However, unless everyone, regardless of racial or ethnic characteristics, is considered a fully valuable human, "equal rights" and "equal obligation" are simply skeletons without flesh because they are then merely ideals without any practical significance. Treating others equally has to do, in part, with empathizing with their human condition, and then acknowledging that their interest in fundamental rights is on a par with one's own. All people have a coextensive right to exercise and enjoy their autonomy, so long as they do not infringe on the liberties of others.[16] Everyone has an innate right to be independent and be bound only to rules and laws that are mutually obligatory on others. This principle comports with the requirement that persons respect the rights of others to the same extent as they would want to be likewise respected.[17]

Duties owed to each social member translate into a collective responsibility to provide people with equal opportunities to fulfill their potential. Egalitarian society provides each person with the option to exercise political volitions and participate in important public decisions. For equality to be meaningful, the government must give the same consideration and deference to all persons living in the community. Democratic societies afford each of their members a voice in collective decisions. Various political offices must also be available to all persons able to meet reasonable qualifying criteria. Requisite qualifications must be congruous with the anticipated duties of office. Persons with the necessary talents, training, and skills may be favored for particular offices, but they should only gain them through fair procedures, such as plebiscite or objective examination.

Putting obstructions against enjoying the right to equal treatment in the way of groups because of their skin pigmentation or ethnic background makes no political or social sense. Egalitarianism decries the use of arbitrary distinctions to promote inequalities. Making a major impact on people's lives based on impertinent factors is simply unfair. Each person, not only the privileged few, has a coequal interest in expressing his or her personhood, so long as he or she does not hamper the self-development of others.

The majority is obliged not to abuse its power and to wield it in such a manner as to honor the right of minorities to be treated equally. Prominent negative images of outgroups make the process of accepting misethnic paradigms almost unconscious and, hence, promote a widespread disregard for their humanity.

Shutting out an identifiable group from full political participation without fair procedural and substantive reasons is a particularly egregious act of injustice. Distinguishing legally between sets of people based on stereotypes that are impertinent to the qualifications of specific individuals is an example of unfair differentiation. Discrimination against minorities is a systematic, broad-based form of prohibition on people's right to live unmolested lives in a participatory democracy. It restricts outgroups' ability to fully express their citizenship because it limits their educational, professional, and political prospects. This manner of degradation treats vulnerable groups as if they are unworthy of sharing the rights of normal people or receiving the bounties of living in a political community.[18] A legally significant inequality, then, is one that affects people in spheres that are essential to engaging with others as fellow citizens. We may put this principle into practical effect by postulating a terse maxim:

All social inequalities that are based on arbitrary criteria ought to be abolished.[19]

Institutional inequality is justified only when it is not maintained to bar persons from social opportunities and when it is to everyone's advantage.[20]

Equity is an indispensable ethical value in a representative democracy committed to human rights. Without institutionalized and reciprocally enforceable mutual obligations, equity rings hollow and is ineffectual. The idea is that persons who have agreed to limit their natural liberties in order to better increase the success rate of social undertakings deserve the same deference from those who have benefited by their sacrifices. Most people will relinquish some of their rights, if burdens are equally allocated and an important community interest is thereby furthered, as when a draft is instituted to repel military aggression.[21] Based on the reciprocal duty of humanity, however, people may not be forced to submit to unprincipled whims. Restrictions on human rights must be based on deliberated decisions carefully crafted to safeguard fundamental and basic rights. Avenues must remain open for individuals to object, through judicial and administrative alternatives, that their rights were unfairly abridged or that a punishment was disproportionately harsh. The state should not make impromptu decisions bearing on persons' lives and liberties; instead, duties and encumbrances should be doled out based on previously enacted laws that apply to everyone whose behavior warrants it, regardless of group affiliations or memberships. While it may be expedient for demagogues and powerful groups to gather support by targeting outgroups and visiting harsh measures on them, it is by no means fair or equitable.

Exploiting people under the guise of law is inequitable because it downplays their humanity and does not empathize with their predicaments.[22] Legislation should protect citizens from deprivation of their liberties before they become prey to oppressors. Moreover, certain laws, such as antidiscrimination statutes, must reflect that certain groups are more vulnerable to victimization because of their traditional positions of weakness in social hierarchies.

Equality of treatment and opportunity are not, however, the ultimate ends of egalitarianism; rather, they are essential means to achieving social well-being, which is its real aim. For there are numerous situations in which unequal distribution is fair, such as different tax burdens for rich and poor and affirmative action to rectify injustices, which leads to the conclusion that certain forms of inequality are appropriate when the ends they are carefully designed to achieve are clearly conducive to the overall good.[23] Equality, like justice, is a vital means without which maximum welfare cannot be achieved. Without it, large groups of people would be systematically excluded from fulfilling rational aspirations, and, thereby, they would be made unhappier. Each person's welfare figures into the overall sum of a community's well-being. Treating persons equally is essential to augmenting the common good. It evinces respect for others, requires that the sources of happiness—for example, jobs and entertainment—be available to all, and shuns unreasonable differentiation.

Egalitarianism's allure to the human conscience lies in its consistency with the intuition that other persons' essential interests, not just one's own, are worthy of preservation and that a tranquil and secure society is more pleasant to live in than one where there is constant infighting. Immediate gratification of individual sensations does not swell welfare to the same extent as fair rules that are reasonably calculated to enhance overall well-being. Persons find more lasting contentment in a society where everyone's rights are secure against arbitrary intrusions than one that limits their pleasures to "bread and circuses." A society that sacrifices the welfare of one group for the good of another raises anxiety both in the harmed group and in society generally wherever persons are no longer sure that the state is committed to impartially protecting their rights.

Persons ought to be treated equally because of their mutual humanity. This rule of rational consistency is an indispensable principle of equality. Personal behavior and legal dictates should be consistent with intuitive ethical rules, established on wise maxims, the substance of which is drawn from experiential data. Slavery, for example, does not maximize the public good because it excludes a whole group of people from its enjoyment, while equal pay for equal work obviously does because it treats persons in significantly similar circumstances equally. Curtailing freedom makes the victims unhappy, while being adequately compensated for diligent labor gives both employer and employee a sense of contentment from just treatment. Policies should be established on these ethical standards, as opposed to privileged racial and ethnic interests, thereby putting the weight of state power behind egalitarianism.

What egalitarian society should cultivate, through a diverse education, is tolerance and cosmopolitanism, and that is just what hate speech opposes and undermines. The attitudes that hate messages elicit, over long periods of time, spurn empathy and benevolence. Most people, it seems, show a greater affection for a small, insular set of humans than for anyone else. Usually their acts of kindness arise from those special feelings.[24] One of the drawing points of destructive messages is that they manipulate historically based prejudices to unify persons belonging to powerful majorities. They help create objects of intimacy and aversion based on skin color and ethnic background, spurning the right of everyone to live an unmolested, good life. This galvanizes ingroups in the attitude that minorities are less worthy of empathy than they. Widespread credence in the ideology of inequality is critical for later sweeping human rights violations. The dissemination of ideas designed to devalue the human worth of minorities is essential to this downward spiral. Hate speech extols injustices, devalues human worth, praises the commission of hate crimes, and influences others to join the ranks in antidemocratic movements.

11

Destructive Messages' Threat to Justice and Equality

Stereotypes help actors legitimize their acts in ways that they would find unfair and inequitable if they themselves were the objects of the vitriol. Moreover, persons who degrade others based on their race or ethnic origin also diminish the general welfare of society by increasing the prevalence of prejudices that deny social goods to persons based on arbitrary characteristics. Therefore, representative democracy should protect minority civil rights by enacting narrowly tailored laws prohibiting instigatory speech that substantially increases the likelihood of discrimination. Lawmakers should be cognizant of historically persecuted groups' concerns about messages that are purposefully spread to harm them, their families, and friends. It is naive, or at least dismissive of historical realities, to believe that all propagandists who spread messages of hate and destruction, except those calling for immediate action, will be content with words.

The premises of hate speech contravene universal fair treatment; they are meant to mark certain persons as unworthy of empathy: these persons become expendable means to advancing the interests of those holding power. This process seeks to invalidate minority aspirations and preferences. Outgroups are viewed as merely instrumental for others, their goals are considered unimportant. Hate speech is intolerant and therefore could never be part of a universal rule of reciprocal action.

Stereotypes do not reflect the truth even when they emerge victorious in the marketplace of ideas, as pro-slavery thought did in the antebellum South or anti-Semitism did in postimperial Germany. Since persons join societies to protect their fundamental rights and to reap the benefits of basic rights, a better test of truth is the extent to which speech seeks, discovers, and establishes institutions conducive for human rights to thrive.[1]

Bigots use derogatory cultural stereotypes to deny outgroups the very rights they find essential and which they expect others to honor. The right to self-expression does not trump other people's dignitary rights.

Destructive messages deny the personhood of minorities. They establish paradigms of thought that are meant to solicit a group's adherents to act inhumanely. Hate speech poses a threat to social stability and individual safety. Infringements of an individual's personhood are intrinsically unjust. The value of such denigrating speech is so low that it pales in comparison to the interests in life, liberty, and self-preservation which it tries to incite others to violate. While hate speech is shrouded in the democratic mantle of freedom of expression, it seeks to undermine a designated group's sense of personal integrity and civic assurance.[2]

To illustrate this point, suppose that some people burn a cross in their community, set up a sign informing Jews they are unwelcome, or design an Internet site committed to instigating a race war. All of these acts, explicitly or subtly, let people know that they are unwelcome, that the acts are designed to terrorize them, and that other community members plan to shun and exclude them. With the added voice of charismatic leaders, devotees of misethnicity become further entrenched in cultural ideologies. Once any social problem—for example, unemployment—is ideologically linked to a particular outgroup, demagogues can offer solutions whose fierceness is commensurate with how entrenched in a culture the evoked stereotypes are.

Our views of the world and perspectives of others are permeated with presumptions and categorizations acquired from the symbols commonly used in our cultures.[3] Language is not only a means for exposing and discerning truth, but also for stifling and misrepresenting it. Derogatory misethnic stereotypes pave the way for harmful social movements because they create a despised class of people. It is difficult to justify injustices because humans have an innate, although surmountable, proclivity for empathy. However, when a salient group is thought to embody undesirable traits—being devoid of human qualities, corrupting society, and posing a threat to women and children—its personhood can be ignored.

The most effective propaganda rejects or disregards the humanity of particular groups of people. Everyone in the outgroup is classed together. They are all deemed subordinate and socially repulsive. Misethnic insults convey "the message that distinctions of race are distinctions of merit, dignity, status, and personhood."[4] Such speech disregards or outright rejects the humanness of its object, making it easier to commit aggressive acts with moral equanimity. It rejects the notion that each individual is intrinsically important and fit for social membership. Once the others have become mere chimeras with purely wicked attributes, they no longer have any fundamental rights, and society, surely, is no longer obliged to protect their basic rights.[5]

To soothe their conscience for exterminating Jews with poisonous gas, Nazis first characterized them as vermin, thereby justifying their fumigation. On a different continent, slave owners shackled slaves hand and foot and sold them into slavery after they were convinced blacks were a species of man inferior to whites. The guilt associated with treating people unfairly can be eviscerated by messages whose effectiveness comes from their protracted potency to indoctrinate large numbers, and sometimes almost an entire nation, of followers. Misethnic insults are meant to establish a basis on which persecution and acts as brutal as murder can be rationalized. Supremacists recruit followers by proclaiming their moral, religious, and cultural superiority relative to weaker groups. Frontier people who forcefully stole Native American lands thought they were doing Indians a favor by "civilizing" and bringing Christianity to them. When outgroups are regarded as parasitic, their right to personal security is not deemed genuine. Without accounting for this part of the equation, the strand uniting ideology with socially acceptable misethnic violence is lost.

Hate groups use destructive messages and deprecations to build up their infrastructure while they wait for their often slow acting poison to act on the body politic.[6] The Nazis could not have come to power if anti-Semitism had not first become acceptable in the preceding years. They incorporated slogans into their *weltanschauung* that had become part of popular culture (e.g., "The Jews Are Our Misfortune") and took them to their logical conclusion: genocide. Likewise, blacks had been degraded since the sixteenth century in parts of the American colonies. The long-standing commitment to slavery made it impossible to get states like South Carolina to ratify the U.S. Constitution without including provisions tolerant of that undemocratic institution. Misethnicity often takes a long time to spread its roots. It was not until the legend of the roaming Indian became popular on a national level that a notorious Indian conqueror, Andrew Jackson, could push the Indian Removal Act through Congress and justify land theft under the guise of law. Hate speech rarely results in only short-term harms. More commonly, it is developed by succeeding generations and becomes part of social interaction and political culture.

The purpose of destructive messages is to perpetuate inequalities in opposition to democratic values. Calumnies reject the validity of outgroup claims to social-compact benefits. Propagandists call on others, and express a personal commitment, to undermining government's obligation to safeguard the well-being of all citizens. Their expressions impair people's ability to realize dreams and to have their rights fully protected. The notion that propaganda is essential to the assent of tyrannical regimes is not new. In *The Republic*, Plato drew attention to the central role charismatic leaders play in a degenerating democracy. He recognized that agitators systematically generate broad support by denigrating their enemies with false accusations. Plato also had the foresight to realize that the freedoms people enjoy in a democracy can be exploited to establish mob rule and, subsequently, tyranny.[7] Demagogues look for colloquialisms and well-established symbols to make their messages more easily understood. This endears them to the masses and drafts others to exploit minority members for ulterior motives.

When orators, especially those with a following, begin speaking of purging society's diversity, the potential for discrimination against outgroups rises. Speakers use historical stereotypes purporting the inferiority of outgroups to incite violence. Hate crimes are not perpetrated in a psychological and social vacuum. Oratory enunciated against outgroups with the explicit intent to harm them can inflame audiences to commit violent actions. Hate speech reinforces existing prejudices and provides the false information necessary to create new ones. The intensification and development of prejudice is a social evil that threatens harmonious democracy.

The repeated expression of racist and ethnocentric invective makes commonplace the view that minorities are innately unworthy of full constitutional rights. It becomes an affront to even suggest there is anything wrong with unjustly treating people who are commonly disparaged. Persons reared on misethnic linguistic paradigms are confused, offended, and even angered by anyone who questions these injustices; after all, they are only committed against those apelike, parasitic, lazy fools whose very presence pulls down all society.

A society cannot simultaneously cultivate discriminatory attitudes and be committed to protecting personal rights. Human integrity is guaranteed only by states where each individual's liberty is viewed as equally precious, no matter how powerful or powerless his or her race and ethnic group may be. Persons living in any organized society with formal laws and rules owe one another a reciprocal duty of humanitarian treatment. This cannot be achieved where persons treat others in ways they would find unfair if treated so themselves, and where hate propaganda is allowed to influence the development of social institutions. The quest for justice entails using reason to arrive at empathic and tolerant customs, rules, and regulations. The libertarian argument that minority rights can best be protected by uninhibited and unrestricted hate propaganda is counterintuitive given the long-term dangers associated with hate speech. Hate messages are opposed to the spirit of social contract theory, which requires respect for the rights of the contractees. Only when everyone's liberty interests are recognized is there hope of ending the sometimes deadly blights of racism and ethnocentrism. Identification with other people's dignity derives best from a cosmopolitan conception of human consciousness and the expression of empathy toward diverse individuals.[8]

Although hate speech does not always lead to organized supremacism, it is a necessary ingredient to that end. Permitting persons or organizations to spread ideology touting a system of discriminatory laws or enlisting vigilante group violence gradually leads to the erosion of democracy.[9] So it was in the Weimar Republic, where the repeated anti-Semitic propaganda of vulgar ideologues like Julius Streicher, who published perverse attacks against Jews in *Der Stürmer*, chipped away at the democratic experiment in pre–World War II Germany. His weekly stories of Jewish ritual murder and rape of Christian children hit their mark: the German psyche. It is truly eerie, now, looking at photographs relating the effectiveness of Nazi propaganda: respectable-looking adults in suits and dresses listening to long lectures on Jewish inferiority; children, barely able to stand on their two feet, raising their right arm in a Nazi salute. So, too, with racism in America. Senator John Calhoun, Congressman Henry Wise, and other powerful racist orators misled the public about the supposedly benevolent slave owner, feeding his slaves and treating them like his own children. Omitted were the reputable accounts of slaves being beaten to death, having their limbs cut off for running away, getting their front teeth knocked out as a form of branding, and other tortures captured in eyewitness books such as *American Slavery As It Is: Testimony of a Thousand Witnesses*. The repeated inculcation of supremacism proved effective in misrepresenting blacks as movable property. Giants of human rights advocacy, such as Theodore Weld, Angelina and Sarah Grimké, Frederick Douglass, and William Lloyd Garrison, were unable to win the country to their abolitionist views. The contradictory, dual American messages—of the legitimacy of human bondage and civil liberty—compromised the ideals of equality.

Free speech is not an absolute right. It is constrained by the rights of others to enjoy their lives and liberties without fear of hate groups expostulating on their inferiority and advocating their enslavement, extinction, or disenfranchisement.

Recognizing ethnic differences is not, of course, in and of itself detrimental. In fact, celebrating diversity facilitates civil interactions. The danger arises when individuals disseminate legitimizing discourse in order to organize exclusionary movements.

Placing no limits on speech—not even on expressions blatantly intended to make life miserable for minorities—preserves the rights of speakers at the expense of targeted groups. One person's right of expression should not infringe on other people's rights. This is a chief principle behind limits on speech via defamation statutes, zoning regulations, and obscenity laws. Everyone's right to develop personally is equally important both to individuals and to society. Successful hate speech, which gains a broad following, has the potential to inhibit the targets from full self-realization and reduces the total available talents in the social pool of abilities. Spain, for instance, hurt itself culturally and economically by expelling its Jewish population in 1492. The Expulsion came after years of Inquisition propaganda, and hurt both the exiled Jews and the remaining Spanish population. Teachings by zealous preachers like Vincent Ferrer, a later-canonized Dominican monk, in the late fourteenth and early fifteenth centuries, brought on a nationwide anti-Jewish hysteria. By ridding the country of Jews, the Spanish monarchs, Ferdinand and Isabella, were carrying out the religious doctrines of the Inquisition. The economic consequences were grave. Many commercial enterprises in Seville and Barcelona, for instance, were ruined. "Spain lost an incalculable treasure by the exodus of Jewish . . . merchants, craftsmen, scholars, physicians, and scientists," wrote the encyclopedic Will Durant, "and the nations that received them benefited economically and intellectually."[10] Anti-Jewish preaching in Spain influenced a wide social segment of the population, and the result was devastating both for the Jews who fled and for the country that renounced them on dogmatic grounds.

The composite good of a society is reduced by the publication of material intent upon instigating pain and suffering for a particular group. Adopting an unrestrictive point of view on free speech assumes the character of dogma, taking a right as an ultimate duty and ignoring the ultimate end of constitutional government, which is the well-being of all social members. Thus, when the speech of some social contractees interferes with the right of others to live contented lives, it is speech, and not the essential rights necessary for well-being, that must be limited.

Speech is not the end of social justice. The First Amendment does not protect all expressions. It is designed to maintain an open dialogue about individual rights and overall welfare. In and of itself, speech is a neutral medium that can just as easily promote fascism as democracy, or justify genocide as civil rights. Ideological declarations that create irrational prejudices will not protect other rights. Hate messages can sway attitudes by their congruity with accepted exclusionary social schemas and linguistic paradigms. They can impress themselves on avowed supremacists and can also recruit young neophytes who, when they become adults, will carry on the tradition of vertical racial and ethnic hierarchies. Misethnic speech increases the reaches and continuity of racism and ethnocentrism in society. The hatreds underlying traditional scapegoating will not always burgeon into action. For that, social strains have to be at a peak. But they will lie dormant until the season is right for the noxious ideas to bud into violence.

Harboring hate speakers poses a threat to personal liberties. It enervates the very democratic ideals from which free speech arises. The overindulging of demagogues, therefore, deteriorates the commitment to fundamental rights that lies at the heart of people's decision to join together and reside in communities. The risks that misethnic propaganda poses to social well-being are enormous. They significantly increase the likelihood that violence will be perpetrated against minorities and that their safety will be jeopardized. Further, propaganda is subversive to social order because it infuses stress into intergroup relations.

Diatribe is intended to communicate aggression and to influence behavior. Hate speakers do not proclaim their views to engage listeners in intellectual debate; rather, they try to gain adherence to their destructive ideals. Hate speech functions to justify social injustices and to champion their rectitude.

The hate message is often meant to curtail inclusiveness and is stated in the context of a historical discourse, which supports existing power structures. It also perpetuates a mindset that views group interactions in the context of insiders with common interests and outsiders undeserving of basic human rights. The political implication of this self-perpetuating system is that it creates a racial identity that artificially classifies persons' mental abilities and moral uprightness on the basis of artificial semantic constructs.[11] The effects of misethnicity, then, go far beyond personal attitudes, seeping into subordinating social structures that limit minority rights.

Knowing the dangerous potentials of hateful diatribe, we ought to be leery about the social-justice claims of a doctrine that extols speech above all other democratic values. Speech that furthers social welfare and justice is on a different par from invectives designed to undermine them. Preserving civility is vital to a diverse society. Hate propaganda, on the other hand, makes it easier to channel aggression and enmity, thereby creating a chimerical enemy and distracting attention from genuine problems. Many politicians, in fact, obtain and retain offices by eliciting fears about historical outgroups and their allegedly evil ways.

The potential that today's fringe groups will gain political ascendency through sustained ideological dissemination calls for legislative vigilance.[12] A democratic state need not tolerate demagogues who manipulate constitutional provisions for spreading deadly ideology designed to enlist followers and eventually enact discriminatory laws. The state need not sit idly by while the freedoms of democracy are exploited by powerful social forces bent on undermining justice and the common good.[13] While the Constitution protects freedom of speech, "it is not a suicide pact."[14]

In a constitutional democracy, each person's rights must be respected as intrinsically valuable. Society and the state must honor and respect each person and protect his or her rights. A democracy is a quilt of individuals sown together by just principles and fair laws. Each person adds color and contributes to its overall pattern. When propagandists undo the threads that bind all the separate parts, the entire structure is weakened and is threatened with decay and collapse.

Destructive messages are contrary to the principles of egalitarian society because they influence people to deny the humanity of outgroups and refuse them equal treatment. Repudiating someone's personhood is in effect denying that the reciprocal duty of humanity and the imperative to empathetic treatment are at all applicable to him or her. Misethnists spread misinformation, invoking traditional images of ethnic stratification, to legitimize arbitrary laws and intolerant private conduct. The followers of racialist ideology seek to deprive minorities of basic needs, such as adequate education and unbiased law enforcement, which are essential for self-realization and personal security.

The more often insulting words about minorities are repeated, the easier it becomes to treat them uncompassionately without incurring much resistance. Hate propaganda, thus, creates not only immediate threats of harm, but also long-lasting residual effects on the entire community where it becomes incorporated into daily conversations, sermons, and political diatribe.[15]

The ramifications of hate speech include elevated anxiety about social stability. It decreases social contentment by denying minorities the opportunity to fulfill their aspirations. Demeaning affronts to minorities are also opposed to numerous constitutional ideals: self-realization, personal security from the tyranny of the majority, an unmolested and good life, secure property rights, and equal say in picking political representatives. Bigotry elicits preconceptions that have led to countless crimes against humanity. It interferes with democratic governments' efforts to achieve harmony among a variegated population. Instead of furthering everyone's interests, hate messages denigrate groups that have been historically vulnerable to victimization. How can it be argued that calls for murder, rapine, and enslavement promote everyone's welfare? Rather than being a means to elicit more political, ethical, and social opinions, which the right to free speech is meant to facilitate, misethnic insults dismiss the opinions of minorities based on no more than mere assertions of their inferiority.[16]

The argument that hate speech furthers democracy is difficult to fathom, given that its very intent is to stifle political debate on the issues and replace it with false accusations and brutal solutions. It presents no ideas of any worth in improving peoples lives, increasing people's knowledge, or furthering the human quest for social justice. Laws and regulations designed to protect democratic mainstays, like procedural and substantive justice, contain counter-majoritarian safeguards. The purveyors of hatred, on the other hand, seek to rationalize why outgroups should not have an equal share of rights in the democratic community. Representative democracies are devoted to protecting the civil rights of their populations; therefore, hate speech, which argues that identifiable outgroups should not equally participate in social institutions and privileges, is incompatible with democracy.[17]

Speech that purposefully tries to undermine minority well-being is contrary to the reciprocal duty of humanity: it rejects the ethical duty to treat others empathically and act for the increase of overall contentment. Instead of developing inclusive institutions, hate propaganda furthers injustices by drawing on a cultural vocabulary that places minority rights below ingroup interests.

Outgroups suffer at the hands of bigots advocating supremacist doctrines. Minorities are impeded in their cultural and social development because of daily uncertainties resulting from their relative political impotence and inability to fully participate in formulating substantive policies. Their safety is compromised by the real potential for violence imbedded in the cultural attitudes that give rise to hate propaganda. Misethnic speech is more than merely offensive to particular people; it carries a historical significance of exclusion and subjugation. Its overtones, therefore, are more sweeping and harmful to the life prospects of whole groups of people than are defamations.[18] The function that free speech plays in opening the political gates to all social contractees is also eviscerated by the constant bombardment of derogatory images which degrade minority political candidates based on irrelevant criteria and elevating persons because of their opposition to equal rights.

Misethnic antagonism that uses propaganda to instill negative attitudes toward outgroups lies along a continuum. Gradually the messages raise popular fury to a fever pitch, adding diatribe that blames traditional scapegoats for contemporary problems. When the stage is set by this preparatory groundwork, demagogues need only wait until social pressures and economic strains increase. It then becomes semantically natural for the ingroup to assign present-day troubles to a group that is supposedly culturally and nationally inimical. All that then remains is to call on the devotees to take the logical next steps: physical violence and persecution. So it was in Germany, where the hyperinflation that swept through the country after World War I catalyzed support for National Socialists. Relying on time-tested and politically refined anti-Semitism, Nazis found it relatively easy to convince most Germans that Jews deserved collective punishment for Germany's postwar woes.

Hate speech continues to play a significant role in degrading vulnerable peoples. For instance, in Mauritania and Sudan, racist common words, phrases, and symbols, which depict blacks as intellectually and religiously subservient to Arabs, perpetuate black slavery. Misethnicity is not merely a secondary social evil, it has been at the vanguard of widespread social movements. During the nineteenth century, anti-Irish sentiments existed throughout the United States. In the early part of that century, a formidable political party, the Know-Nothing Party, developed a large following through slogans denouncing immigrants and Roman Catholics. Racism against the Irish was then popular, as is evident from cartoons depicting them as apes and referring to them as "savages."[19] Hate speech seeds the ground for fascist and racist institutions. It is a vital ingredient in any political movement fixated on inflicting maximum harm against outgroups.[20]

Fomentation of misethnic attitudes and exhortation to commit discriminatory actions is diametrically opposed to the orderly and beneficent running of a representative democracy.[21] Misethnicity is inimical to the hopes of persons already straining under the weight of institutionalized racism and ethnocentrism. A multicultural society like the United States is strengthened and adorned by the equal treatment of different racial, ethnic, religious, and national groups. Cultural differences nourish society with unique perspectives about the empirical world and human relationships. On the other hand, hate speech promotes intergroup animosities. It disregards the personal qualities of its victims, discounts their capabilities, and augments social discontent.

While the major danger comes from state-sponsored prejudices, private groups and individuals who spread destructive messages also pose a danger, especially when they increase their power and presence through supremacist recruitment. Democracy is not only compromised by inequitable governmental actions but also by unchecked private conduct.

As social actors in a political state, persons enjoy correlative rights in respect to other citizens. Individuals living in communities established on a social contract and cooperative laws have the same right as any other contractees to advance themselves and obtain desirable resources and political offices. Laws must impartially protect social players' right to attain their desired goals. Destructive messages embed themselves in the social psyche, making it harder for minorities to achieve equal political status. Casting aspersions on outgroups is not a legitimate form of political discourse. Disparaging persons is an affront to the targets' dignity as free, conscious individuals. Moreover, such rhetoric is often accompanied by calls to perpetuate exclusionary cultural norms.

The right to spread hate propaganda freely does not outweigh the right to equal treatment. Personal autonomy is not an absolute right; rather, it is limited by the right of all social players to live secure lives and the overarching aim to attain social well-being. If personal liberty were an absolute right, persons could defame, assault, batter, or murder others at will. The principle of equality does not mean that everyone should be allowed to do anything he or she wishes, including insulting outgroups and calling on people to persecute them. Instead, that principle stands for the equal right to express one's personhood and live a good life. The common good is essential for those ends; otherwise, persons would be as unprotected against others' harmful whims as they would be in a state of nature.

The substantial role hate propaganda plays in elevating intergroup animosity and in sanctioning hate crimes requires that there be some limits on demagoguery. The dangers associated with destructive messages are connected to their historical contexts. Symbols representing white supremacist and Nazi ideologies are dehumanizing predicates that can—as they have in the past—promote violent acts and beliefs in the future even if they do not have this immediate effect.

Judges evaluating the potential dangers of racist declarations should be aware of a minority's history with discrimination. Without such recognition they will probably see destructive messages as nothing worse than personal defamations. It is improbable that statements against ingroup participation in political and cultural life will have any effect on their social status; however, in the case of an outgroup the situation is different.

A diverse egalitarian democracy will be improved by vigorous debate on how best to integrate the variegated groups residing there. Inclusive speech, then, will hold the preeminent position, and other forms of expression will not be so highly valued. A society need not be neutral when it comes to preferring expressions that are likely to promote freedom and justice over ones with a substantial likelihood of undermining them.[22] Taking an absolutist approach to free speech fails to acknowledge and integrate other rights, such as autonomy and life. A stand-alone theory of speech fails to account for the diverse and pluralistic aims of representative democracy. Although limitations on speech carry some danger of being abused, so too does any other law touching upon constitutional rights. The devastating potential effects of hate speech, which we have reviewed throughout this book, warrant the careful crafting of policies and laws drafted in the least restrictive way to protect individual rights and increase overall well-being.[23]

Bigotry is not cathartic; it is inflammatory. The longer a group goes unopposed in communicating its aggressive hatred of minorities, the more it becomes habituated in defamatory statements and unjust acts.[24] Social attitudes are embedded in negative images and stereotypes about outgroups; these are reinforced in popular dialogue incorporating stereotypes into puns and expletives. Once individuals perceive members of identifiable groups as legitimate targets for aggression, their personal dislikes are reinforced by negative rationalizations. When stereotypes are culturally established and personally internalized through oft-repeated fallacies about outgroup characteristics, they facilitate arbitrary discrimination. Hate propaganda embellishes negative social mores and habits. It also passes malignant stereotypes, misethnic semantics, and other expressive devices, such as juxtapositions, on to children.

Placing hate speech on the level of political discourse, as Justice Scalia did in *R.A.V. v. St. Paul*, legitimizes hate group participation in the political process.[25] This decision is full of potentially dangerous consequences. Who could have accurately predicted that the Weimar Republic—which at one point even had a Jewish foreign minister, Walther Rathenau—would one day be ruled by the vociferous Nazis? The Republic fell to anti-Semitic forces who distributed their ideas throughout Germany's major institutions, including schools, the military, judiciary, and political associations.[26] Scalia failed to reflect on any similar historical evidence about the danger hate speech poses to democracy.

Hate speech is elicited to agitate intolerance and guide adherents to fulfill violent solutions. Systematic murder, genocide, and enslavement are justified through aspersive discourse about the alleged dangers outgroups pose to society. Orators tell and retell the myth of inferiority using the framework of accepted and popularized discourse, thus desensitizing common people to the plight of victimized minorities and justifying unequal treatment of them.

Without constitutional and legislative checks on power, the majority can run roughshod over the minority's fundamental and basic rights. An unregulated system of speech, in which more powerful forces have greater access and control over informational distribution systems, might produce what Justice Holmes called a "proletarian dictatorship."[27] But it is an abuse of representative democracy to manipulate its institutions to destroy the foundations on which it is established.

Hate groups pose a threat, though not always an immediate one, to representative democracy. They use slogans that have been successfully employed to recruit and incite crowds against outgroups. Through repeated exposure to bigotry, the populace is likely to become so desensitized that it will accept oppression as a matter of course, as has happened in the past.

Violent hate speech not only advocates antidemocratic ideals, it is an intrinsic part of an overall scheme to weaken democratic institutions by attacking pluralism and inciting injustices. Unrestricted transmission of these messages threatens to undermine the political influence of diverse groups whose participation is critical to the popular-input aspect of the democratic process. The very purpose of bigotry is to exclude weaker groups from political debate.[28] Aspersions are intended to reduce participation in governmental discourse, and destructive messages are meant to intimidate and injure. Racial hierarchies, working to the disadvantage and detriment of the less powerful, are maintained, reinforced, and revivified by a state that legitimates the use of racist and ethnocentric dialogue, especially when that dialogue makes no secret about its ultimate goal to victimize outgroups.

Representative governments are obligated to prevent incitement against a whole group of people. The legislature should act before hate propaganda endears itself into the popular culture. Tolerance and egalitarianism should not be sacrificed at the altar of an absolutist free speech doctrine. Herd mentality is best avoided by strong laws, making clear society's disapprobation of inequality and injustice. Legislation can help assure that minorities will not be tyrannized and exploited by powerful interests. Hate speech statutes will display social disapprobation for hate speech and distinguish it from legitimate forms of political dialogue. Hate speech does not further political discourse; instead, it escalates the threat to law and order.

12

But Will It Work?

Regulation of Hate Propaganda in Other Countries

Many countries have determined that their societies are better served by laws prohibiting expressions designed to instigate hatred against minorities than they would be by the virtually unlimited license for hate speech in the United States. A general consensus among nations holds that hate propaganda perpetuates misethnicity and threatens both outgroup participation in democracy and minority rights. Countries that have enacted laws penalizing the dissemination of hate speech include Austria, Belgium, Brazil, Canada, Cyprus, England, France, Germany, India, Israel, Italy, Netherlands, and Switzerland.[1] Their legislative enactments and judicial opinions frankly weigh orators' interests in the right to free expression against the potential dangers victims encounter as a result of destructive messages.

International treaties also place limits on misethnic diatribe. The almost universal recognition that anti-Semitic propaganda facilitated both the Nazi rise to power and the Holocaust spurred a movement to prohibit inciteful speech. On December 9, 1948, the United Nations General Assembly adopted the Convention on the Prevention and Punishment of the Crime of Genocide. Among other obligations, signatory states agreed to punish "[d]irect and public incitement to commit genocide."[2] The European Convention on the Protection of Human Rights and Fundamental Freedoms, adopted on November 4, 1950, affirmed the commitment of twenty-three party states to protecting the rights to free expression and opinion but tempered them by acknowledging other social interests: "The exercise of these freedoms . . . may be subject to such formalities, conditions, restrictions or penalties as are prescribed by law and are necessary in a democratic society, in the interests of . . . public safety, for the prevention of disorder or crime, for the protection of health or morals, for the protection of the reputation or rights of oth-

180

ers."[3] The European Convention was enacted, in part, to prevent the rise of totalitarian regimes unconcerned for the rights of minorities.[4]

Then, in 1960, after a series of anti-Semitic incidents around the world, the United Nations passed the U.N. Convention on the Elimination of All Forms of Racial Discrimination. Article 4 of the Convention committed governments to rigorously uprooting hateful messages:

> States Parties condemn all propaganda and all organizations which are based on ideas or theories of superiority of one race or group of persons of one colour or ethnic origin, or which attempt to justify or promote racial hatred and discrimination in any form, and undertake to adopt immediate and positive measures designed to eradicate all incitement to, or acts of, such discrimination, and to this end, with due regard to the principles embodied in the Universal Declaration of Human Rights and the rights expressly set forth in Article 5 of this Convention, *inter alia*:
>
> (a) Shall declare an offence punishable by law all dissemination of ideas based on racial superiority or hatred, incitement to racial discrimination, as well as all acts of violence or incitement to such acts against any race or group of other persons of another colour or ethnic origin, and also the provision of any assistance to racist activities, including the financing thereof;
>
> (b) Shall declare illegal and prohibit organizations, and also organized and all other propaganda activities, which promote and incite racial discrimination, and shall recognize participation in such organizations or activities as an offence punishable by law;
>
> (c) Shall not permit public authorities or public institutions, national or local, to promote or incite racial discrimination.[5]

Several countries adopted the resolution in 1959 and 1960; however, it did not enter into force until 1969.[6] The United States signed on in 1966, but the Senate did not ratify the Convention until 1994, coupling it with numerous eviscerating reservations to preserve U.S. hate speech jurisprudence.[7] On the other hand, most signatories conform their domestic hate speech laws to the ratified terms of the Convention.[8]

Another international agreement, the International Covenant on Civil and Political Rights, was adopted on December 16, 1966. The 115 covenanted parties recognized that the freedoms of thought and expression are tempered by certain "duties and responsibilities" such as respect for others' reputations. Article 20(2) was the most substantive, enjoining states to enact legislation against "[a]ny advocacy of national, racial or religious hatred that constitutes incitement to discrimination, hostility or violence."[9]

International conventions have increasingly become incorporated by European states in formulating and interpreting their laws. For example, Austria enacted §283 of its Penal Code and a special constitutional provision in furtherance of the Convention on the Elimination of All Forms of Racial Discrimination. Section 283 makes it a criminal offense, punishable by up to two years' imprisonment, to "jeopardize the public order" by inciting hostilities against religious, racial, ethnic, or national groups. Furthermore, it is an offense to stir up hatred against those groups or violate "their human dignity" by slandering them and holding them in contempt.[10] France ratified the convention on July 28, 1971. A law passed there in July 1972 criminalizes incitement to discrimination, defamation based on a person's origin, and injurious conduct based on a person's racial, national, ethnic, or religious group. France further buttressed its efforts to proscribe racism, anti-Semitism, and xenophobia with the passage of another law in July 1990. Among other provisions, the 1990 Act makes it an offense to falsify contemporary history publicly or privately.[11] Italy also officially ratified the convention with the enactment of Law 205 of June 25, 1993 (replacing the previous incitement law, article 3 of Law No. 654 of 1975). The Italian Decree-Law 122 criminalizes the dissemination of ideas that are based on superiority and racial or ethnic discrimination. It also prohibits persons from inciting others to violence or committing violence based on racial, ethnic, national, or religious grounds.[12]

England has long recognized the dangers inherent in misethnic speech. The Public Order Act of 1936 was enacted at a time of increasingly volatile anti-Semitic fascist rallies. In response to violence committed by Sir Oswald Mosley's blackshirts, the act forbade persons from wearing uniforms at public demonstrations. Article 5 provided that an offender could be convicted "if it can be shown that the accused deliberately intended to provoke a breach in the peace or, regardless of his intention, due to his actions a breach of the peace would be likely."[13] The law was subsequently strengthened, and in 1965 section 6 of the British Race Relations Act prohibited persons from intentionally publishing written materials or giving public speeches that were threatening, abusive, or insulting and likely to stir up racial hatred.[14] The 1965 act removed a previous provision under the Public Order Act of 1936, which permitted police to interfere only upon a finding of probable breach of peace. Nine years later, the Race Relations Act of 1976, which amended the 1965 act, became incorporated into the Public Order Act of 1936. The major alteration to the 1976 act was its removal of the requirement that prosecutors prove the speaker's intent to incite persons to racial hatred. It was sufficient, then, to prove that the speech or publication was "threatening, abusive or destructive," and "having regard to all the circumstances hatred is likely to be stirred up against any racial group in Great Britain." Even inflammatory scientific and religious works became subject to prosecution.[15]

The most recent addition to Great Britain's legislative arsenal against hate speech is the Public Order Act of 1986. This criminal law balances the right to free speech with the right to live free of trepidation from effective prejudice. Section 17 of the act defined "racial hatred" to mean "hatred against a group of persons in Great Britain defined by reference to colour, race, nationality (including citizenship) or ethnic or national origins." Constables can arrest persons they reasonably suspect of violating the act. Persons guilty of the offense either intend to stir up racial hatred, or "having regard for all the circumstances, racial hatred is likely to be stirred up thereby." Adjudicators can issue warrants if there are reasonable grounds to believe contraband is within a particular location. Two weaknesses in the act are its exemption of broadcast and cable program materials and its inapplicability to persons who "inside a dwelling" advocate hatred toward the designated groups. These leave untouched racist broadcasts and orators using residential houses to organize their minions.[16]

British antidiscriminatory speech laws have prohibited expressions tending to lead to violence and social disorder, regardless of whether they pose an immediate danger. Instead they have been guided by the view that countenancing misethnic speech can contribute to the spread of racism and ethnocentrism and, eventually, undermine representative democracy.[17]

Canada has enacted one of the most comprehensive schemes designed to thwart the proliferation of misethnic speech. Article 1 of the Canadian Charter recognizes that fundamental freedoms, such as free expression, are "subject only to such reasonable limits prescribed by law as can be demonstrably justified in a free and democratic society."[18] The Canadian Criminal Code contains a cause of action against the public incitement of others to hatred:

"Every one who, by communicating statements in any public place, in- cites hatred against any identifiable group where such incitement is likely to lead to a breach of the peace is guilty of (a) an indictable of- fence and is liable to imprisonment for a term not exceeding two years; or (b) an offence punishable on summary conviction."[19] Further, under §319(2), the penalty for persons willfully promoting hatred through public statements against an identifiable group is up to two years impris- onment.[20] Incitement to commit genocide is punishable by up to five years imprisonment.[21] So important are the social interests involved that, when there are reasonable grounds to believe hate propaganda is kept on premises within a court's jurisdiction, a judge is required to issue a warrant authorizing its seizure.[22]

The Canadian Human Rights Act prohibits telephonic communication of discriminatory hatred against a person or group.[23] The Supreme Court of Canada upheld the constitutionality of that legislative provision in *Canada (Human Rights Commission) v. Taylor*. Taylor helped finance a telephone service with a prerecorded dial-up message. Callers heard about an alleged Jewish conspiracy to get rich by causing unemployment, inflation, and race mixing. The Canadian Supreme Court concluded that hate propaganda threatens society and undermines the dignity and self- worth of victimized groups "by eroding the tolerance and open-minded- ness that must flourish in multi-cultural society which is committed to the idea of equality."[24]

The Supreme Court of Canada has affirmed the constitutionality of Canada's hate propaganda laws in some other opinions. In a seminal case, *Regina v. Keegstra*, the Court found that §319(2), which bars the willful promotion of hatred, is constitutional. The case involved a social studies teacher who was teaching his high school students that Jews were "child killers," "treacherous," "power hungry," "moneyloving" people who fabricated the Holocaust. Students who mimicked his views on their examinations received high marks, and those who did not were given low grades. Keegstra maintained that §319(2) violated his right to free speech. The Court held that it was legitimate to criminalize this type of speech since it harms both individual victims and society as a whole. It could be anticipated that targeted persons would be humiliated and de- graded by hate propaganda because it would negatively affect their sense of human dignity and belongingness to a community. The long-term ef- fects of hate speech were not lost on the Court: "Even if the message of hate propaganda is outwardly rejected, there is evidence that its premise of racial or religious inferiority may persist in a recipient's mind as an idea that holds some truth, an incipient effect not to be entirely discounted." Violence might then ensue from the attendant discrimination that could become endemic in Canadian society. Moreover, the Court found, that based on international human rights instruments such as the International Convention on the Elimination of All Forms of Racial Discrimination, to which Canada is a signatory, §319(2) effectuated international commitment to human rights, principles of equality, and personal dignity. Therefore, the Court concluded, the statute reduced racial, ethnic, and religious tensions by suppressing the expression of intolerance. Hate propaganda seeks to subvert the democratic process and is therefore "inimical to the democratic aspiration of the free expression guarantee." Section 319(2) was a narrowly tailored restriction on speech, with a "*mens rea* requirement, either necessitating intent to promote hatred or knowledge of the substantial certainty of such," that was neither overbroad nor vague.[25]

The Supreme Court of Canada reaffirmed the constitutionality of §319(2) in *Regina v. Andrews*. The Court upheld the conviction of two white nationalists who published the *Nationalist Reporter*, promoting "the theory of white supremacy." Their publication contained messages like "Nigger go home," "Hoax on the Holocaust," "Israel Stinks," and "Hitler was Right. Communism is Jewish." An Ontario District Court judge thought the degree of hatred the defendants expressed against Jews could only be characterized as "rubbish and offal." In *Andrews*, the Canadian Supreme Court held that the guarantee to the freedom of speech in the Charter of Rights is not absolute, and limitations on hate propaganda are constitutional and compatible with a free democratic society. The Supreme Court affirmed the conclusion of Ontario Appellate Court Justice Cory and quoted parts of his reasoning. Cory determined that although the free speech protections found in Canada's Charter of Rights & Freedoms are more "comprehensive" than those in the First Amendment, hate propaganda is not protected by them. Cory relied on the findings of the Special Committee on Hate Propaganda in Canada. It found that the rise of Nazism in Germany through "loathsome messages of Nazi propaganda" enabled a fringe Nazi minority in the Weimar Republic to become the dominant political party that held power and pursued a genocidal policy. Based on the empirical evidence of how hate speech spilled over into heinous actions, the Supreme Court concluded that it was justifiable to restrain the promotion of hatred against identifiable groups.[26]

The Internet, with its cross-border capabilities, has caused Canada, and other countries with laws against misethnic incitement, particular problems. In order to enforce laws against hate propaganda, the Commissioner of the Canadian Human Rights Commission, Max Yalden, has declared that the Commission can prevent Internet sites from transmitting hate messages, even when the source servers are based in other countries. Canada considers that it has jurisdiction over such cases so long as people receive Internet signals in Canada, regardless of where the messages originate.[27] The Commission on Human Rights has found that recent technological advances have made it more difficult for law enforcement agencies to prevent the dissemination of hate messages. The Commission has already investigated inciteful Web sites like those maintained by Ernst Zundel and Heritage Front. To pursue these and other propagandists, Canada enacted the Canadian Human Rights Act in 1999, which prohibits the technological distribution of hate materials. The Act prohibits persons or groups from using telecommunications to expose any identifiable group to hatred or contempt or to incite others to discriminate.[28] Canadian judges may issue warrants to confiscate computer hard drives, CD ROMs, and computer disks that were used to spread propaganda punishable under §319.[29]

Unlike the U.S. Supreme Court precedents, which only place restrictions on hate speech that presents an imminent threat of harm, the Canadian criminal provisions are not so restrictive. Promotion of misethnicity, regardless of when the speaker intends it to be carried out, is criminally punishable. In making these laws, the Canadian legislature realized the long-term harmful influence of hate propaganda. What's more, Canada, unlike the United States, has not saddled its jurisprudence with an unequivocal ban of content-based hate speech legislation. Canadian laws, instead, recognize how detrimental hate speech is to democracy and aim to protect identifiable groups from heinous and inhumane crimes. Canadian cases find that the private interest in promulgating misethnic virulence is significantly less than are the interests of identifiable groups to maintain their sense of self-dignity and common humanity and of multicultural society to guard racial and ethnic harmony. The crux of this reasoning is that hate speech can undermine the common good, while narrowly drafted restrictions on it can be conducive to egalitarianism.

Many other democratic countries have enacted their own hate speech legislation. Germany is particularly vigilant in recognizing, prescribing, and penalizing the social menace posed by destructive messages because of its experience with how effective Nazi propaganda was in organizing a nationwide movement devoted to liquidating Jews. While Germany is fundamentally committed to preserving freedom of expression, its laws preclude totalitarianism from reasserting its choke hold on the nation. The German Basic Law, upon which its constitutional system is based, includes a provision, Article 5, guaranteeing freedom of expression. Article 5(1) covers the right to freedom of speech via "audiovisual media" like television broadcasts and Internet messages. It asserts a commitment to freedom of the press and to "the right freely to express and disseminat[e]" ideas. However, this constitutional right is not absolute, but subject to "limitations in the provisions of general legislation, in statutory provisions for the protection of youth and the citizen's right to personal respect."[30]

Germany has passed several laws designed to allay the short- and long-term risks of unchecked hate speech. Individuals and groups are subject to imprisonment for attacking the human dignity of others by (1) inciting people to hate particular segments of the population; (2) advocating "violent or arbitrary measures against them"; and (3) insulting them, "maliciously exposing them to contempt or slandering them."[31] Further, it is criminal to publically distribute or supply any "writings that incite to race hatred or describe cruel or otherwise inhuman acts of violence against humans in a manner which glorifies or minimizes such acts of violence or represents the cruel or inhuman aspects of the occurrence in a manner offending human dignity."[32]

Other German laws also balance the right to free speech against the preservation of democratic institutions. Most of these have been passed to stem the tide of the persistent xenophobia and anti-Semitism in Germany. Article 18 enumerates:

> Those who abuse their freedom of expression, in particular freedom of the press, freedom of teaching, freedom of assembly, freedom of association, privacy of correspondence, posts and telecommunications, property, or the right of asylum in order to undermine the free democratic basic order, shall forfeit these basic rights. Such forfeiture and the extent shall be pronounced by the Federal Constitutional Court.[33]

Notably, Germany, unlike England, recognizes that the press and private discourse are potential sources of hate propaganda that should not be immune from the state's commitment to stable democracy.

The German Criminal Code forbids persons from using "flags, insignia, parts of uniforms, slogans and forms of greeting" to propagate undemocratic political parties like the National Socialist party. Article 21.2 of the Basic Law bans political parties that pose a threat to democratic order. Nonpolitical organizations are also banned from overthrowing the constitutional order.[34]

The German Constitutional Court has reaffirmed the constitutionality of such laws. One case arose when the National Democratic Party of Germany (NPD) met and heard a speech by Holocaust revisionist David Irving. The German government acted under the authority of the Public Assembly Act, which prohibits meetings where the planned speeches constitute criminal violations. The Court held that the Act did not violate article 5(1) of the Basic Law which protects publicly uttered opinions. "If the [assumed facts] are demonstrably untrue, freedom of expression usually gives way to the protection of personality." Thus, contrary to Justice Oliver Wendell Holmes's Social Darwinistic definition of "truth" as the opinion of the most powerful, the German Constitutional Court made its decision based on objective evidence. It examined Holocaust denial against historical facts, eyewitness accounts, and documentation, finding David Irving's spurious comments unprotected by the Basic Law. Holocaust denial was found insulting to Jews. Others had "a special moral responsibility" to respect that ethnic group's historical sensibility. Denial of this event amounted to rejecting the "personal worth" of the Jewish people and continuing discrimination against them.[35] Among numerous other German judicial opinions upholding the constitutionality of hate propaganda laws was a 1994 case, decided by the Constitutional Court, which ruled that freedom of speech was not a defense available to groups propagating the "Auschwitz lie." Then, a Berlin state court, in 1995, convicted a leader of Germany's neo-Nazi movement for spreading racial hatred and denigrating the state by telling persons visiting the Auschwitz concentration camp that the Holocaust was a fiction.[36] On the other hand, the state may not suppress the recitation of an interpretive opinion, such as the belief that Germany was not at fault for starting World War I.[37]

German content-based legal measures are aimed at protecting the population against expressions of hatred and incitements to violence, regardless of whether the threat of harm is imminent. They are designed to protect people's fundamental rights against those persons who abuse their freedoms to undermine democracy.

Other Western democracies have enacted comparable legislation. The Federation for Swiss Jewish Communities succeeded in convincing Switzerland to ban anti-Semitic books because they were insulting to Jews. A January 1, 1995 referendum to the Criminal Code (article 261bis) punishes public incitement to racial hatred or discrimination, spreading racist ideology, denying crimes against humanity, and refusing to supply a service intended for the public on grounds of race, ethnic origin, or religion.[38]

Another notable example of laws designed to prevent persons from instigating misethnicity through speech is Article 269(1) of the Hungarian Penal Code. It prohibits persons from communicating incitements to large gatherings and thereby adjuring them to hate persons based on nationality, creed, or race. The Hungarian Constitutional Court upheld the constitutionality of that criminal law in a 1992 decision. The ruling declared Article 269(1) a legitimate restriction on the freedoms of expression and press set forth in Article 61.[39] The Court began by observing how important freedom of speech is to "social justice and human creativity." Therefore, any legislative restrictions on that fundamental right had to be balanced and proportional. Those objectives could only be met by "the least restrictive means available," nonarbitrary limits on content, and reflections on democratic norms.[40]

Like the U.S. Supreme Court in *Beauharnais v. Illinois*, the Hungarian Constitutional Court rendered its decision after reflecting on evidence which indicated speech can "subject . . . certain groups in a population to denigrating and humiliating treatment." Comparing communications to fire, which provides illumination and warmth but can also rage out of control and result in misery and devastation, the Court wrote:

> To afford constitutional protection to the incitement of hatred against certain groups under the guise of the freedom of expression and freedom of press would present an indissoluble contradiction with the value system and political orientation expressed in the Constitution: the democratic rule of law, the equality of human beings, equality of dignity, as well as the prohibition of discrimination, the freedom of religion and conscience, the protection of national and ethnic minorities—as recognized by the various Articles of the Constitution.[41]

Inciteful speech poses a danger to individual rights and public tranquility. "[F]or the concept of incitement it is totally immaterial whether the stated facts are true or not; what matters is that they, true or false, are capable of arousing hatred."[42] A May 12, 1999 resolution of the Hungarian Constitutional Court amended Article 269 to reflect the decision. It now reads as follows:

> A person who incites to hatred before a general public gathering against (a) the Hungarian Nation; (b) any national, ethnic, religious, or racial group or certain groups of the population, commits a felony and shall be punishable with imprisonment for up to three years.[43]

The effort against hate speech was further strengthened in March 1996.

The Hungarian Parliament then passed a law criminalizing the organizing or providing of finances for any event which may provoke violence against a national, ethnic, racial, religious, or other group, hatred or incitement against the Hungarian nation, or any national, ethnic, racial, or religious group.[44]

Unlike the United States, then, Hungary prohibits misethnic incitement regardless of whether or not it poses an imminent threat of harm or clear and present danger. The critical issue is whether the words threaten democratic order. However, just as in Germany, merely offensive words are not criminalized.[45]

Israel, too, has enacted legislation to battle misethnicity. The Knesset, Israel's parliament, enacted legislation in 1985 restricting political candidates for national office to persons who do not (1) incite others to racism; (2) negate the democratic state of Israel; or (3) deny the valid existence of the State of Israel.[46] Realizing the grave need, especially in the volatile Middle East, to guard against both anti-Semitic and anti-Arab messages, the Knesset in 1986 passed amendments to the Penal Law, defining racism as "persecution, humiliation, degradation, manifestation of enmity, hostility or violence, or causing strife toward a group of people or parts of the population—because of color, affiliation with a race or national-ethnic origins." Persons publishing material "with the purpose of inciting to racism" risk being imprisoned for up to five years. Anyone possessing these materials for later distribution is subject to up to one year of imprisonment. No religious utterance is classified as an offense unless it is expressed for "the purpose of inciting to racism." Interestingly, whether there is any truth in a purposefully racist publication is irrelevant under Israeli legislation, just as it is in Hungary.[47]

Israeli prosecutors must prove the *mens rea* element, making conviction more difficult. There is no comparable option to proving the speaker's purpose as there is in the British Public Order Act of 1986, which allows prosecutors to choose between proving an orator's intent and the likelihood that she or he will stir up racial hatred.[48]

Incitements to hatred are also prohibited in Scandinavian countries. Article 266b of the Danish Penal Code criminalizes racist statements, making it illegal "to utter publicly or deliberately, for the dissemination in a wider circle, a statement or another remark, by which a group of people are threatened, derided or humiliated."[49] Finland prohibits agitational expressions: "A person who spreads statements or other notices among the public where a certain race or national, ethnic or religious group or a comparable group is threatened, slandered or insulted shall be sentenced for ethnic agitation to a fine or to imprisonment for a maximum of two years."[50] There is a mandatory two-year term of imprisonment in Sweden for "agitation against a national or ethnic group." Chapter 16, §8, of the Swedish penal code forbids persons to spread any statement or communication that "expresses contempt for a national, ethnic or other such group of persons with illusion to race, colour, national or ethnic origin or religious belief."[51] Article 135a of the Norwegian Penal Code Number 10 of 1902, which continues to be the governing law, prohibits propaganda and incitement to racial, xenophobic, ethnocentric, and homophobic hatred which is directed against specific groups or individuals, but it is not punishable to merely express racist ideas.[52] In 1996, eight of the eighty-six trials on discrimination charges brought in the Netherlands were against persons for allegedly inciting others to hatred, discrimination, or violence.[53]

In the East, India adopted §153A into its Penal Code, thereby demonstrating its commitment to tolerance and public tranquility. It punishes persons who "by words, either spoken or written or by signs or by visible representations or otherwise, promotes or attempts to promote, on grounds of religion, race, place of birth, residence, language, caste or community or any other ground whatsoever, disharmony or feelings of enmity, hatred or ill-will between different religious, racial, language or regional groups or castes or communities" with up to three years' imprisonment, a fine, or both.[54] Although the statute nowhere specifies a *mens rea*, Indian courts have determined that speakers can be found culpable only if they purposefully try to "promote feelings of enmity," regardless of whether or not they are successful. Intent can be determined both by the content of words and the circumstances in which they are said.[55] "If the language is of a nature calculated to produce or to promote feelings of enmity or hatred the writer must be presumed to intend that which his act was likely to produce. This was the principle laid down . . . in dealing with a case of seditious libel and the same principle clearly applies to the case of a publication punishable under section 153A, I.P.C."[56] Section 153A has been an important tool for maintaining order in India's multiethnic society.

These international examples demonstrate that the United States' pure speech jurisprudence is anomalous. A broad consensus holds that inciting others to hatred is detrimental to society. Democracies generally recognize that preserving human rights supersedes a bigot's desire to spread venomous messages. Granting unrestricted verbal freedom at the expense of outgroup members' rights weakens representative government because all members of the society cannot share equally in its benefits. Increased suffering in one segment of the population decreases the overall happiness of the political community. Speech intended to deny civil rights to outgroups is meant to suppress, not further, pluralistic and multicultural ideals. The history of racism in the United States, from Native American dislocations, to slavery, to Japanese internment, makes clear that here, as in other democracies, intolerance and persecution can exist in spite of the socially held ideals of fairness and equality. Even though the Declaration of Independence promises liberty and justice for all, not all groups have shared equally in that bounty. Safeguards against the realistic effects of hate speech should be enacted to prevent the forces of bigotry from harnessing resources to strengthen socially regressive movements.

13

Regulating Hate Speech

Developing a Policy Dealing with Hate Speech

Overwhelming historical, psychological, and sociological evidence demonstrates that hate speech has been and continues to be instrumental in initiating and perpetuating great human injustices. Before the Holocaust, the enslavement of blacks, and Native American dislocations, stereotypes depicted these outgroup members as subhumans, unworthy of civil rights. Contrary to many Western democracies, which have recognized the prolonged dangers of hate speech, the United States has maintained a head-in-the-sand approach to historical realities by refusing to acknowledge that any but the most immediate dangers can result from words targeting identifiable outgroups.

Hate propagandists aim to instill fear in outgroups and make them too timid to assert their constitutional rights. The purveyors of hatred endeavor to rationalize why minorities should not have an equal share of rights in the democratic community, put outgroup members in fear for their safety, decrease social welfare, and limit the diversity of people contributing to the policies of a multiethnic society. Hate speech is an obstacle to the extension of civil rights. Bigots seek to devalue the common humanity of an identifiable group of people. Bigotry lays the groundwork for future oppression, persecution, enslavement, genocide, and forceful expropriations. "As all fascists know, it is just a matter of time, after hate propaganda and disparagement have done their work, that violence will follow."[1] Before committing massive human right violations, hate groups systematically develop and disseminate a linguistic paradigm that becomes part of daily communications. With the unrestricted propagation of hate speech, animosity toward outgroups becomes more sophisticated and poised for destructive actions.

Unrestricted hate speech poses a significantly greater danger to democracy than do limits preventing demagogues from spewing vitriol. Thus, there is a compelling interest to regulate hate speech, even though that involves curbing the contents of some messages.[2] The libertarian argument that hate speech should be tolerated regardless of its potentially injurious consequences to vulnerable groups depreciates minority rights to life, liberty, and self-preservation. Misethnic speech does not merely harm individuals. It causes a maximum amount of damage to the lives of minorities. Its instruments are not simply personal dislikes but stereotypes that draw from shared, historical consciousness. Outgroups are typically the objects of intolerance because their relative sociopolitical position makes them more susceptible to group defamations than other segments of the population. Racism and ethnocentrism establish parameters of thought that help justify violent actions.[3] The continued ability of persons across racial and ethnic lines to benefit from equal rights and freedoms outweighs the interest of individuals to make false and divisive speeches aimed at destroying egalitarianism. Hate speech perpetuates racial and ethnic stereotypes that are both meant to maintain discriminatory practices and, ultimately, to provoke hate crimes.

Inciteful hate speech falls into a graver category than merely offensive words that cause no injury. The First Amendment of the U.S. Constitution protects persons who express abstract opinions about the inferiority of specific groups as long as such speech does not advocate present or future persecution. For example, scientific or anthropological arguments, which do not call for violence against outgroups, should not be criminally censured.[4] Such ideas pose little danger to society and are outside the purview of criminal laws. On the other hand, speech used to incite people to commit belligerent actions is not benign and its damages are not illusory.

The legislation proposed in this chapter is designed to protect outgroups against the threat of hate propaganda. There is no less restrictive alternative to preventing the many social harms that follow in the wake of hate speech than to punish its more dangerous manifestations. The premise of this book is that destructive messages against minorities are not innocuous; they are crucially linked to the perpetration of misethnic crimes. As the populations of most Western countries have become more diverse through immigration and intermarriage, the risks of prejudice have multiplied. They threaten not only individuals and targeted groups but the well-being of society in general.[5]

It goes almost without saying that no identifiable groups, including those that have never been targeted by hate mongers, should ever be persecuted. It is important to realize, however, that traditional scapegoats are more likely to suffer such a fate. United States common law recognizes that, given the history of intolerance, government has a more compelling interest in preventing discrimination based on race, ethnicity, and national origin than discrimination based on membership in other identifiable groups.[6] Thus, special legal protections for historically persecuted minorities are not a novelty here. Likewise, in the First Amendment arena, courts should apply principles of suspect classification to persons victimized by widely circulated stereotypes.[7] As we saw in chapter 8, Justice Blackmun, in his concurrence to *R.A.V. v. St. Paul*, recognized that governmental entities can legitimately prohibit the use of racially inflammatory symbols such as burning crosses. Justice Stevens, in a separate concurrence in *R.A.V.*, argued that the city of St. Paul could determine which fighting words to regulate based on the different social harms caused by them.[8]

An abundance of excellent articles have been written about regulating hate speech through a torts-based approach. Several of these scholarly studies offered constructive solutions for formulating a civil cause of action against racist and ethnocentric dignitary harms.[9] My focus in setting out policy guidelines and a legislative scheme is on guarding against the social harms, not just the individual, dignitary injuries, of destructive messages. Governmental enactments against bigotry could impel a move away from misethnicity because they would signify social denunciation of organizations that thrive on derisive attitudes toward outgroups.

As discriminatory laws make prejudice more socially acceptable, so, too, outlawing discriminatory practices could decrease the reach of prejudice.[10] Some authors have insisted that prohibiting the spread of virulently hateful messages strengthens bigots in their resolve. Therefore, they argue against enacting laws against hate speech.[11] This viewpoint does not consider that the same argument could be made against the enforcement of the Thirteenth, Fourteenth, and Fifteenth Amendments to the U.S. Constitution, or any other civil rights legislation.[12] The enforcement of those provisions has significantly decreased the occurrence of unequal treatment in housing and employment, eliminated laws that prohibited blacks from voting, and generally decreased the incidence of racism and discrimination in the United States. As Justice Felix Frankfurter wrote: "That the legislative remedy might not in practice mitigate the evil, or might itself raise new problems, would only manifest once more the paradox of reform. It is the price to be paid for the trial-and-error inherent in legislative efforts to deal with obstinate social issues."[13]

Further, the contention that hate speech legislation should not be enacted because it would increase demagogues' popularity loses sight of the fact that all defamation suits tend to increase the audience of a fallacy, and trials provide speakers with a platform to parade their ideas. That, however, is no reason to do away with causes of action for defamation. Trials on those issues expose the fallacies of libels and slanders. They do not legitimize them. Likewise, putting racist and ethnocentric orators on trial might make them popular in the eyes of fringe groups, but for most people exposure of the error will make it more untenable and less beguiling.[14]

Legislation can also be an effective factor in changing attitudes because it sets out which behaviors are socially and ethically tolerable. In a representative democracy, laws establish parameters for reciprocal respect and equal treatment. No matter how many times these laws are changed, they can never stay true to social contract principles and simultaneously permit involuntary servitude or systematic genocide. Corrections away from misethnic institutions sway public opinion through equitable administration of justice and the promotion of all citizens' well-being.[15] Emile Durkheim, the pioneer French sociologist, explained the pattern of social enlightenment through criminal law: "[Criminal law's] true function is to maintain social cohesion intact, while maintaining all its vitality in the common conscience . . . it serves to heal the wounds made upon the collective sentiments. . . . Without this necessary satisfaction, what we call the moral conscience could not be conserved . . . [I]t functions for the protection of society."[16] Criminal laws have the effect of inhibiting persons from committing antisocial conduct. On the one hand, they threaten to dole out punishment for unfair behavior and, on the other hand, they establish positive norms for interhuman, cooperative conduct. Criminal law, then, is both preventative and instructional. Societies can avert harms and exhort citizens to be respectful toward each other by criminalizing virulent hate propaganda. Federal or state laws can deter future persecutions and augment intergroup empathy.[17]

Restrictions on misethnic speech communicate society's disapprobation with movements that aim to harm vulnerable minorities. They indicate the government's commitment to preserving fundamental fairness. While increased tolerance may not immediately follow the passage of laws, it raises public sensitivity to some of the risks posed by racist and ethnocentric orators. Thereafter, membership in a hate organization is less likely to be taken as a legitimate civic choice. Hate speech laws can therefore change misethnic attitudes. Even where they cannot effect such a change, legal restraint on misethnic expressions will probably deter the incidence of hate crimes. [18]

The constitutionality of civil rights legislation and affirmative action programs evinces that laws need not always be neutral. They can reflect the awareness that targeting people based on their outgroup characteristics is more likely to cause reverberating harm than personal attacks are. Even laws such as those prohibiting employers from firing employees based on race might be found unconstitutional under the viewpoint neutrality doctrine that Justice Scalia pronounced in *R.A.V.*[19]

Some writers, like Nadine Strossen, have argued that criminal laws against inciteful hate speech will be ineffective. But just as with other First Amendment restrictions, the difficulty of obtaining a conviction does not speak against enacting and enforcing laws. Prosecutors have, for example, found it difficult to convince juries that sexually explicit materials that appeal to purely prurient interests are patently offensive and have no significant social value.[20] The complexities of proving obscenity cases have not, however, reduced society's determination to curb those materials because there is "at least an arguable correlation between obscene material and crime."[21] Legislatures cannot be absolutely certain that enacted laws will eradicate the blight of racism, but the preservation of human rights and the common good require the adoption of laws reasonably calculated to prevent violent incitements against vulnerable minorities.

In evaluating the constitutionality of hate speech statutes, courts should consider whether or not the legislation protects or disturbs individual rights and the common good. Hate propaganda degrades individuals, denying their right to equal treatment and legitimizing oppression by spreading misconceptions and outright fabrications. Active state participation in furthering democratic ideals should not be misconstrued as an abuse of power. People join and live in a community because they expect to be happier there than elsewhere; therefore, it is one of government's primary missions to prevent others from inducing unjust harms that are deleterious to social contentment.[22]

Laws against destructive messages are compatible with other constitutional principles, like substantive and procedural due process, because their overarching aim is promoting social welfare. U.S. political ethics and jurisprudence recognize that individuals have an inalienable interest against arbitrary infringement of their humanity. This crucial component of fairness is a source of laws against unreasonable searches and seizures, involuntary servitude, poll taxes, and cruel and unusual punishments. Hate propaganda contravenes the reciprocal duty of humanitarian treatment by advocating and incrementally furthering disrespectful behavior against identifiable groups.[23]

Justice is furthered when positive law reflects painful minority experiences with hateful messages and is drafted to prevent disparaging stereotypes from ingraining themselves in the social conscience. Misethnic propaganda tends to undermine minorities' right to fair treatment and to diminish their social standing. Racist and ethnocentrist statements are the most dangerous when they are part of long-standing, accepted doctrines.

Misethnic ideology teaches that natural, racial, and ethnic hierarchies must be maintained, if necessary by force. Members of the minority seeking equal treatment are viewed as usurping the supposedly rightful place of the dominant group, and repressive actions toward them are considered justified.[24] Comprehending the oft-repeated pattern of hate speech leading to social stratification and, eventually, to persecution ought to guide legislators in drafting anti–hate speech statutes. Inductive reasoning is instructive for finding practical legislative methods and fulfilling egalitarian ideals.

Holding misethnists legally responsible for instructing others to harm outgroups will deter grave injustices. Government should not passively sit by while racist and ethnocentric forces develop their ideologies, animate their following, and methodically prepare to harm minorities.[25] The sparks of misethnicity should be extinguished before they burn out of control to consume the edifice of representative democracy.

Five Policy Considerations

In order to maintain the integrity of its constitutional system, government must safeguard both equal administration of justice and free expression. Fair treatment of the populace is significantly more important to sustaining and nurturing constitutional principles than permitting hate speech to prevail in the bazaar of ideas. The value of political dialogue should be measured by the extent to which it advances evenhanded administration of justice, not simply by quantifying how much speech goes unregulated.

The dissemination of hatred and calls to commit violence against out-groups promote political unfairness.[26]

Therefore, hate speech poses a potential threat to American democracy and should be kept in check by federal and state legislation. Based on principles inherent in the Fourteenth Amendment to the U.S. Constitution, the Supreme Court has repeatedly recognized the need to protect persons with immutable characteristics, such as race, color, and ethnicity, against the tyranny of the majority.[27] Analogously, hate speech aimed at harming persons with immutable characteristics should be prohibited when, based on analysis of sociolinguistics, psycholinguistics, and historic patterns of misethnicity, it has a realistic probability of inciting discrimination or violence.

Hate speech has played a significant role in fostering organized and systematic persecutions. It is therefore critical to enact a statute that is tailored narrowly enough to protect First Amendment rights, but which is also sufficiently farseeing to prevent future harms to identifiable outgroups. The legislation should only prohibit speech that, in its virulent expression of hatred, poses a threat to individual rights and social goods. The following issues should be considered in formulating such a policy.

Whether the Speaker Targeted a Group That Has Historically Been Persecuted

Hate speech directed at historically oppressed groups is suspect and is antithetical to representative democracies. United States courts regularly apply a heightened standard of judicial review to cases involving historically disadvantaged, discrete, insular minorities.[28] As the famous fourth footnote to *United States v. Carolene Products, Co.*, pointed out, prejudices against salient and identifiable outgroups "tend to seriously . . . curtail the operation of those political processes ordinarily . . . relied upon to protect minorities."[29] Regulating speech that is designed to undermine personal freedoms, equality, and the common good turns on normative purposes of political communities. It will be more difficult for minorities to receive equal treatment and demand the reciprocal duty of respect if society does not recognize and address the inherent dangers of hate speech. The brunt of countenancing hate speech naturally falls upon the already bruised backs of groups that have historically been disadvantaged.

The semantic meaning of hate propaganda draws from historical experiences that psychologically and sociologically affect an entire group. The derogatory cultural content and virulence of destructive messages directed at victimized groups cannot be matched by insults about powerful groups. Prejudices serve as conceptual models for dominant forces to organize the commission of degrading actions against less powerful social members.[30] The perpetrated injustices are enlivened by widely disseminated projections, displacements, and justifications. Hate speech regulation is part of a scheme that appreciates the potential risks to weaker groups from concentrated and exclusionary majoritarian power. A prohibition against incitement is not averse to free speech nor to human rights. Rather, it is an enlightened balancing between speakers' rights to express their opinions and the governments' obligation to preserve social contentment. The interest of citizens to assert their right of influencing and enlightening others through discourse does not trump individuals' claims to live safely, without being terrorized by supremacist organizations.[31]

Rather than enlightening listeners through accurate depiction of its subjects, hate speech menaces outgroups through false characterizations and aggressive ideology. Owen Fiss, a leading constitutional scholar, has pointed out that even if we accept the primacy of free speech above other constitutional values, laws prohibiting hate speech are nevertheless legitimate. Not only do misethnic exhortations influence like-minded people to commit crimes against others based on their racial or ethnic group, they also stifle minority voices. With destructive propaganda swirling around them in popular media, print, and speeches, outgroups feel they are unwelcome strangers in their own communities. They see that society places greater value on the ability of purveyors of hate to speak their minds than it does on preventing misethnic attitudes from spilling over into violence. Minority sensitivities are effectively silenced, while the prerogatives of those who deprecate their humanity are elevated. Enacting content-based laws recognizes that widespread misethnicity keeps outgroup ideas, concerns, and wisdom out of political discourse.[32]

The Thirteenth Amendment prohibits all indicia of slavery, regardless of how they are manifested.[33] Threatening signs, such as swastikas and burning crosses, have historical connotations that draw upon and enhance the "badges" and "symbols" of servitude, discrimination, oppression, and persecution.[34] Racial and ethnic threats draw upon and buttress social hierarchies and age-old schemata that have been used for perpetuating enslavement, exploitation, and subjugation. Statements that disparage outgroups often draw their points of view from supremacist ideologies that regard minorities less worthy of respect and happiness than powerful ingroups. These paradigms count members of the majority, no matter how criminal, more worthy of humane treatment than the most altruistic minorities.[35]

These forms of symbolic speech portend the perpetration of future or imminent destructive acts. Persons expressing themselves in these menacing ways may not contemporaneously have the resources to commit their stated desires. However, those utterances may not be benign. They can implant themselves into the social attitudes and accepted practices. What is more, they can motivate individuals. If calls to future violent actions are left unchecked, the seeds of hatred, planted and nurtured in the fertile hearts of bigots, can—at opportune moments—blossom into violent outbreaks. Failing to take these dangers seriously downgrades the vitality of rights like life, liberty, and equality, and overextends the place of speech.

The potential of hate speech to bring injustices to fruition makes it vital to enact legislation limiting the lawful use of intolerant symbols to nonaggressive purposes, such as memorabilia collections or historical analyses. Persons who defame an individual commit civil liability. However, persons who target minorities cause an injury not only to the insulted individuals, but to the victim's entire group. There is a compelling reason for prohibiting hate speech since it has historically proven to be a catalyst for violence, committed against susceptibly weak outgroups. A more significant reduction in the public sense of safety results from misethnic slurs than from personal insults. The state, therefore, has a significant interest in prosecuting persons who target outgroups.

When evaluating which expressions to prohibit, lawmakers should empathize with the historical consciousness of outgroups. A prejudicial remark may not be perceived as dangerous unless it is contextualized in the historic experience of the targeted outgroup. For example, if someone were to say that whites should be disempowered or killed because they control and manipulate the world's financial markets or that whites should be segregated because they are intellectually inferior and morally corrupt, the remarks would be crass but probably innocuous. Yet, if those same statements referred to Jews and blacks, respectively, they would potentially cause great harms because they are based on inflammatory stereotypes of Jews as greedy and blacks as bestial. Those stereotypes have in the past agitated bigots to violate the human rights of outgroups, and, if their expression is not restricted, they will likely cause further harms during times of social upheaval. Legislative proposals should be advanced against the type of stereotypes that in the past have led their adherents to violate outgroups' human rights.

Whether It Is Substantially Probable or Reasonably Foreseeable That Dissemination of Racially or Ethnically Derogatory Remarks Will Elicit Discrimination, Violence, Persecution, or Oppression against Targeted Outgroups

Statutes should prohibit epithets when it is substantially probable or reasonably foreseeable that they will elicit violence, vandalism, or discrimination against identifiable groups. How substantial a threat vilifications pose must be determined by both the content and context within which they are enunciated.[36] "Context" refers to the circumstances surrounding particular messages. "Content" refers to the words' linguistic placement and cultural connotations. Among the crucial issues that courts must analyze in order to determine the probability that expressions will cause harms are (a) the syntax and semantics of the language in which they were uttered; (b) the time and place when the statements were spoken; (c) the audience to which they were said; (d) the speaker's intent; (e) whether or not the targeted group has been historically persecuted; (f) whether the speaker and audience belong to a group that perpetrated previous injustices against the targeted group; and (g) whether or not the remarks were invocations to action or abstract statements. These questions all go to determining whether there is reason to believe that the invective has a significant probability of infringing on the targets' rights. The findings should be established on empirically verifiable facts, derived through multidisciplinary analysis. The significance of particular speech and its potential to lead to destructive behaviors should be determined on a case by case basis.[37]

Depictions that minimize the social value and depreciate the accomplishments of outgroups gradually deteriorate democracy and make degradation more socially tolerable. By depicting outgroups as subhumans, it becomes easier for bigots to commit uncensored acts of violence. Traditional scapegoats are more easily attacked and disparaged because the general population becomes indoctrinated in supremacism from an early age, making it more probable that disrespect and overgeneralization will lead to spirited abuse. It is easier to deprive groups of their property and jobs, when they are perceived not as equals but as chimerical representatives of evil. In Part I of this book, we saw how dehumanizing stereotypes made it possible to gradually deprive minorities of their rights. The methodical dissemination of unfair characterizations variously led to the Holocaust, the U.S. Civil War, the Indian Removal Act, and Mauritanian slavery. These empirical findings indicate that hate speech is substantially more dangerous than other defamations. Labels that artificially rob outgroups of their humanity increase the likelihood that words will turn into widespread attitudes which, then, will lead to intolerance and catastrophe for minorities and society as a whole. Therefore, charismatic leaders should be prohibited from harnessing racist, xenophobic, and anti-Semitic ideologies to further discrimination and achieve ruinous objectives. Criminal statutes can deter prejudice and prevent the deterioration of social mores toward outgroups.

Even during times of social and fiscal tranquility, when no imminent threat of grand-scale racial and ethnic intolerance looms, legislative policy should still prohibit hate speech and reflect the potential of moral and economic deterioration. Often during national crises, misethnicity draws persons who were formerly only ideologues to vehemently and sadistically oppress members of despised outgroups. The substantial possibility that misethnic speech that might be relatively benign today can later take on a malignant form should not be overlooked.[38]

Whether the Speaker Intended the Declarations to Incite Criminal Acts against an Outgroup[39]

The Supreme Court has determined that in incitement cases it is material for courts to consider a speaker's intent. In *Schenck v. United States*, the Court upheld the defendant's conviction for printing and distributing a pamphlet that equated conscription with involuntary servitude.[40] The Court found that by mailing the pamphlet, Schenck manifested the intent to obstruct the government from conscripting soldiers.[41]

Pursuant to the majority holding in *Schenck*, an element of future hate speech legislation should require proof that the speaker intentionally encouraged persons to commit inhumane acts against an identifiable outgroup. By adding a *mens rea*, criminal intent, element to hate speech legislation, lawmakers assure that theoretical utterances and personal opinions will not be punished. This intent requirement protects First Amendment rights while punishing utterances outside First Amendment protections.

Speech is not merely a retelling of facts, it is also a vehicle of communicating dogma and influencing others. Misethnists interact with persons in their group, with whose attitudes they identify and whose conduct they can affect.[42] Hate speech that is intended to elicit violent responses from bigots can be dangerous both at the time it is uttered and in the future. When the statement is made, the menace may be in its developmental stage, but the ultimate intended ends—inhumane acts and civil rights abuses—materialize after systematic development. It is unpredictable how far the hateful flames produced by one ember of bigotry can spread.[43] It is only reasonable for the government to extinguish bigotry before it burns out of control and consumes society in the flames of authoritarianism. A law prohibiting speech that is intended to raise a following of people willing to act inimically is not arbitrary, but rather conscious of historical examples in which racist, ethnocentric, and anti-Semitic rhetoric led to violence, enslavement, dislocation, and genocide. The common good is served by preventing orators from exploiting bigoted sentiments for the purpose of enlisting persons to commit hate crimes. The government should not stand idly by while intentionally volatile speech consolidates the forces of bigotry to infringe upon autonomy rights and to trample democratic ideals; instead, it should "suppress the threatened danger in its inception."[44]

A speaker who intends listeners to commit a brutal plan against a group of people should be held criminally responsible because state inaction may compromise public safety. There is a continuum of racist antagonism that starts with hateful speech.

Eventually, a protagonist is likely to cross a juncture whereupon his or her hate speech succeeds in inciting followers to hurt or tyrannize outgroups. Bigots intending their words to be part of an incremental plan to efface equal rights should be prosecuted to deter future molestations. Propaganda aimed at the long-term development of racial and ethnic animus is even more dangerous than hate speech posing only an immediate threat of harm. The deliberate orchestration of prejudice whittles away those social mores that are based on justice and equality. Systematic incitement is easier to marshal and sustain than utterances calling for immediate, singular acts of violence. Forward-looking hate propaganda can elicit greater harms against humanity than speech that poses only a concurrent risk.

Whether the Social or Individual Benefit from the Message Is Outweighed by Its Realistic Potential to Disrupt the Social Order and
Infringe on Fundamental Rights

Judges should balance the various constitutional interests of orators and
victims of hate speech. Free speech does not exist in a vacuum. They are
connected to other constitutional guarantees. An outgroup's right to live
in peace, without having to fear for its safety, outweighs a bigot's right to
express racist vitriol.

Balancing the values of representative democracy against the values
promoted by hate speech is integral to establishing rational public policy.
This process includes evaluating the speaker's interests in pronouncing
the message; whether the victims' fundamental and basic rights are affected; and whether the social interest of advancing the common good is
furthered by hate speech law. These factors must be analyzed to determine whether a restriction on speech is the least restrictive and best alternative for protecting civil rights. This proposal integrates various constitutional principles. Instead of taking the narrow approach of automat-
ically placing the right to free expression ahead of other essential rights,
such as autonomy and self-dignity, it recognizes that they are all essential
to social well-being.

The freedom to speak may be limited so long as the restriction increases vulnerable people's autonomy and augments general welfare. The
restraint on expression must be necessary to protect pluralistic discourse,
justice, and equality.[45]

Speakers' rights are limited to the extent that they substantially infringe on the rights of others. A scheme that permits fascist forces to com-
mandeer the institution of free speech is incompatible with social contract
principles because it hinders some citizens from fully participating in the
civic life of their community and from accomplishing unintrusive personal aspirations. Laws that criminalize virulent misethnicity are of
greater import to the vitality of democracy than are false declarations
about historically oppressed peoples.

If the Speech Involves Religious Beliefs, Then Incitement Laws
Must Be Neutral

Religion has been misused in many cultures to spread intolerant hatred.
The institution of slavery was justified on the basis of religious ideology,

and Islamic extremism continues to foment modern terrorism. While protecting the right to freely exercise religious convictions, the state should also adopt a set of legal guidelines to prohibit the abuse of creeds as catalysts for oppression. Since the state has a compelling interest in protecting the well-being of its citizens against the incitement to ethnic hatred, it can enact narrowly drafted laws that prohibit religious hate speech.[46]

United States courts traditionally refuse to "approve, disapprove, classify, regulate, or in any manner control sermons delivered at religious meetings."[47] The proscription against governmental meddling in religious tenets and institutions ought to be maintained. However, hate speech couched in religious terminology should be banned when it poses a significant danger to public welfare. The victim of a hate crime suffers no less if his or her persecutors are religious rather than secular misethnists. Determinations about which forms of religious speech are dangerous to outgroups should be neutral. That is, the restriction must be such that if the specifically religious elements were removed from the utterance, the call to violence would nevertheless threaten social stability and individual rights. Laws passed to prevent religiously inspired hate speech should not discriminate against any specific religion. Furthermore, no policy should be adopted to regulate or limit religious speech that does not threaten the human rights of identifiable groups of people.

Hate speech that is nominally couched in doctrinal tenets should not be protected simply because it uses religious terminology. Courts should evaluate expert witness testimony, the content of the message, and whether a substantially similar message, expressed in like circumstances, has previously incited people to commit acts of violence or oppression against the targeted outgroup. First Amendment protections are not absolute, and they should be weighed against the right of individuals to enjoy their lives without realistically foreseeable threats of religious intolerance.

Delimiting Restrictions on Hate Speech

I set out two model criminal laws against the use of hate propaganda. They are virtually identical except that the first is preferable because it recognizes the special vulnerabilities of outgroups, while the second reflects Justice Scalia's requirement in *R.A.V. v. St. Paul* that fighting words statutes be neutral. I recommend the first alternative for European countries whose experience with the dangerous effects of misethnic messages is extensive. However, in the United States, where Scalia's opinion continues to dominate the arena of incitement speech jurisprudence, there is a greater likelihood of passing the second.

I.

(1) Anyone inciting others to discriminate, persecute, oppress, or commit any similar acts against members of a historically persecuted group;

(2) where it is substantially probable or reasonably foreseeable, based on the content and context of the message, that its dissemination will elicit such acts; and

(3) where the speaker intended the message to promote destructive behavior;

(4) shall receive a term of imprisonment of at least three months and not exceeding three years;

(5) in addition to the term of imprisonment, the court may impose up to four hundred hours of community service.

(6) Defenses: No one shall be convicted under this law if: the statement was uttered as an expression of opinion on a neutral scientific, academic, or religious subject and/or the statement was made to eliminate the incidence of hatred toward a historically persecuted group.

II.

(1) Anyone inciting others to discriminate, persecute, oppress, or commit any similar acts against members of an identifiable group;

(2) where it is substantially probable or reasonably foreseeable, based on the content and context of the message, that its dissemination will elicit such acts; and

(3) where the speaker intended the message to promote destructive behavior;

(4) shall receive a term of imprisonment of at least three months and not exceeding three years;

(5) in addition to the term of imprisonment, the court may impose up to four hundred hours of community service.

(6) Defenses: No one shall be convicted under this law if: the statement was uttered as an expression of opinion on a neutral scientific, academic, or religious subject and/or the statement was made to eliminate the incidence of hatred toward an identifiable group.

Democracy is not a license for absolute liberty. Protecting individuals' desire to freely disseminate hate propaganda should be counterbalanced against the more important egalitarian, social values: civil rights and human happiness. The First Amendment should not protect hate speech intended to cause the oppression of specific groups of people. Hate speech, U.S. Supreme Court Justice White said, is politically "worthless and undeserving of constitutional protection."[48] Bigots, throughout the world, have repeatedly used destructive messages to spread stereotypes about outgroups. Once the stereotypes became part of the collective cultural psyche, disparaged outgroups were discriminated against, enslaved, and systematically murdered.

Some writers argue that it is unnecessary to create laws in the United States to punish any but the most imminently dangerous forms of hate speech. According to this line of thought, the United States, unlike countries such as Germany, does not have a long history of bigotry; therefore, it is unnecessary to punish hate speech here except in those instances when it poses an immediate threat to public order.[49] Its proponents base this argument on abstract legal theory that is not grounded in empirical and historical evidence. Hate speech is not only dangerous when it calls for immediate action. History is replete with examples of extensive, organized manipulation of propaganda that, over a long term, became part of the accepted social dialogue, making misethnic movements popularly attractive. The propagation of affective stereotypes helped establish a schema of social mores that justified and perpetuated expropriations, dislocations, and cruelties against Native Americans and sanctioned black slavery and disenfranchisement. The widespread dissemination of anti-Semitic rhetoric in Germany prior to and until the rise of the Nazi Party demonstrates how quickly bigotry can flare into a virtually uncontrollable conflagration.[50]

An absolutist free speech doctrine should not trump egalitarian ideals. Narrowly tailored laws that distinguish legitimate forms of political dialogue from hate speech are in the public interest. False statements about identifiable groups do nothing to further mutual respect for inalienable rights. Language plays a significant role in structuring social relationships. Hate crimes are almost inevitable in a society that allows orators to interweave bigotry into everyday speech. To avoid the recurrence of the greatest crimes against humanity, laws should be adopted prohibiting persons from intentionally disseminating substantially dangerous racist and ethnocentric invective.

Notes

NOTES TO CHAPTER 1

1. I refer to "hate speech" variously throughout the book, including "hate propaganda," "destructive messages," and "biased speech." These terms refer to antisocial oratory that is intended to incite persecution against people because of their race, color, religion, ethnic group, or nationality, and has a substantial likelihood of causing such harm. This definition does not include verbal attacks against individuals who incidentally happen to be members of an outgroup.

2. *See* R. Delgado & D. H. Yun, *Pressure Valves and Bloodied Chickens*, 82 CALIF. L. REV. 871 (1994).

3. See U.S. CONST. art. I, §2, cl. 3; art. I, §9, cl. 1, *amended by* U.S. CONST. amends. XIII, XIV, and XV.

4. Delgado & Yun, *supra*, at 881–82.

5. *See* P. Gilroy, AGAINST RACE 230 (2000).

NOTES TO CHAPTER 2

1. *See* S. Ettinger, *Origins of Modern Anti-Semitism*, *in* 2 NAZI HOLOCAUST 180 (M. R. Marrus ed., Meckler 1989).

2. The massacres spread through Röttingen, Franconia, and Bavaria. *See* M. Rubin, *Imagining the Jew*, *in* IN & OUT OF THE GHETTO (D. Junker ed., 1995).

3. R. GUTTERIDGE, OPEN THY MOUTH FOR THE DUMB! 3 (1976).

4. M. LUTHER, *On the Jews and Their Lies*, in 47 LUTHER'S WORKS 268–69 (H. T. Lehmann & Franklin Sherman eds., Martin H. Bertram trans., Concordia Pub. House 1971) (1543).

5. 47 *id.* at 286.

6. *See* L. S. DAWIDOWICZ, THE WAR AGAINST THE JEWS 1933–1945 23 (1975). *See also* M. S. Allen, *Right Old Wrong*, HOUS. CHRON., Oct. 9, 1993, at 1. The Evangelical Lutheran Church in America has issued a statement rejecting Luther's anti-Semitism. *Id.* It has recognized that Luther's words are still used by hate groups like the Ku Klux Klan and the Aryan Nation. *Id.*

7. K. Marx, A World without Jews 45 (D. D. Runes trans., 1959) (1843).

8. *The Bower* had 400,000 subscribers. Its pages were often filled with reactions to Germany's economic depression.

9. *Quoted in* J. Weiss, Ideology of Death 98 (1996).

10. *Id.* 84.

11. There is some disagreement about when this book was first published, with some authors placing it in 1873 and others in 1879.

12. *Quoted in* M. Zimmerman, Wilhelm Marr 69 (1986).

13. *Quoted in* J. Katz, From Prejudice to Destruction 260 (1980).

14. *Quoted in* Weiss, *supra*, at 98.

15. P. Massing reproduced Stoecker's speech, "What We Demand of Modern Jewry," *in* Rehearsal for Destruction 279–87 (1949).

16. Weiss, *supra*, at 91; *see also* Dawidowicz, *supra*, at 34–35.

17. The quotes are found in F. Stern, Politics of Cultural Despair 61–63 (1961).

18. H. v. Treitschke, History of Germany in the Nineteenth Century 256, 105–6 (E. & C. Paul trans., U. of Chicago Press 1975) (1879).

19. *See* Katz, *supra*, at 263.

20. *Quoted in* Der Berliner Antisemitismusstreit 13 (H. v. W. Boehlich ed., Insel Verlag 1988) (1879).

21. *Quoted in* Dawidowicz, *supra*, at 36.

22. *Quoted in* L. Poliakov, Aryan Myth (E. Howard trans., Sussex U. Press 1974) (1971).

23. S. E. Bronner, Rumor about the Jews 34 (2000).

24. Protocols of the Learned Elders of Zion, *quoted in* Bronner, *supra*, at 12.

25. *Id.* at 17.

26. J. Parkes, Antisemitism 51 (1963); *see also* K. D. Bracher, German Dictatorship 35 (J. Steinberg trans., Praeger Press 3d prtg. 1972).

27. B. W. Segel, A Lie & a Libel 118 (Richard S. Levy trans., U. of Nebraska Press 1995) (1926).

28. *Quoted in* N. Cohn, Warrant for Genocide 136–37 (1967).

29. *Quoted in* Dawidowicz, *supra*, at 71.

30. *Quoted in id.* at 71–72.

31. *See id.* at 57, 60, 91.

32. "An entire generation of Germans had absorbed generous doses of anti-Semitism in the *Gymnasium* and the university." W. T. Angress, *Prussia's Army & the Jewish Reserve Officer Controversy before World War I, in* Imperial Germany 114 (James J. Sheehan ed., New Viewpoints 1976).

33. *See* Weiss, *supra*; D. J. Goldhagen, Hitler's Willing Executioners (1997) (discussing the crucial role that ordinary Germans played in the Holocaust).

34. *Quoted in* M. Broszat, *Genesis of the Final Solution*, 13 YAD VASHEM STUDIES 73, 88 n.20 (1979).

35. *Id.* at 107 n.33.

36. *Quoted in* Andreas Hillgruber, *War in the East & Extermination of the Jews*, 3 THE NAZI HOLOCAUST, *supra*, at 111.

37. R. GUTTERIDGE, OPEN THY MOUTH FOR THE DUMB! 315 (1976).

38. *Id.* at 227.

39. *Quoted in* H. Krausnick, *The Persecution of the Jews, in* ANATOMY OF THE SS STATE 44 (R. Barry et al. trans., Walker 1968).

40. *See* GOLDHAGEN, *supra*, at 168–77.

41. *See* LIFTON, *supra*.

42. *See e.g.* Brandenburg v. Ohio, 395 U.S. 444, 447 (1969) (per curiam).

43. "[P]rolonged and intense verbal hostility always precedes a riot." G. W. ALLPORT, THE NATURE OF PREJUDICE 60 (3d ed. 1979) (1954).

NOTES TO CHAPTER 3

1. I use the term "blacks" rather than the currently popular Afro-Americans or African Americans because the latter terms are both over- and underinclusive. They are overinclusive because they include persons like white South Africans, whose ancestors were never persecuted in the United States. They are underinclusive because they do not include persons, such as the indigenous people of Papua New Guinea whose characteristics resemble people of African ancestry, and who could, therefore, be targeted by racists.

2. *See* W. D. JORDAN, WHITE OVER BLACK: AMERICAN ATTITUDES TOWARD THE NEGRO, 1550–1812 44 (1968); C. N. Degler, *Slavery & the Genesis of American Race Prejudice*, 2 COMP. STUD. IN SOC'Y & HIST. 49, 50 (1959).

3. "When slavery did become embodied in law, it could not help but reflect the folk bias within the framework of which it developed." C. N. DEGLER, OUT OF OUR PAST 30 (1959). *But see* O. & M. F. Handlin, *Origins of Negro Slavery, in* ORIGINS OF AMERICAN SLAVERY & RACISM (D. L. Noel ed., Merrill 1972) (1950).

4. *See* W. D. Jordan, *Modern Tensions & the Origins of American Slavery, in* BLACKS IN WHITE AMERICA BEFORE 1865 113 (R. V. Haynes ed., D. Mckay 1972).

5. *In* R. HAKLUYT, 7 PRINCIPAL NAVIGATIONS VOYAGES TRAFFIQUES & DISCOVERIES OF THE ENGLISH NATION 263–64 (James MacLehose & Sons 1904) (1578).

6. S. SEWELL, SELLING OF JOSEPH A MEMORIAL 83–87; J. SAFFIN, BRIEF & CANDID ANSWER TO A LATE PRINTED SHEET, ENTITULED [*sic*], THE SELLING OF JOSEPH 251–56, *in* G. H. MOORE, NOTES ON THE HISTORY OF SLAVERY IN MASSACHUSETTS (D. Appleton & Co. 1866).

7. *See* W. S. JENKINS, PRO-SLAVERY THOUGHT IN THE OLD SOUTH 6–7 (1935).

8. C. MATHER, THE NEGRO CHRISTIANIZED 2–3 (1706).

9. JENKINS, *supra*, at 13.

10. M. GODWYN, NEGRO'S & INDIANS ADVOCATE 3 (1680).

11. G. BERKELEY, WORKS OF GEORGE BERKELEY 244 (A. C. Fraser ed., Oxford 1871) (sermon of Feb. 18, 1731).

12. FORENSIC DISPUTE ON THE LEGALITY OF ENSLAVING THE AFRICANS 31 (1773).

13. JENKINS, *supra*, at 7.

14. The centrality and leadership of Quakers in helping to develop an anti-slavery movement cannot be overstated. However, it was not until 1758 that Quakers forbade their own members from owning slaves and 1776 when they disowned slave owners. Before then, many Quakers owned slaves and amassed wealth through the institution.

15. *See* J. N. NORWOOD, SCHISM IN THE METHODIST EPISCOPAL CHURCH, 1844 (1923).

16. *See* O. REISS, BLACKS IN COLONIAL AMERICA 98 (1997).

17. *See* Degler, *Slavery & the Genesis of American Race Prejudice, supra*, at 19 & 24.

18. MATHER, *supra*, 5, 23, 25.

19. J. Quincy, *Two Dialogues on the Man-trade, in* A. BENEZET, SHORT ACCOUNT OF THAT PART OF AFRICA, INHABITED BY NEGROES 31 (1762).

20. PERSONAL SLAVERY ESTABLISHED 18–19 (1773).

21. *Id.* at 3, 5–7.

22. [E. LONG], HISTORY OF JAMAICA 360, 365, 370 (L. Lowndes, 1774).

23. G. JAHODA, IMAGES OF SAVAGES 228 (1999); *but see* W. D. JORDAN, WHITE MAN'S BURDEN 15 (1974) (arguing that the speculative connection between apes and blacks was aroused because the English discovered the existence of the two at about the same time).

24. 2 HISTORY OF JAMAICA, *supra*, at 353–54.

25. B. ROMANS, CONCISE NATURAL HISTORY OF EAST & WEST FLORIDA 105 (1775).

26. [A. LEE], ESSAY IN VINDICATION OF THE CONTINENTAL COLONIES OF AMERICA 30 (1764).

27. T. JEFFERSON, NOTES ON VIRGINIA, *in* COMPLETE JEFFERSON 665 (S. K. Padover, ed., Tudor Pub. 1943) (1785).

28. CONG. GLOBE, 33rd Cong., 1st Sess., Appendix 230 (Feb. 24, 1854).

29. The voices of public speakers who rebelled against the libels could not change the contemporary system of oppression. Among those progressive thinkers were Benjamin Rush, John Quincy Adams, Abigail Adams, and others who decried the hypocrisy and unfairness of slavery throughout the early days of

the republic. Rush penned a passionate appeal against the use of pro-slavery pro-paganda as an excuse to commit brutal crimes:

> The vulgar notion of their being descended from Cain, who was supposed to have been marked by this colour, is too absurd to need a refutation. . . . Their master's name is now marked upon their breasts with a red-hot iron. . . . [B]ehold an Over-seer approaches them—In vain they sue for pity.—He lifts up his whip, while streams of blood follow ever stroke. Neither age nor sex are spared. . . . [L]et us . . . see the various modes of arbitrary punishments inflicted upon them by their masters. Behold one covered with stripes, into which melted wax is poured—another tied down to a block or a stake—a third suspended in the air by his thumbs.

B. Rush, Address to the Inhabitants of the British Colonies in America, upon Slave-Keeping 4, 19 (1775).

30. *See* G. Vassa, Life of Olaudah Equiano, the African, *in* Great Documents in Black American History 47 (G. Ducas ed., Praeger Publishers 1970) (1789).

31. 1 Documents Illustrative of the History of the Slave Trade to America 129 (E. Donnan ed., Carnegie Inst. of Wash. 1930). Alexander Falcon-bridge, an English ship surgeon, left an account of the conditions aboard slave-trading vessels. Slave merchants inspected the hardiness of the Africans. Merchants took onboard persons they deemed capable of arduous work. Traders rejected, beat, and sometimes killed captives whom they found too weak or infirm for their purposes. Those who were taken on as human cargo had so little space in the sleeping compartments that it was virtually impossible for them to rest in any other manner than side by side. The enslavers provided them with conical buckets to relieve themselves. These they often placed too far for some of the captives, forcing them to urinate and defecate where they lay, thus creating a disease-filled environment. Ship captains guarded against deterioration of their cargo and threatened those who refused to eat with red-hot coals and sometimes burned them with melted lead. The poor ventilation in the sleeping quarters made the air rife for the transmission of infectious agents. During stormy weather, when the ship and its inhabitants were jarred, the floor where the Africans slept was coated with mucus and blood. Driven by greed for lucre, slave traders sometimes over-loaded their ships with mortal results. In one case, a Liverpool ship took on so many captives that they were forced to lie one on top of another, causing the death of half of them during the voyage. *See* A. Falconbridge, Account of the Slave Trade on the Coast of Africa (1788) (visited Jan. 27, 2001) <http://web-cr05.pbs.org/wgbh/aia/part1/1h281t.html>.

32. J. Hammond, *Letter to an English Abolitionist, in* The Ideology of Slavery 191–92 (1981).

33. JENKINS, *supra*, at 47.

34. FORENSIC DISPUTE ON THE LEGALITY OF ENSLAVING THE AFRICANS (1773).

35. *Quoted in* JENKINS, *supra*, at 76.

36. T. R. Dew, *Review of the Debate in the Virginia Legislature, in* SLAVERY DEFENDED 20–33 (E. L. McKitrick ed., Prentice Hall 1963) (1832).

37. C. CRAWFORD, OBSERVATIONS UPON NEGRO-SLAVERY 21 (1784) (quoting a "religious author").

38. D. COOPER, SERIOUS ADDRESS TO THE RULERS OF AMERICA, ON THE IN-CONSISTENCY OF THEIR CONDUCT RESPECTING SLAVERY 17–18 (1783).

39. Ironically, George Mason, who delivered the most fiery anti-slavery speech at the Constitutional Convention, never freed his own slaves, bequeathing them to his children.

40. B. M. PALMER, RIGHTS OF THE SOUTH DEFENDED IN THE PULPITS (1860).

41. SAFFIN, *supra*, in MOORE, *supra*, at 251–52 (1866).

42. For an interesting discussion on the developments of colonial racism, *see* S. B. VICKERS, NATIVE AMERICAN IDENTITIES 26–27 (1998).

43. G. S. SAWYER, SOUTHERN INSTITUTES 193 n.3 (Negro U. Press reprint 1969) (1858).

44. S. Cartwright, *Prognathous Species of Mankind, in* SLAVERY DEFENDED, *supra*, at 20–33 (1857).

45. *Quoted in* SAWYER, *supra*, at 195 (Negro U. Press, reprint 1969) (1858). There has never been definitive proof, even using contemporary measuring methods like magnetic resonance imaging, between brain size and intelligence. Much of brain size is based on diet and nutrition. Scientists are not yet even clear whether "to measure brain size by absolute mass, brain-to-body ration, or some other formula." Even during the twentieth century an accurate way to measure the brain size of living subjects was not developed, and cadavers' brains shrivel and lose weight as they dry. *See* J. W. KALAT, BIOLOGICAL PSYCHOLOGY 173–76 (5th ed. 1995).

46. SAFFIN, *supra*, in MOORE, *supra*, at 256 (1866) (1701).

47. T. R. R. COBB, INQUIRY INTO THE LAW OF NEGRO SLAVERY IN THE UNITED STATES OF AMERICA 39 (Negro U. Press, 1968) (1858).

48. W. J. GRAYSON, HIRELING & THE SLAVE, *in* SLAVERY DEFENDED, *supra*, at 64 (1856).

49. 2 WORKS OF JOHN C. CALHOUN 631–32 (R. K. Crallé ed., D. Appleton 1888) (Feb. 7, 1837).

50. *5 id.* at 204 (Feb. 4, 1836).

51. J. C. Calhoun, *Speech on the Reception of Abolition Petitions, in* SLAVERY DEFENDED, *supra* 13 (Feb. 6, 1837).

52. See CONG. GLOBE, 25th Cong., 3d Sess. 177 (Feb. 18, 1839).

53. *Id.*, 35th Cong., 1st Sess. (Mar. 4, 1858), quoted in JENKINS, supra at 286.

54. CONG. GLOBE, 27th Cong., 2nd Sess., Appendix, 337 (Apr. 15, 1842).

55. *Id.*, 27th Cong., 2nd Sess., 173 (Jan. 26, 1842).

56. J. Davis, JEFFERSON DAVIS CONSTITUTIONALIST 49 (Dunbar Rowland ed., Miss. Dept. of Archives and Hist. 1923) (March 2, 1859).

57. *See* W. L. MILLER, ARGUING ABOUT SLAVERY (1996).

58. CONG. GLOBE, 33rd Cong., 2nd Sess., Appendix 230 (Feb. 23, 1855).

59. *See* H. Greeley, *Freeing the Slaves Should Be the Primary War Aim, in* SLAVERY 260–64 (1992) (1862).

NOTES TO CHAPTER 4

1. *See e.g.* A. M. JOSEPHY, JR., INDIAN HERITAGE OF AMERICA 49–52, 87 (revised ed., 1991) (early agriculture); H. E. DRIVER, INDIANS OF NORTH AMERICA 244–64 (1961) (tenancy and land ownership); A. L. KROEBER, CULTURAL & NATURAL AREAS OF NATIVE NORTH AMERICA 143–46, 218–21 (1939) (natural resources and agriculture).

2. J. WINTHROP, 2 WINTHROP PAPERS 141 (1931) (1629); R. F. BERKHOFER, JR., WHITE MAN'S INDIAN 113–14 (1978); H. Knox to G. Washington, in AMERICAN STATE PAPERS: INDIAN AFFAIRS 53–54 (2d prtg. 1998) (July 7, 1789).

3. *Nova Brittania*, 1 TRACTS & OTHER PAPERS RELATING PRINCIPALLY TO THE ORIGIN, SETTLEMENT, & PROGRESS OF THE COLONIES IN NORTH AMERICA no. 6, 11 (Peter Force ed., Peter Force 1836).

4. K. O. KUPPERMAN, INDIANS & ENGLISH 3 (2000).

5. S. PURCHAS, 19 HAKLUYTUS POSTHUMUS OR PURCHAS HIS PILGRIMES 231 (1906) (1625).

6. H. Hawks, *Relation of the Commodities of Nova Hispania . . . , in* Richard Hakluyt, 9 PRINCIPAL NAVIGATIONS VOYAGES TRAFFIQUES & DISCOVERIES OF THE ENGLISH NATION 386 (James MacLehose & Sons 1904) (1572).

7. *Quoted in* G. JAHODA, TRAIL OF TEARS 135 (Random House 1995) (1975).

8. *See* BERKHOFER, *supra*, at 23–25.

9. W. ROBERTSON, 1 HISTORY OF AMERICA 282–83 (1777). Robertson considered all aboriginal peoples savages except the Incas and Aztecs.

10. *Quoted in* W. T. HAGAN, AMERICAN INDIANS 15 (3d ed. 1992).

11. WINTHROP, 3 *supra* 167 (May 22, 1634).

12. *See* W. S. Simmons, *Cultural Bias in the New England Puritans' Perception of Indians*, 38 WILLIAM & MARY Q. 56, 70 (1981).

13. R. BEVERLEY, HISTORY & THE PRESENT STATE OF VIRGINIA (L. B. Wright ed., U. of North Carolina Press 1947) (1705).

14. *See* Letter from W. Penn to Committee of Free Society of Traders, *in* White on Red 50–54 (N. B. Black & B. S. Weidman eds., 1976) (1683).

15. *See* B. Franklin, *Savages of North America, in* COMPLETE WORKS OF BENJAMIN FRANKLIN 25–31 (G. P. Putnam's Sons 1888) (1784).

16. *Quoted in* Hagan, *supra*, at 15.

17. T. Jefferson, *Hints on the Subject of Indian Boundaries*, 17, *in* Writings of Thomas Jefferson 374 (Andrew A. Lipscomb ed., 1905) (Dec. 29, 1802).

18. *See* R. H. Pearce, Savages of America 66 (1965).

19. 21 U.S. 543 (1823).

20. *Id.* at 590. Subsequently, the right to conquest was only allowed in cases of "defensive wars" or those fought for a "just cause." Worcester v. Georgia, 31 U.S. (6 Pet.) 515, 545 (1832).

21. Johnson, 21 U.S. at 590.

22. *Id.* at 591.

23. S. Scheckel, Insistence of the Indian 27 (1998).

24. *Quoted in* F. P. Prucha, The Great Father 324 (U. of Nebraska Press 1984) (1852).

25. T. L. McKenney, 1 Memoirs, Official and Personal 233 (1846).

26. Letter from Rev. S. Stoddard to Gov. J. Dudley, Ser. 4, 2, Collections of the Mass. Hist'l Soc'y 235 (1854) (Oct. 22, 1703).

27. *Quoted in* Puritan Tradition in America 1620–1730 66 (A. T. Vaughan, ed., U. of South Carolina Press 1972).

28. C. Eby, "That Disgraceful Affair," The Black Hawk War 248–59 (1973).

29. H. H. Brackenridge, Indian Atrocities 62 (V. P. James 1867) (1782).

30. *See e.g.* Letter from A. Jackson to J. Monroe & letter from Jackson, D. Meriwether, & J. Franklin to W. Crawford, *both in* 4 Papers of Andrew Jackson 50, 65 (1994) (July 9, 1816 & Sept. 20, 1816).

31. A. Jackson, 2 Compilation of the Messages & Papers of the Presidents 458 (James D. Richardson ed., Bureau of Nat'l Literature and Art 1902) (Dec. 8, 1829).

32. R. N. Satz, American Indian Policy in the Jacksonian Era 55 (1975).

33. Key to Taney, *in Letters to Francis Scott Key to Roger Brooke Taney, and Other Correspondence*, 5 Md. Hist. Mag. 28 (March 1910) (Nov. 6, 1833).

34. A. Jackson, 2 *supra*, at 522 (2d Annual Message, Dec. 6, 1830).

35. J. Hall, *Essay on the History of North American Indians, in* 3 T. L. McKenney & J. Hall, Indian Tribes of North America 83 (John Grant 1934) (1842).

36. Reg. Deb., 21st Cong., 1st Sess., 327 (Apr. 15, 1830).

37. *Life of Black Hawk*, 40 N. Am. Rev. 68, 85 (Jan. 1835).

38. F. J. Grund, Americans, in Their Moral, Soc., & Pol. Rel. 228 (1837).

39. *Quoted in* Satz, *supra*, at 17, 28–29.

40. *Quoted in* Jahoda, *supra*, at 45 (speaking about the so-called Five Civilized Tribes).

41. Reg. Deb., 21st Cong., 1st Sess., 312 (Apr. 9, 1830).

42. Article III, section 4 of the Constitution of the Cherokee Nation stated: "No person who is of negro or mulatto parentage, either by the father or mother side, shall be eligible to hold any office of profit, honor, or trust in this Governement." *Quoted in* L. Filler, Rise & Fall of Slavery in America 72 (1980).

43. *Quoted in* A. K. Weinberg, Manifest Destiny 83 (1958).

44. "[N]o new State shall be formed or erected within the Jurisdiction of any other State . . . without the consent of the Legislatures of the States concerned as well as of the Congress." U.S. Const. art. IV, §3.

45. *Quoted in* Speeches on the Passage of the Bill for the Removal of the Indians 84 (1973) (May 15, 1830) (appearing in Representative Henry R. Storrs's speech).

46. 30 U.S. 1 (1831).

47. *Id.* at 16–17.

48. Letter from J. J. Marshall to J. J. Story, *quoted in* G. E. White, Marshall Court & Cultural Change 714 (1988).

49. 31 U.S. 515 (1832).

50. *Found* in G. Foreman, Indian Removal 244 (9th prtg. 1982).

51. Approximately 4,000 Cherokees remained in the hills after the roundup, thereby avoiding the Trail of Tears.

52. G. Bancroft, 3 History of the United States 302 (17th ed. 1862).

53. 1 *id.* at 382 (1st ed. 1834).

Notes to Chapter 5

1. *See* Worldwide Slavery: Hearing before the Senate Foreign Relations Committee (Sept. 28, 2000) (statement of Professor Kevin Bales).

2. J. Fleischman, Mauritania's Campaign of Terror 91–92 (1994).

3. *See* S. Cotton, Silent Terror 25–28 (1998); K. Bales, Disposable People 109 (1999).

4. (Visited July 29, 2001) <http://www.hrw.org/reports/2001/Africa/Mauritania/Mauritania.html>.

5. B. Lewis, Race & Slavery in the Middle East 22, 56–57, 92, 95 (1990).

6. Fleischman, *supra*, at 86.

7. *Id.* at 90.

8. L. Surette, *New Laws to Curb Hate on Internet?*, The Gazette (Montreal), Mar. 24, 1999, at A12.

9. T. Perry & K. Murphy, *White Supremacist*, L.A. Times, Nov. 11, 2000, at A20.

10. (Visited Sept. 4, 2000) <http://www.nsm88.com/magazine.html>.

11. *See* Alexander Tsesis, *Hate in Cyberspace: Regulating Hate Speech on the Internet*, 38 San Diego L. Rev. 817 (2001).

12. *See e.g.* R. Weintraub-Reiter, Note, *Hate Speech over the Internet*, 8 B.U. PUB. INT. L.J. 145, 173 (1998).

13. R. Gearty, *Filter Bars Web Hate*, DAILY NEWS, Nov. 12, 1998, at 11.

14. *See* Censorware Project, Blacklisted by Cyber Patrol (visited October 24, 2000) <http://www.spectacle.org/cwp/ada-yoyo.html>.

15. *Smith on Video*, ASSOCIATED PRESS, July 7, 1999, at State and Regional Section.

16. M. Manuel, *Neo-Nazis Next Target of Lawyer Who Broke Klan*, ATLANTA J. & CONST., Mar. 5, 1999, at 1C.

17. C. Burritt, *Klan Role in S.C. Arson Costs It $37.8 Million*, ATLANTA J. & CONST., July 25, 1998, at 1A.

18. M. Kakutani, *Critic's Notebook*, N.Y. TIMES, Apr. 30, 1993, at C1.

19. *See* T. B. Edsall, *Barr Spoke to White Supremacy Group*, WASH. POST, Dec. 11, 1998, at A23; D. Lease, *Hate Group with Local Origins Makes National News*, SARASOTA HERALD-TRIB., Mar. 1, 1999, at 8A; E. O. Hutchinson, *Viewpoint, Bob Barr*, NEWSDAY, Dec. 28, 1998, at A30. H. B. Price, Commentary, *To Be Equal*, COPELY NEWS SERV., Jan. 20, 1999.

20. Derrick Z. Jackson, Editorial, *Ashcroft's Flirtations with the Racist Right*, B. GLOBE, Jan. 10, 2001, at A19.

21. *Muslim Program*, FINAL CALL, Mar. 16, 1999; *Duke Seeks Ex-Rep. Livingston's Seat*, CHI. TRIB., Mar. 19, 1999, at 23.

22. D. L. Schaefer, Commentary, *Farrakhan's Vilifying Videos Don't Belong in High School Classrooms*, TELEGRAM & GAZETTE, Mar. 27, 1998, at A11; *Farrakhan Show*, WASH. POST, Aug. 1, 1984, at A23.

23. K. Merida, *Black Leaders Call on Farrakhan to Repudiate Controversial Remarks by Aide*, WASH. POST, Jan. 26, 1994, at A3.

24. Bond recently discussed the importance of strengthening the relationship between blacks and Jews at the Anti-Defamation League's Annual Leadership Conference. *See New NAACP Head Seeks to Improve Weathered Black/Jewish Relations*, JACKSONVILLE FREE PRESS, Apr. 15, 1998, at 2. At a conference held at Yeshiva University, King spoke out against racism and anti-Semitism, stating that "[e]ven passive toleration of anti-Semitism serves the evils of prejudice and bigotry my father fought against." A. Dickter, *Mixed Messages on Blacks and Jews*, JEWISH WEEK, May 1, 1998, at 8.

25. An Anti-Defamation League study found, in 1998, that 34 percent of blacks harbored anti-Semitic views, as compared to 9 percent of whites. *See* F. Eltman, *More Blacks Found to Be Anti-Semitic*, ASSOCIATED PRESS, Nov. 24, 1998.

NOTE TO PART II

1. *See* T. A. v. DIJK, COMMUNICATING RACISM 191–93 (2d prtg. 1989).

NOTES TO CHAPTER 6

1. *See* T. W. ADORNO ET AL., AUTHORITARIAN PERSONALITY 5 (1950).

2. *See* J. PARKES, ANTISEMITISM 10–12 (1963).

3. *See* E. Frenkel-Brunswick, *Comprehensive Scores & Summary of Interview Results, in* ADORNO, *supra*, at 474.

4. *See* R. DELGADO & J. STEFANCIC, MUST WE DEFEND NAZIS? 4–5 (1997).

5. *See* R. Delgado and J. Stefancic, *Ten Arguments against Hate-Speech Regulation: How Valid?*, 23 N. KY. L. REV. 475, 478 (1996).

6. *See* G. E. SIMPSON & J. M. YINGER, RACIAL & CULTURAL MINORITIES 64 (4th ed. 1972).

7. *See* H. J. EHRLICH, SOCIAL PSYCHOLOGY OF PREJUDICE 21 (1973).

8. *See* D. L. Hamilton & T. K. Trolier, *Stereotypes & Stereotyping, in* PREJUDICE, DISCRIMINATION & RACISM 143–44 (J. F. Dovidio & S. L. Gaertner eds., 1986).

9. *See* J. KOVEL, WHITE RACISM 96–97 (1970).

10. E. J. DINGWALL, RACIAL PRIDE & PREJUDICE 212–13 (1946).

11. F. FANON, BLACK SKIN, WHITE MASKS 147–48 (C. L. Markmann trans., Grove Press 1967) (1952).

12. *See* DELGADO & STEFANCIC, *supra*, at 7.

13. *See* R. E. Money-Kyrle, *On Prejudice—A Psychoanalytical Approach*, 33 BRIT. J. MED. PSYCHOL. 205, 205, 207 (1960).

14. *See* M. A. Chesler, *Contemporary Sociological Theories of Racism, in* TOWARDS THE ELIMINATION OF RACISM 31–32 (P. A. Katz ed., 1976).

15. *See* EHRLICH, *supra*, at 39.

16. W. Lippmann, PUBLIC OPINION 126 (Transactional Publisher 1991) (1922).

17. *See* E. J. DINGWALL, RACIAL PRIDE & PREJUDICE 217–18 (1946).

18. SIMPSON & YINGER, *supra*, at 71.

19. *See* ADORNO, *supra*, at 630.

20. *Quoted in* A. MITSCHERLICH & F. MIELKE, DEATH DOCTORS 265 (James Cleugh trans., Elek Books 1962) (1949).

21. *See* A. KARDINER & L. OVESEY, MARK OF OPPRESSION 379 (1951).

22. FANON, *supra*, at 122.

23. *See* SIMPSON & YINGER, *supra*, at 76.

24. *See* ADORNO ET AL., *supra*, at 485.

25. *See* SIMPSON & YINGER, *supra*, at 154.

26. M. J. Matsuda, *Public Response to Racist Speech*, 87 MICH. L. REV. 2320, 2373 (1989).

27. *See* J. Spurlock, *Some Consequences of Racism for Children, in* RACISM & MENTAL HEALTH 150 (C. V. Willie et al. eds., U. of Pittsburgh Press, 2d ed. 1973).

28. *See* M. L. KING JR., WHY WE CAN'T WAIT 81–82 (1964).

29. DELGADO & STEFANCIC, *supra*, at 5.

30. FANON, *supra*, at 191–92.

NOTES TO CHAPTER 7

1. *See* J. B. Thompson, *Introduction* to P. BOURDIEU, LANGUAGE & SYMBOLIC POWER 5 (G. Raymond and M. Adamson trans., Harvard U. Press 1991).

2. *See* R. Delgado & D. H. Yun, *Pressure Valves and Bloodied Chickens*, 82 CALIF. L. REV. 871, 882 (1994).

3. M. KLEG, HATE PREJUDICE & RACISM 177 (1993).

4. *See* P. BOURDIEU, LANGUAGE & SYMBOLIC POWER 105–6 (G. Raymond and M. Adamson trans., Harvard U. Press 1991).

5. *See* R. STACKELBERG, HITLER'S GERMANY 42 (1999).

6. G. JAHODA, IMAGES OF SAVAGES 233 (1999).

7. G. MYRDAL, AMERICAN DILEMMA 72 (2d ed., 1962).

8. *See* G. W. ALLPORT, THE NATURE OF PREJUDICE 57 (3d ed. 1979) (1954).

9. *See* T. A. v. DIJK, COMMUNICATING RACISM 11 (2d prtg. 1989); KLEG, *supra* at 175.

10. *See id.* at 179–80.

11. E. YOUNG-BRUEHL, ANATOMY OF PREJUDICES 347 (1996).

12. *See* P. BOURDIEU, LANGUAGE & SYMBOLIC POWER 119, 121 (G. Raymond and M. Adamson trans., Harvard U. Press 1991).

13. I think of reality as a unified whole that can be broken down into parts through the imagination.

14. *See* v. DIJK, *supra*, at 182–83.

15. *See* D. A. J. RICHARDS, FREE SPEECH & THE POLITICS OF IDENTITY 105, 129 (1999).

16. *See* H. Tajfel, *The Roots of Prejudice: Cognitive Aspects, in* PSYCHOLOGY & RACE 86–87 (Peter Watson ed., 1973).

17. *See* H. Proshansky & P. Newton, *Colour: Nature and Meaning of Negro Self-Identity, in* PSYCHOLOGY & RACE, *supra*, at 179.

18. *See* P. A. Katz, *Acquisition of Racial Attitudes in Children, in* TOWARDS THE ELIMINATION OF RACISM 148 (P. A. Katz ed., 1976).

19. *See* G. E. SIMPSON & J. M. YINGER, RACIAL & CULTURAL MINORITIES 161–62 (4th ed. 1972).

20. *See* Thompson, *supra*, at 13–14.

21. P. GILROY, AGAINST RACE 281 (2000).

22. *See* P. L. Roux, *Growing up an Afrikaner, in* GROWING UP IN A DIVIDED SOCIETY 198 (S. Burman & P. Reynolds eds., 1990) (1986).

23. *See* SIMPSON & YINGER, *supra*, at 153–54.

24. *See* ALLPORT, *supra*, at 60.

25. *Id.* at 15.

26. *See* FANON, *supra*, at 146.

27. *See* SIMPSON & YINGER, *supra*, at 305–7.

28. H. J. EHRLICH, SOCIAL PSYCHOLOGY OF PREJUDICE 41–42 (1973).

29. G. W. Allport & B. M. Kramer, *Some Roots of Prejudice*, 22 J. OF PSYCHOLOGY 9, 37 (1946).

30. *See* EHRLICH, *supra*, at 137.

31. *See* M. A. Chesler, *Contemporary Sociological Theories of Racism, in* TOWARDS THE ELIMINATION OF RACISM 31–32 (P. A. Katz ed., 1976).

32. *See John* 8:31–44.

33. *See* J. KATZ, FROM PREJUDICE TO DESTRUCTION 264 (1980).

34. *See* R. DELGADO & J. STEFANCIC, MUST WE DEFEND NAZIS? 7 (1997); T. W. ADORNO ET AL., AUTHORITARIAN PERSONALITY 653 (1950).

35. *See* A. KARDINER & L. OVESEY, MARK OF OPPRESSION 383 (1951).

36. *See* ADORNO, *supra*, at 620 (discussing the objectification and persecution of Jews).

37. *See* N. Sanford, *Roots of Prejudice, in* PSYCHOLOGY & RACE 66 (Peter Watson ed., 1973) (discussing D. J. Levinson's views on ethnocentrism in AUTHORITARIAN PERSONALITY, *supra*).

38. *See* v. DIJK, *supra*, at 394.

NOTES TO PART III

1. *See* F. M. Lawrence, *Resolving the Hate Crimes/Hate Speech Paradox*, 68 NOTRE DAME L. REV. 673, 680 (1993).

2. Wisconsin v. Mitchell, 508 U.S. 476 (1993).

3. R.A.V. v. St. Paul, 505 U.S. 377 (1992).

NOTES TO CHAPTER 8

1. 249 U.S. 47 (1919).

2. 249 U.S. 204 (1919).

3. 249 U.S. 211 (1919).

4. Schenck, 249 U.S. at 52.

5. Frohwerk, 249 U.S. at 208–9.

6. *Id.* at 206.

7. 250 U.S. 616 (1919).

8. *See* S. M. NOVICK, HONORABLE JUSTICE 329–32 (1989).

9. *See e.g.* Debs, 249 U.S. at 216 ("We should add that the jury were most carefully instructed that they could not find the defendant guilty for advocacy of any of his opinions unless the words used had as their natural tendency and reasonably probable effect to obstruct the recruiting service, &c., and unless the defendant had the specific intent to do so in his mind").

10. *Id.* at 628 (Holmes, J., dissenting).

11. *See id.* at 629–30 (Holmes, J., dissenting). The Supreme Court has repeatedly reaffirmed the rule that there is a constitutional difference between mere advocacy of abstract theories justifying the use of violence and actual preparations taken in furtherance of such theories. *See e.g.* Noto v. United States, 367 U.S. 290, 297–98 (1961).

12. Abrams, 250 U.S. at 630 (Holmes, J., dissenting).

13. 268 U.S. 652 (1925) (Holmes, J., dissenting).

14. *Id.* at 654.

15. *Id.* at 659.

16. 505 US. 377 (1992).

17. Gitlow, 268 U.S. at 669.

18. *Id.* at 673 (Holmes, J., dissenting).

19. *See* Whitney v. California, 274 U.S. 357, 376 (1927) (Brandeis, J., concurring), *overruled on other grounds*, Brandenburg v. Ohio, 395 U.S. 444 (1969).

20. *See id.* at 377.

21. *See id.* at 375. Brandeis failed to mention that some of the very founders who believed that liberty is a moral end and a moral means also condoned slavery.

22. *Id.* at 376.

23. *Id.*

24. *Id.* at 375.

25. 315 U.S. 568 (1942).

26. *See* Cohen v. California, 403 U.S. 15, 20 (1971).

27. Chaplinsky, 315 U.S. at 572.

28. 395 U.S. 444 (1969) (per curiam).

29. *See* O. Fiss, Irony of Free Speech 8 (1996).

30. *See id.* at 446–49. The film also depicted hooded persons setting fire to a cross and carrying firearms. *See id.* at 445.

31. 505 U.S. 377 (1992).

32. St. Paul, Minn., Legis. Code §292.02 (1990), *cited in R.A.V.*, 505 U.S. at 380.

33. *R.A.V.*, 505 U.S. at 387.

34. *Id.* at 395–96.

35. *Id.* (White, J., concurring).

36. *See id.* at 402, 411.

37. *See id.* at 416 (Blackmun, J., concurring).

38. *Id.* at 423 (Stevens, J., concurring).

39. *See id.* at 425, 434, 436.

40. Texas v. Johnson, 491 U.S. 397, 414 (1989).

41. For the views of several Supreme Court justices on this point, see R.A.V. v. St. Paul, 505 U.S. at 377 (discussing First Amendment jurisprudence involving a form of hate speech, and including several concurring opinions).

Notes to Chapter 9

1. Gertz v. Robert Welch, Inc., 418 U.S. 323, 344 n.9 (1974).
2. *See* Gompers v. United States, 233 U.S. 604, 610 (1914).
3. Dennis v. United States, 341 U.S. 494, 523–24 (Frankfurter, J., concurring).
4. *See* Kleindienst v. Mandel, 408 U.S. 753, 777 (1972) (Marshall, J., dissenting); NAACP v. Button, 371 U.S. 415, 438–39 (1963); Gibson v. Florida Legislative Investigation Committee, 372 U.S. 539, 546 (1963).
5. *See* Reno v. ACLU, 521 U.S. 844, 874 (1997).
6. *See* J. S. MILL, ON LIBERTY 89 (Pelican Classics 1980) (1859).
7. Abrams v. United States, 250 U.S. 616, 630 (1919) (Holmes, J., dissenting).
8. P. L. Gregg, *Pragmatism of Mr. Justice Holmes*, 31 GEO. L.J. 262, 294 (1943).
9. *See* Letter from O. W. Holmes to F. Pollock (April 23, 1910) *in* O. W. HOLMES, I HOLMES-POLLOCK LETTERS 163 (1941).
10. J. Dewey, *Justice Holmes & the Liberal Mind, in* MR. JUSTICE HOLMES (F. Frankfurter ed. 1931).
11. *See* O. W. Holmes, *Natural Law*, 32 HARV. L. REV. 40, 40 (1918) (writing that "[d]eep-seated preferences can not be argued about . . . and therefore when differences are sufficiently far reaching, we try to kill the other man rather than let him have his way").
12. *See* Gitlow v. New York, 268 U.S. 652, 673 (1925) (Holmes, J., dissenting).
13. *See* [O. W. Holmes], *Gas-Stokers'Strike*, 7 AM. L. REV. 582, 583 (1873).
14. O. W. HOLMES, COLLECTED LEGAL PAPERS 258 (1920).
15. *See id.* 238, 239.
16. *See* [Holmes], *Gas-Stokers' Strike, supra*, at 584.
17. O. W. Holmes, *Book Review*, 6 AM. L. REV. 593 (1871), *reprinted in* 44 HARV. L. REV. 788 (1931); *see* American Banana Co. v. United Fruit Co., 213 U.S. 347, 356 (1909).
18. Letter from Holmes to Pollock (Jan. 19, 1928) *in* 2 HOLMES-POLLOCK LETTERS, *supra*, at 212.
19. *See* J. C. Ford, *Fundamentals of Holmes' Juristic Philosophy*, 11 FORDHAM L. REV. 255, 257 (1942) (stating that Holmes's doctrine "is logically a step to the proposition that might makes right"). "The fact that Holmes was a polished gentleman who did not go about like a storm-trooper knocking people down and proclaiming the supremacy of the blonde [*sic*] beast should not blind us to his legal philosophy that might makes right." B. W. Palmer, *Hobbes, Holmes and Hitler*, 31 AM. BAR ASSOC. J. 569, 571 (1945).

Holmes's view that laws are made at the discretion of the powerful is reminiscent of Friedrich Nietzsche's theory that the *Übermensch* (roughly translated "Higher Man" or "Superman") must reevaluate orthodox views of good and evil.

See e.g. F. NIETZSCHE, THUS SPAKE ZARATHUSTRA 101 (R. J. Hollingdale trans., Penguin Classics 1964) (1883–85) (stating that the images of good and evil should not be referred to as sources of knowledge); *see* R. A. Posner, *Jurisprudence of Skepticism*, 86 MICH. L. REV. 827, 885–86 (1988) (comparing the similarity of Nietzsche's convictions on morality to Holmes's views that the relative worth of laws is based on the views of the dominant group).

Holmes's ideas on morality and law are not, however, identical to Nietzsche's. For example, the former believed that the "dominant forces of a community" should be given the opportunity to establish the institutions of government. *See* Gitlow, 268 U.S. at 673 (stating that the "dominant forces of a community" should be given the opportunity to establish a "proletarian dictatorship" if they so desire). Nietzsche, on the other hand, mocked herd mentality and extolled excellence and individual thought. *See* F. NIETZSCHE, BEYOND GOOD AND EVIL 111, 114 (M. Cowan trans., Gateway Editions 1955) (1886) (writing disparagingly about herd mentality and extolling an "independent intellect").

20. F. E. Lucey, *Holmes-Liberal-Humanitarian-Believer in Democracy?* 39 GEO. L.J. 523, 534 (1951).

21. Letter from Holmes to Pollock (Feb. 1, 1920) *in* 2 HOLMES-POLLOCK LETTERS, *supra*, at 36.

22. Letter from O. W. Holmes to J. Wu (Aug. 26, 1926) *in* O. W. HOLMES, HIS BOOK NOTICES & UNCOLLECTED LETTERS & PAPERS 187 (H. C. Shriver ed. 1936).

23. HOLMES, COLLECTED LEGAL PAPERS, *supra*, at 314.

24. *See* [Holmes], *Gas-Stokers' Strike*, *supra*, at 583.

25. *See* Letter from Holmes to Wu (June 21, 1925) *in* HIS BOOK NOTICES & UNCOLLECTED LETTERS & PAPERS, *supra*, at 197.

26. *See* Buck v. Bell, 274 U.S. 200, 207 (1927) (upholding law requiring the mentally ill to undergo sterilization).

27. Letter from Holmes to Wu (July 21, 1925) *in* HIS BOOK NOTICES AND UNCOLLECTED LETTERS AND PAPERS, *supra*, at 181.

28. *See* Letter from Holmes to Pollock (Feb. 1, 1920) *in* 2 HOLMES-POLLOCK LETTERS, *supra*, at 36 (writing skeptically about the effectiveness of the League of Nations).

29. [Holmes], *Gas-Stokers' Strike*, *supra*, at 584.

30. Holmes's nihilistic relativism might be understood to manifest a speculative view whose practical application he would have abhorred. Other philosophers who have held skeptical views have nevertheless moderated their ideas when it comes to everyday life. *See e.g.* D. HUME, TREATISE OF HUMAN NATURE 183, 269 (L. A. Selby-Bigge ed., Oxford 1978) (1739) (writing that although he maintained a skeptical philosophy, he nevertheless lived his daily life as if he had a degree of certainty about his knowledge of empirical reality).

31. Letter from Holmes to Wu (Aug. 26, 1926) *in* His Book Notices and Uncollected Letters and Papers, *supra*, at 187.

32. *See* Gitlow, 268 U.S. at 673 (Holmes, J., dissenting).

33. *See* A. Meiklejohn, Free Speech and Its Relation to Self-Government 87 (1948).

34. *See* C. R. Sunstein, *First Amendment in Cyberspace*, 104 Yale L.J. 1757, 1762 (1995).

35. *See* H. O. Hunter, *Problems in Search of Principles*, 35 Emory L.J. 59, 132 (1986).

36. *See* Whitney v. California, 274 U.S. 357, 376, 377, 375 (1927) (Brandeis, J., concurring), *overruled on other grounds* by Brandenburg v. Ohio, 395 U.S. 444 (1969).

37. New York Times v. Sullivan, 376 U.S. 254, 270 (1964).

38. Chaplinsky v. New Hampshire, 315 U.S. 568, 572 (1942) (establishing the fighting words doctrine).

39. *See* H. H. Wellington, *Freedom of Expression*, 88 Yale L.J. 1105, 1130, 1132 (1979).

40. *See* Brandenburg v. Ohio, 395 U.S. 444, 447 (1969) (per curiam); Abrams v. United States, 250 U.S. 616, 628 (1919) (Holmes, J., dissenting).

41. G. W. Allport, The Nature of Prejudice 57 (3d ed. 1979) (1954).

42. *See* K. E. Mahoney, *Hate Speech*, 1996 U. Ill. L. Rev. 789, 801 (1996); S. H. Shiffrin, *Racist Speech, Outsider Jurisprudence, and the Meaning of America*, 80 Cornell L. Rev. 43, 80 (1994).

43. *See* K. Lasson, *Holocaust Denial & the First Amendment*, 6 Geo. Mason L. Rev. 35, 70 (1997).

44. *See* Dennis v. United States, 341 U.S. 494, 509 (1951) (clarifying that government need not wait to act "until the putsch is about to be executed, the plans have been laid and the signal awaited").

45. *See* T. A. v. Dijk, Communicating Racism 267 (2d prtg. 1989).

46. *See* Gitlow, 268 U.S. at 669 (regarding revolutionary utterances).

47. Chapter 13 discusses these issues in detail.

48. *See* R.A.V. v. St. Paul, 505 U.S. 377, 386 (1992).

49. *See id.* at 415–16 (Blackmun, J., concurring).

50. *See id.* at 423–34 (Stevens, J., concurring).

51. *Id.* at 424–25 (Stevens, J., concurring).

52. J. P. Stevens, *Freedom of Speech*, 102 Yale L.J. 1293, 1296 (1993).

53. *See* Renton v. Playtime Theaters, Inc., 475 U.S. 41 (1986); Watts v. United States, 394 U.S. 705 (1969); Burson v. Freeman, 504 U.S. 191 (1992); Friedman v. Rogers, 440 U.S. 1 (1979); United States v. O'Brien, 391 U.S. 367 (1968); Miller v. California, 413 U.S. 15 (1973).

54. *See* C. J. Ogletree Jr., *The Limits of Hate Speech*, 32 Gonz. L. Rev. 491, 502 (1996–97).

55. Chaplinsky, 315 U.S. at 572.

56. *See* R. DELGADO & J. STEFANCIC, MUST WE DEFEND NAZIS? 43 (1997) (discussing the favoritism of First Amendment exceptions to powerful interests).

57. *See R.A.V.*, 505 U.S. at 395.

58. *See* A. R. Amar, *Case of the Missing Amendments*, 106 HARV. L. REV. 124, 151, 152–53 (1992).

59. *See* R. Delgado, *Toward a Legal Realist View of the First Amendment*, 113 HARV. L. REV. 778, 778 (2000).

60. Chaplinsky v. New Hampshire, 315 U.S. 568, 571 (1942).

61. *See* A. E. Taslitz, *Hate Crimes, Free Speech, & the Contract of Mutual Indifference*, 80 B.U. L. REV. 1283, 1288 (2000).

62. Kennedy v. Mendoza-Martinez, 372 U.S. 144, 159–60 (1963).

63. *See* J. A. Powell, *As Justice Requires/Permits*, 16 LAW & INEQ. J. 97, 109 (1998).

64. *See* T. M. Scanlon, *What We Owe to Each Other* 199–200 (1998).

65. *See* Barenblatt v. United States, 360 U.S. 109, 126 (1959).

66. Dennis v. United States, 341 U.S. 494, 524–25 (1951) (Frankfurter, J., concurring).

67. *See* A. KOPPELMAN, ANTIDISCRIMINATION LAW & SOCIAL EQUALITY 204 (1996).

68. *See* Powell, *supra*, at 109.

69. *See* Beauharnais v. Illinois, 343 U.S. 250, 258, 258–59 (1952).

70. *Id.* at 252.

71. *See id.* at 254–63.

72. *Id.* at 263.

73. *See id.* at 266.

74. *See id.* at 267–75 (Black, J., dissenting).

75. *See id.* at 277–84 (Reed, J., dissenting).

76. *See id.* at 284–85 (Douglas, J., dissenting).

77. *See id.* at 299–305 (Jackson, J., dissenting).

78. *See R.A.V.*, 505 U.S. at 382–83.

79. 376 U.S. 254 (1964). Another sign of Beauharnais vitality came in 1978. The Seventh Circuit Court of Appeals then questioned whether "Beauharnais would pass constitutional muster today." Collin v. Smith, 578 F.2d 1197, 1204, *cert. denied*, Smith v. Collin, 436 U.S. 953 (1978). In their dissent from a denial of writ of certiorari in that case, Justices Blackmun and Rehnquist stated that "Beauharnais has never been overruled or formally limited in any way." *Id.* (Blackmun & Rehnquist, JJ., dissenting). *See also* R. DELGADO & J. STEFANCIC, MUST WE DEFEND NAZIS? 71–72, 89 (1997). T. D. JONES, HUMAN RIGHTS 90–97 (1998).

80. "Leaving aside the special considerations when public officials are the target, *New York Times Co. v. Sullivan* . . . a libelous publication is not protected by

the Constitution. *Beauharnais v. Illinois,* 343 U.S. 250 (1952)." Ferber v. New York, 458 U.S. 747, 763 (1982).

81. New York Times, 376 U.S. at 279–80.

NOTES TO CHAPTER 10

1. I do not mean to imply that people owe no obligations to other living beings, such as animals and trees, but I do not discuss the matter here because it is simply not pertinent to the topic at hand.

2. Note that, unlike John Locke, I have excluded "property" from this list. The right to property arises only when persons become part of a social entity whence they begin to have better claims than others to some material objects. Therefore, property rights are derivative from the existence of interrelations but they are not fundamental. *But see* J. LOCKE, TWO TREATISES OF GOVERNMENT 2: §87 (P. Laslett ed., Mentor Press 3d prtg. 1965) (1689).

3. J. A. Powell, *As Justice Requires/Permits: Delimitation of Harmful Speech in a Democratic Society,* 16 LAW & INEQ. 97, 118 (1998).

4. *See* A. E. Taslitz, *Hate Crimes, Free Speech, & the Contract of Mutual Indifference,* 80 B.U. L. REV. 1283, 1300–1301 (2000).

5. The Three-Fifths Clause reduced blacks to three-fifths the value of whites for purposes of representation, while the Fugitive Slave Clause prohibited non-slaveholding states from emancipating runaway slaves and required their return to slave owners. *See* U.S. CONST. art. I, §2, cl. 3, *partly repealed by* U.S. CONST. amend. XIV, §2; *id.* art. IV, §2, cl. 3, *affected by* U.S. CONST. amend. XIII.

6. *See* J. RAWLS, *Priority of Right & Ideas of the Good, in* COLLECTED PAPERS 450 (1999).

7. After tying up some more lose ends, I will delineate the substance of those imperatives both on an individual and public levels.

8. *See* LOCKE, *supra,* at 2: §124.

9. *See* B. J. Diggs, *Contractarian View of Respect for Persons, in* SOCIAL CONTRACT THEORY 218–19 (Michael Lessnoff ed., 1990).

10. Obligations owed to people, furthermore, are not exclusively due to other citizens. Whomever a person can effect, regardless of whether he or she is an alien or native, possesses a congruous respectability regardless of the object's social standing or status. Commonsense morality identifies each person as equally worthy of respect.

11. *See* J. G. MURPHY & J. L. COLEMAN, PHILOSOPHY OF LAW 77 (1984).

12. *See* R. Taylor, *Justice & the Common Good, in* LAW & PHILOSOPHY 91 (2d prtg. 1970).

13. This maxim, just as the ideas of several philosophers discussed *supra,* is a refinement on the "golden rule." *Leviticus* 19:18 ("[l]ove your neighbor as

yourself"); *Matthew* 7:12 ("[w]hatever you would want people to do to you, so do unto them likewise"); *see* I. KANT, FUNDAMENTAL PRINCIPLES OF THE METAPHYSIC OF MORALS 47 n.14 (T. K. Abbott trans., 21st ed. 1981) (1785) (discussing the relation of the golden rule to the categorical imperative); *see* J. S. MILL, UTILITARIANISM *in* UTILITARIANISM, ON LIBERTY, AND CONSIDERA-TIONS ON REPRESENTATIVE GOVERNMENT 16 (H. B. Acton ed., J. M. Dent & Sons Ltd. 1972) (1861) 16 (stating that golden rule is spirit of utilitarianism); *see* SIDGWICK, *supra*, at 379–80 (criticizing the imprecision of the golden rule). Some version of the golden rule was found both in ancient Western and East-ern cultures. *See Shabbat* 31a (Jacob Neusner trans., U. of Chicago 1991) (first-century Rabbi Hillel) (stating that all of Judaism could be described as "What-ever you would want people to do to you, so do unto them likewise"); CON-FUCIUS, ANALECTS *in* A SOURCE BOOK IN CHINESE PHILOSOPHY 15.23 (Wing-Tsit Chan trans. & ed., Princeton U. Press 1973) (6th or 5th century B.C.E.) ("[d]o not do to others what you do not want them to do to you"); *id.* at 5.11, 4.15.

14. *See* L. L. WEINREB, NATURAL LAW & JUSTICE 167–69 (1987); S. I. Benn, *Egalitarianism & Equal Consideration of Interests, in* EQUALITY 70 (J. R. Pen-nock & J. W. Chapman eds., 1967).

15. *See* R. DWORKIN, SOVEREIGN VIRTUE 5–6 (2000).

16. *See* RAWLS, *Distributive Justice, supra*, at 133.

17. I. KANT, SCIENCE OF RIGHT, *in* 42 *Great Books of the Western World* 401 (W. Hastie trans., Encyclopaedia Britannica Inc., 1952) (1790).

18. *See* C. R. Sunstein, *Words, Conduct, Caste*, 60 U. CHI. L. REV. 795, 800–801 (1993).

19. *See* H. A. Bedau, *Egalitarianism & the Idea of Equality, in* EQUALITY, *supra*, at 70.

20. *See* RAWLS, *Distributive Justice, supra*, at 133.

21. *See* LUCAS, *supra*, at 12.

22. *See* B. Spinoza, THEOLOGICO-POLITICAL TREATISE 208 (R. H. M. Elwes trans., Dover Publications 1951) (1670).

23. In spite of the general injunctions of equal treatment, socially con-scious programs may be made racially or ethnically specific in recognition of past and continuing discrimination and the effort to overcome it. Affir-mative action programs, for example, acknowledge the pervasiveness of in-stitutionalized racism and seek to end it by recognizing that democratic government has the obligation to end social inequalities. Unfortunately, space does not permit an adequate discussion on this point in this book. *See* R. DWORKIN, *Bakke's Case: Are Quotas Unfair?, in* MATTER OF PRIN-CIPLE 360 (1985).

24. *See* SIDGWICK, METHODS OF ETHICS, *supra*, at 433–34.

NOTES TO CHAPTER 11

1. *See* S. H. Shiffrin, *Racist Speech, Outsider Jurisprudence, & the Meaning of America*, 80 CORNELL L. REV. 43, 87–88 (1994).

2. *See* S. J. Heyman, *Righting the Balance*, 78 B.U. L. REV. 1275, 1375–76 (1998).

3. *See* J. A. Powell, *As Justice Requires/Permits*, 16 LAW & INEQ. J. 97, 129 (1998).

4. R. Delgado, *Words That Wound*, 17 HARV. C.R.-C.L. L. REV. 133, 136 (1982).

5. *See* A. Huxley, *Words & Behavior, in* ABOUT LANGUAGE 463 (M. J. Clark et al. eds., 2d ed. 1975).

6. *See* K. E. Mahoney, *Hate Speech*, 1996 U. ILL. L. REV. 789, 792.

7. *See* PLATO, REPUBLIC *in* THE DIALOGUES OF PLATO 820–24 (562–66) (B. Jowett trans., Random House 1937) (5th or 4th century B.C.E.).

8. *See* P. Gilroy, AGAINST RACE (2000).

9. *See* Heyman, *supra*, at 1375–76.

10. WILL DURANT, 6 STORY OF CIVILIZATION 220 (1957). Durant further discusses Spain's economic loss caused by the Muslim expulsion from Castile and León.

11. *See* Powell, *supra*, at 126.

12. *See* D. Kretzmer, *Freedom of Speech and Racism*, 8 CARDOZO L. REV. 445, 464, 480 (1987).

13. *See* M. E. Gale, *On Curbing Racial Speech*, 1 RESPONSIVE COMMUNITY 47, 48–49 (1990–91).

14. Kennedy v. Mendoza-Martinez, 372 U.S. 144, 160 (1963) (concerning draft evasion).

15. *See* C. MACKINNON, ONLY WORDS 13, 31 (1993).

16. *See* K. Lasson, *Holocaust Denial and the First Amendment*, 6 GEO. MASON L. REV. 35, 71–72 (1997).

17. *See* K. E. Mahoney, *Hate Speech*, 1996 U. ILL. L. REV. 789, 797 (1996).

18. *See* C.R. SUNSTEIN, DEMOCRACY & THE PROBLEM OF FREE SPEECH 186 (1993).

19. *See* L. S. Gould, *Mixing Bodies and Beliefs*, 101 COLUM. L. REV. 702, 752 n.329 (2001); J. F. PEREA, *Introduction* to IMMIGRANTS OUT!: THE NEW NATIVISM AND THE ANTI-IMMIGRANT IMPULSE IN THE UNITED STATES 2 (J. F. Perea ed., 1997).

20. *See* Kretzmer, *supra*, at 447, 463.

21. *See* I. Cotler, *Racist Incitement, in* FREEDOM OF EXPRESSION AND THE CHARTER 254 (D. Schneiderman ed., 1991).

22. *See* O. M. Fiss, *Supreme Court & the Problem of Hate Speech*, 24 CAP. U. L. REV. 281, 285 (1995).

23. M. J. Matsuda, *Public Response to Racist Speech*, 87 MICH. L. REV. 2320, 2381 (1989).

24. *See* G. W. ALLPORT, THE NATURE OF PREJUDICE 354–66, 497 (3d ed. 1979) (annunciating the view that "the display of aggression is not a safety valve, rather it is habit-forming—the more aggression one shows, the more he has").

25. *See* 505 U.S. 377 (1992); R. Delgado & D. H. Yun, *Pressure Valves and Bloodied Chickens*, 82 CALIF. L. REV. 871, 878–79 (1994).

26. *See* D. J. GOLDHAGEN, HITLER'S WILLING EXECUTIONERS 82–85 (1997).

27. Gitlow v. New York, 268 U.S. 652, 673 (Holmes, J., dissenting).

28. *See* B. Neuborne, *Ghosts in the Attic*, 27 HARV. C.R.-C.L. L. REV. 371, 390 (1992).

NOTES TO CHAPTER 12

1. *See* K. E. Mahoney, *Hate Speech*, 1996 U. ILL. L. REV. 789, 803 (1996); K. Lasson, *Holocaust Denial and the First Amendment*, 6 GEO. MASON L. REV. 35, 72 n.286 (1997); T. D. JONES, HUMAN RIGHTS 189–224, 259–313.

2. Art. 3(c), 78 U.N.T.S. 277.

3. Art. 10, 312 U.N.T.S. 22, E.T.S. 5, as amended by Protocol No. 3, E.T.S. 45, Protocol No. 5, E.T.S. 55, & Protocol No. 8, E.T.S 118.

4. *See* S. Farrior, *Molding the Matrix*, 14 BERKELEY J. INT'L L. 3, 65–68 (1996).

5. *Quoted in* N. LERNER, U.N. CONVENTION ON THE ELIMINATION OF ALL FORMS OF RACIAL DISCRIMINATION 43 (1980).

6. *See* LERNER, *supra*, at 1.

7. *See* H. J. Richardson, III, "Failed States," *Self-Determination, and Preventive Diplomacy*, 10 TEMP. INT'L & COMP. L.J. 1, 23 (1996); L. Henkin, *U.S. Ratification of Human Rights Conventions*, 89 AM. J. INT'L L. 341 (1995).

8. *See* D. A. J. RICHARDS, FREE SPEECH & THE POLITICS OF IDENTITY 5 (1999).

9. *See* Art. 18–20, 999 U.N.T.S. 171.

10. *Quoted in* United Nations Committee on the Elimination of Racial Discrimination, *Reports Submitted by States Parties under Article 9 of the Convention: Thirteenth Periodic Report of States Parties Due in 1997, Austria* (visited Apr. 26, 2001) <http://www.hri.ca/fortherecord1999/documentation/tbodies /cerd-c-319-add5.htm>.

11. *See* Act No. 72-546 of July 28, 1972 & Act No. 90-615 of 1990 (Fr.) *cited in* United Nations, *Core Document Forming Part of the Reports of States Parties: France*, HRI/CORE/1/Add.66 (Oct. 7, 1996) (visited Apr. 29, 2001) <http:// www.hri.ca/fortherecord2000/documentation/coredocs/hri-core-1-add17-rev1.htm>; E. BARENDT, FREEDOM OF SPEECH 164–65 (New York: Oxford 1985).

12. *See* Report of Secretary-General to the United Nations General Assembly, *Status of the Protocols Additional to the Geneva Convention of 1949 & Relating to the Protection of Victims of Armed Conflicts*, A/55/173 5 (July 24, 2000) (visited May 1, 2001) <www.un.org/law/cod/sixth/55/english/a55_173e.pdf> (Italy);

Committee on the Elimination of Racial Discrimination, *United Nations International Convention for the Elimination of All Forms of Racial Discrimination, Eleventh Periodic Reports of States Parties Due in 1997: Italy,* CERD/C/317/Add.1 (July 20, 1998) (visited Apr. 29, 2001) <http://www.unhchr.ch/tbs/doc.nsf/(Symbol)/CERD.C.317.Add.1.En?Opendocument>.

13. *See* Public Order Act 1936 (U.K.), 1 Edw. 8 & 1 Geo. 6, ch. 6; Kenneth Lasson, *Racism in Great Britain,* 7 B.C. THIRD WORLD L.J. 161, 165 (1987).

14. *See* Race Relations Act, 1965, ch. 73 (Eng.).

15. *See* S. J. Roth, *Curbing Racial Incitement in Britain by Law,* 22 ISRAEL Y.B. HUM. RTS. 193, 201 (1992); Lasson, *supra,* at 170–71; BARENDT, *supra* at 163–64.

16. The Public Order Act of 1986 §§17–29 (U.K.) are quoted in Lasson, *supra,* at 173–77; *see also* W. J. Wolffe, *Values in Conflict,* 1987 PUB. L. 85.

17. *See* BARENDT, *supra,* at 161.

18. *See* CANADIAN CHARTER OF RIGHTS AND FREEDOMS §§1, 2. Fundamental freedoms set out in section 2 of the Charter include: "freedom of thought, belief, opinion and expression, including freedom of the press and other media of communication . . . [and] freedom of association."

19. *See* Criminal Law, R.S.C., ch. C-46, §319(1) (2000) (1985) (Can.).

20. *See id.* §319(2).

21. *See id.* §318(1) (2000).

22. *See id.* §320(1).

23. Canadian Human Rights Act, R.S.C., ch. H-6 (1985).

24. Canada (Human Rights Commission) v. Taylor, 3 Can. SCR 892, 904, 919 (1990).

25. *See* 3 S.C.R. 697, 713–14, 744–86 (1990) (Can.). The Supreme Court of Canada reaffirmed its commitment to this case in Regina v. Keegstra, 1 S.C.R. 458 (Canada) (1996).

26. 3 S.C.R. (Canada) 870, 874, 875, 878–83, 885 (1990).

27. *See Hearings Ordered into Web Hatred Complaints,* CALGARY HERALD, Nov. 23, 1996, at A9.

28. *See* Canadian Hum. Rts. Act, ch. H-6, §13(1) (1999) (Can.).

29. Department of Justice Canada, Information Technology Security Strategy (ITSS) Legal Issues Working Group, Integrity and Accuracy of Published Government Information (Nov. 8, 1996) (visited on May 2, 2001) <http://canada2.justice.gc.ca/en/ps/ec/chap/ch06.txt>.

30. Article 5 of the Basic Law provides:

(1) Everyone shall have the right freely to express and disseminate his opinion in speech in writing or visually and to obtain information from generally accessible sources without hindrance. Freedom of the press and freedom of reporting through audiovisual media shall be guaranteed. There shall be no censorship.

(2) These rights are subject to limitations in the provisions of general legislation, in statutory provisions for the protection of youth and the citizen's right to personal respect.

(3) Art and scholarship, research and teaching shall be free. Freedom of teaching shall not absolve anybody from loyalty to the constitution.

Art. 5.1-3 GG, *reprinted in* 7 CONSTITUTIONS OF THE COUNTRIES OF THE WORLD: GERMANY 107 (A. P. Blaustein & G. H. Flanz eds., official trans., 1994).

31. *See* §130 STRAFGESETZBUCH (StGB) (F.R.G.) *reprinted in* J. Wetzel, *Judicial Treatment of Incitement against Ethnic Groups and of the Denial of National Socialist Mass Murder in the Federal Republic of Germany, in* UNDER THE SHADOW OF WEIMAR 105 n.12 (1993).

32. §131 STRAFGESETZBUCH (StGB) (F.R.G.) *reprinted in* E. Stein, *History against Free Speech*, 85 MICH. L. REV. 277, 322–23 (1986).

33. Art. 18 GG, *reprinted in* 7 CONSTITUTIONS OF THE COUNTRIES OF THE WORLD: GERMANY, *supra*, at 113–14 (citations omitted).

34. *See* §86a STRAFGESETZBUCH (StGB) (F.R.G.) *reprinted in* Wetzel, *supra*, at 104–5 n.11 (1993) (appearing in section of German Criminal Code entitled "Crimes That Endanger the Democratic Legal State" (§§84–91 StGB) (F.R.G.); Art. 21.2 GG, *reprinted in* 7 CONSTITUTIONS OF THE COUNTRIES OF THE WORLD: GERMANY, *supra*, at 115 ("[p]arties which by reason of their aims or the conduct of their adherents seek to impair or do away with the free democratic basic order . . . shall be unconstitutional"); *see* Art. 9.2 GG, *reprinted in id.* at 109.

35. *See* Holocaust Denial Case 90 BVerfGE 241 (1994), *translated in* D. P. KOMMERS, CONSTITUTIONAL JURISPRUDENCE OF THE FEDERAL REPUBLIC OF GERMANY 382–87 (1997).

36. *See* K. Lasson, *Holocaust Denial & the First Amendment*, 6 GEO. MASON L. REV. 35, 76 (1997); E. Stein, *History against Free Speech*, 85 MICH. L. REV. 277, 289–99 (1986) (providing synopsis of German case law).

37. *See* Historical Fabrication Case 90 BVerfGE 1 (1994), translated in CONSTITUTIONAL JURISPRUDENCE OF THE FEDERAL REPUBLIC OF GERMANY, *supra*, at 387–88. For general analysis of German constitutional case law, *see* R. Hofmann, *Incitement to National and Racial Hatred, in* STRIKING A BALANCE 159, 167–70 (1992).

38. *See* Council of Europe (Committee of Ministers), *European Commission against Racism & Intolerance: Switzerland* I.C.6 (Jan. 9, 1998) (visited May 1, 2001) <http://cm.coe.int/reports/cmdocs/1997/97cm213ad.html>.

39. *See* Decision No. 30/1992 (V.18) AB, Constitutional Court of the Republic of Hungary, in 2 EAST EUROPEAN CASE REPORTER OF CONSTITUTIONAL LAW 8–26 (1995). In the second part of its decision, the Court struck down a subsection of the law (269(2)) that forbade using offensive language in front of crowds to denigrate people based on nationality, creed, or race.

40. *See id.* at 13.

41. *Id.* at 16.

42. *Id.* at 21.

43. *Translation via* telephone interview with Akash Kara, Legal Adviser at the Hungarian Ministry of Justice (May 11, 2001).

44. *See* United Nations, *Convention for the Rights of the Child, Consideration of Reports Submitted by States Parties: Hungary*, CRC/C/8/Add.34 (Sept. 24, 1996) (visited Apr. 29, 2001) <http://www.hri.ca/fortherecord1997/documentation/tbodies/crc-c-8-add34.htm>.

45. *See* A. Sajo, *Hate Speech for Hostile Hungarians*, 3 E. EUR. CONST. REV. 82, 84–85 (Spring 1994).

46. Basic Law: The *Knesset* (Amendment No. 9) Law, 1985, *quoted in* D. Kretzmer, *Racial Incitement in Israel*, 22 ISRAEL Y.B. ON HUM. RTS. 243 (1992).

47. Penal Code (Amendment No. 20), *quoted in* Kretzmer, *supra*, at 249.

48. *See* Kretzmer, *supra*, at 250; E. Lederman & M. Tabory, *Criminalization of Racial Incitement in Israel*, 24 STANFORD J. INT'L L. 55, 81 (1988).

49. *Quoted in* James D. Wilets, *International Human Rights Law & Sexual Orientation*, 18 HASTINGS INT'L & COMP. L. REV.1, 82 (1995).

50. Penal Code of Finland & Related Laws, ch. 11 §8, *quoted in* PREVENT GENOCIDE INTERNATIONAL (visited Apr. 22, 2001) <http://www.preventgenocide.org/fi/rikoslaki.htm>.

51. Swedish Penal Code, *On Crimes against Public Order*, Chapter 16, §8 (Law 1988:835) (Swedish Ministry of Justice trans.). (Visited Apr. 22, 2001) <http://justitie.regeringen.se/propositionermm/ds/pdf/Penalcode.pdf>.

52. *See* Council of Europe (Committee of Ministers), *European Commission against Racism & Intolerance: Norway* I.C.5 (Jan. 9, 1998) (visited May 1, 2001) <http://cm.coe.int/reports/cmdocs/1997/97cm213ad.html>.

53. *See* U.S. Department of State, *The Netherlands Country Report on Human Rights Practices for 1997* (visited Apr. 30, 2001) <http://www.state.gov/www/global/human_rights/1997_hrp_report/netherla.html>.

54. Indian Penal Code, Ch. VIII, §153A, *quoted in* T. D. JONES, HUMAN RIGHTS 213 (1998).

55. *See* P. K. Chakravarty v. Emperor, 1926 A.I.R. (Cal.) 1133, 1135.

56. *Kali Charan Sharma*, 1972 A.I.R. 649, 652.

NOTES TO CHAPTER 13

1. K. E. Mahoney, *Hate Speech*, 1996 U. ILL. L. REV. 789, 792 (1996).

2. Laws directed at the content of speech receive greater judicial scrutiny than those incidentally affecting the message. *See* M. H. *Redish, Content Distinction in First Amendment Analysis*, 34 STAN. L. REV. 113, 113 n.3 (1981) (citing case law).

3. *See* T. A. v. DIJK, COMMUNICATING RACISM 211 (2d prtg. 1989).

4. *See* M. J. Matsuda, *Public Response to Racist Speech*, 87 MICH. L. REV. 2320, 2364–65 (1989).

5. *See* v. DIJK, *supra*, at 383.

6. *See* Palmore v. Sidoti, 466 U.S. 429 (1984) (ruling that in child custody decisions laws favoring one parent over another solely based on race are suspect); Loving v. Virginia, 388 U.S. 1 (1967) (determining that marriage laws containing racially based restrictions are subject to strict scrutiny); Korematsu v. United States, 323 U.S. 214 (1944) (finding that laws classifying persons by race are suspect and subject to strict scrutiny); Strauder v. West Virginia, 100 U.S. 303 (1879) (holding a law unconstitutional that was facially discriminatory against blacks).

7. *See* D. A. J. RICHARDS, FREE SPEECH & THE POLITICS OF IDENTITY 40 (1999).

8. *See* 505 U.S. 377, 416 (1992) (Blackmun, J., concurring); *see id.* at 436 (Stevens, J., concurring).

9. *See e.g.* R. Delgado, *Words That Wound*, 17 HARV. C.R.-C.L. L. REV. 133 (1982); J. C. Love, *Discriminatory Speech and the Tort of Intentional Infliction of Emotional Distress*, 47 WASH. & LEE L. REV. 23 (1990); R. G. Hartman, *Revitalizing Group Defamation as a Remedy for Hate Speech on Campus*, 71 OR. L. REV. 855 (1992); S. H. Yen, REDRESSING THE VICTIM OF RACIST SPEECH AFTER R.A.V. v. ST. PAUL, 26 COLUM. J.L. & SOC. PROBS. 589 (1993).

10. *See* G. W. ALLPORT, THE NATURE OF PREJUDICE 469 (3d ed. 1979).

11. *See e.g.* B. Neuborne, *Ghosts in the Attic*, 27 HARV. C.R.-C.L. L. REV. 371, 380 (1992); D. E. Lively, *Racist Speech Management*, 1 VA. J. SOC. POL'Y & L. 1, 35–36 (1993).

12. U.S. CONST. amend. XIII (prohibiting slavery and involuntary servitude), XIV (source of state due process equal protection guarantees), XV (ensuring voting rights regardless of race, color, or former status of servitude).

13. Beauharnais v. Illinois, 343 U.S. 250, 262 (1952) (supporting the principle that government is a "science of experiment").

14. *See* T. D. JONES, HUMAN RIGHTS 102 (1998).

15. *See* H. SIDGWICK, METHODS OF ETHICS 457–59 (7th ed. 1907) (1874).

16. E. DURKHEIM, DIVISION OF LABOR IN SOCIETY 108–9 (George Simpson trans., Free Press 1933) (1893).

17. *See* JONES, *supra*, at 152.

18. *See* N. Sanford, *Roots of Prejudice, in* PSYCHOLOGY & RACE 73 (1973) (discussing how laws against racist expressions can be effective against persons with authoritarian personalities).

19. *See* C. R. Sunstein, *Words, Conduct, Caste*, 60 U. CHI. L. REV. 795, 827–28 (1993).

20. *See* Miller v. California, 413 U.S. 15, 25–26.

21. Paris Adult Theatre I v. Slaton, 413 U.S. 49, 58, 59–60 (1973).

22. *See* O. FISS, IRONY OF FREE SPEECH 6, 11, 26 (1996).

23. *See* R. DELGADO & J. STEFANCIC, MUST WE DEFEND NAZIS? 8–9 (1997).

24. *See* DELGADO & STEFANCIC, *supra*, at 84.

25. *See* D. Kretzmer, *Freedom of Speech and Racism*, 8 CARDOZO L. REV. 445, 456 (1987).

26. *See* I. Cotler, *Racist Incitement, in* FREEDOM OF EXPRESSION & THE CHARTER 256–57 (D. Schneiderman ed., 1991); S. H. Shiffrin, *Racist Speech, Outsider Jurisprudence, & the Meaning of America*, 80 CORNELL L. REV. 43, 87–88 (1994).

27. *See* Holland v. Illinois, 493 U.S. 474, 496 (1990) (Marshall, J., dissenting) (asserting that immutable characteristics include race and ethnic background); Kahn v. Shevin, 416 U.S. 351, 357 (1974) (Brennan, J., dissenting) (stating that race, national origin and alienage are immutable characteristics).

28. A "history of purposeful discrimination" is an indicia of membership in a suspect class of people. *See* San Antonio Indep. Sch. Dist. v. Rodriguez, 411 U.S. 1, 28 (1973). *See also* L. H. Tribe, AMERICAN CONSTITUTIONAL LAW 1465–66, 1521–27, 1544–46 (2d ed. 1988) (concerning suspect classification).

29. 304 U.S. 144, 152 n.4 (1938) ("It is unnecessary to consider now whether . . . similar considerations enter into the review of statutes directed at particular religions, or national, or racial minorities: whether prejudice against discrete and insular minorities may be a special condition, which tends seriously to curtail the operation of those political processes ordinarily to be relied upon to protect minorities, and which may call for a correspondingly more searching judicial inquiry").

30. *See* v. DIJK, supra, at 211.

31. *See* R. Delgado, *Toward a Legal Realist View of the First Amendment*, 113 HARV. L. REV. 778, 796–98 (2000).

32. *See* O. M. Fiss, *Supreme Court & the Problem of Hate Speech*, 24 CAP. U. L. REV. 281, 287–88 (1995) (criticizing Scalia's opinion in R.A.V. v. St. Paul, 505 U.S. 377 (1992)).

33. *See* Civil Rights Cases, 109 U.S. 3, 35–36 (1883) (Harlan, J., dissenting) (arguing that certain "burdens and disabilities" are the substantive and visible forms of slavery and they are therefore prohibited by the Thirteenth Amendment).

34. *See* A. R. Amar, *Case of the Missing Amendments*, 106 HARV. L. REV. 124, 157 (1992).

35. *See* R. Delgado & D. Yun, *Neoconservative Case against Hate-Speech Regulation*, 47 VAND. L. REV. 1807, 1823 (1994); R. Delgado and J. Stefancic, *Ten Arguments against Hate-Speech Regulation*, 23 N. KY. L. REV. 475, 482 (1996).

36. *See* Justice J. P. Stevens, *Freedom of Speech*, 102 YALE L.J. 1293, 1310 (1993).

37. *See* J. T. Nockleby, *Hate Speech in Contest: The Case of Verbal Threats*,

42 BUFFALO L. REV. 653, 672 (1994). For an example of how the Supreme Court has applied a contextual assessment of speech, *see* Watts v. United States, 394 U.S. 705 (1969) (overturning a conviction for alleged threats against the President of the United States).

38. Another important issue, which is beyond the scope of this book, concerns the need to redress emotional harms suffered by outgroup members when they are targeted by hate speech. *See* K. N. Hylton, *Implications of Mill's Theory of Liberty for the Regulation of Hate Speech and Hate Crimes*, 3 U. CHI. L. SCH. ROUNDTABLE 35, 52 (1996).

39. Reckless oratory that has a realistic potential of causing harm to a historically oppressed group might also be sufficient for culpability.

40. 249 U.S. 47, 49–50, 53 (1919).

41. *See id.* at 51.

42. *See* v. DIJK, *supra*, at 24.

43. *See* Gitlow v. New York, 268 U.S. 652, 669 (1925) (discussing the dangers of revolutionary speech).

44. *See id.*

45. *See* C. S. NIÑO, CONSTITUTION OF DELIBERATIVE DEMOCRACY 61 (1996).

46. *See* Widmar v. Vincent, 454 U.S. 263, 269–70 (1981) (stating that to regulate content-based religious speech, the state must have a compelling interest and the law must be drafted as narrowly as possible to achieve the desired end).

47. Fowler v. Rhode Island, 345 U.S. 67, 70 (1953) (reversing and remanding the conviction of a Jehovah's Witness for preaching at a public meeting).

48. R.A.V. v. St. Paul, 505 U.S. 377, 401 (1992) (White, J., concurring).

49. *See e.g.* Floyd Abrams, *Hate Speech*, 37 VILL. L. REV. 743, 754 (1992) ("There are no current risks of the communal violence that has plagued India . . . no history, fortunately, such as that of Germany").

50. The Nazi Party received only 2.61 percent of the total vote in the May 20, 1928 German elections. By July 1932, the National Socialist Party received 37 percent of the vote. Then, on January 30, 1933, Hitler became Chancellor of Germany, and the fate of the six million Jews who died in the Holocaust was sealed. *See* W. L. SHIRER, RISE AND FALL OF THE THIRD REICH 118, 185, 187 (1960).

Index

New York Times v. Sullivan, 146
Nietzsche, Friedrich, 225n. 19
Norway, 191
Noto v. United States, 224n. 11
Nott, Josiah C., 42
Nuremberg Laws, 102, 110, 139

Obscenity laws, 171, 197
Oklahoma City Federal Building bombing, 5, 75
Oliver Twist (Dickens), 111
Olmsted, Frederick, 45
Otis, James, 40
Our Mutual Friend (Dickens), 111

Paine, Thomas, 40
Palmer, Benjamin M., 41
Pamphlets: abolitionist, 32; anti-Semitic, 12, 18, 20, 23; in hate crimes, 5; pro-slavery, 41
Parsons, Theodore, 31
Patrick Henry On-Line, 71
Penn, William, 31, 54
Pequot War, 57
Personality, 85
Physical stereotypes, 66
Pierce, William, 75
Platform for Internet Content Selection (PICS), 73
Plato, 169
Ploetz, Alfred, 15
Political compacts, 150, 154
Political discourse. *See* "Marketplace of ideas" doctrine
Political organizations, 18, 20, 76–77, 109–10, 175–76
Positive good theory, 44–46
Posters, 25
Prejudice, 81. *See also* Misethnicity
Preventative laws, 151
Projection (in psychology), 85
Property rights, 44, 154, 229n. 2
Protocols of the Elders of Zion, 20–23
Public Assembly Act (Germany), 188
Public Order Acts (Great Britain), 182–83, 191
Punishments, 151
Puns, 177
Purchas, Samuel, 51
Puritans, 53, 56–57

Quakers, 31–32

Race Relations Act (Great Britain), 182–83
Racial differentiation. *See* Stratification, racial and social
Racism, 2, 81, 194. *See also* Misethnicity
Rational consistency, rule of, 164
R.A.V. v. St. Paul, 5, 119, 124, 126–28, 140–43, 145–47, 178, 195, 197, 207
Reciprocal beneficence, 158–60
Reciprocal duty of humanity, 148–59, 163, 170, 173–74, 198
Reed, Joseph, 146
Regina v. Andrews, 185
Regina v. Keegstra, 184
Religious ideologies: blacks and, 29–32, 41–42, 47, 68–69, 71, 108–9; Jews and, 11–12, 25–26, 91, 102, 110–11, 113, 170; model laws and, 205–6; Native Americans and, 31, 50, 53, 57, 108–9, 168
Rhode Island, 40
Riehl, Wilhelm, 13
"Right of dominant powers" doctrine, 133–34
Rights: basic, 149, 151, 154, 156, 166; equality of, 115, 159–65, 176–77, 186, 197–98; fundamental, 2, 5, 149–51, 153–57, 159, 166, 172; property, 44, 154, 229n. 2. *See also* Good, public or common
Robertson, William, 52
Rockwell, George Lincoln, 78
Romans, Bernard, 35
Ross, John, 64
Rush, Benjamin, 214n. 29
Russia, 23, 92. *See also* Soviet Union

Saffin, John, 30, 41, 43
Sanford, Edward Terry, 124
Sawyer, George S., 41
Scalia, Antonin, 5, 127, 140–43, 146–47, 178, 197, 207
Scapegoating, 85–98, 109–10, 172, 195; against Jews, 20, 22–23, 114, 116, 175
Schenck v. United States, 121, 203
Scott, Winfield, 64
Segel, Binjamin, 21
Self-defense mechanisms, 91, 116
Self-esteem, 88–90, 93–95, 97, 104
Seminoles, 62
Separatism, 77–78
Sewell, Samuel, 30
Sexual exploitation, 91–92
Shakespeare, William, 111

About the Author

Alexander Tsesis is a Visiting Scholar at the University of Wisconsin—Madison, School of Law, Institute for Legal Studies, as well as an Assistant Corporation Counsel for the city of Chicago.